THE CONFESSIONS OF HENRY LEE LUCAS

The Dodge died again. Sandra maneuvered it out of traffic and coasted to the side of the highway.

A pair of headlights came behind Sandra's car.

Two men got out and started walking toward her. Both were smiling. One man was tall and heavyset, the other shorter and thinner. The smaller man, who was also the older of the two, had a droopy, dead-looking eye that didn't move when his other one did.

The taller of the two men told Sandra the engine was burned up. The engine didn't smell hot, and she hadn't seen a heat indicator on, but she knew she needed to get a mechanic out to take a look under the hood. She said she should get to a telephone.

"Okay, come on and get in," the older man said, motioning toward the station wagon.

The moment the short, dark-haired man pulled into traffic, Sandra realized she'd made a terrible mistake. The younger, taller man casually reached under the front seat. In disbelief, Sandra saw his hand emerge with a long knife. Then it was pressing against her pounding throat . . .

THE CONFESSIONS OF HENRY LEE LUCAS

MIKE COX

POCKET STAR BOOKS

New York   London   Toronto   Sydney   Tokyo   Singapore

An *Original* Publication of POCKET BOOKS

 A Pocket Star Book published by
POCKET BOOKS, a division of Simon & Schuster Inc
1230 Avenue of the Americas, New York, NY 10020

ISBN: 978-1-5011-0995-9

First Pocket Books printing August 1991

10 9 8 7 6 5 4 3 2 1

For Linda

Preface

About the only thing going on in the press room of the Austin Police Department that summer morning in 1983 was the steady emptying of the coffeepot. No news is good news for the police, but city editors never like hearing from their police reporter that "nothing's going on over here."

Maybe Lt. Robert Wisian, a former homicide detective, might have felt sorry for me, or maybe he was just making conversation, but after the second or third cup of coffee, he said, "I hear they've got a guy up in north Texas somewhere who claims he kills women and then has sex with their bodies."

I checked around and found out that the man Wisian was talking about was in custody in Montague County, north of the Dallas–Fort Worth area. Then I pitched the story to the city desk. As soon as I had that afternoon's paper taken care of, I was on a plane to Dallas with a photographer. We rented a car and got to Montague shortly before 5 P.M.

My strategy was to get to the district attorney as soon as possible and interview him for a story to run in the morning paper. But I found that would have to wait until after the suspect was arraigned.

I saw Henry Lee Lucas for the first time when he was escorted from the county jail to the courthouse. I went inside to watch the proceedings, more interested in how soon I could talk to the D.A. than in watching a routine courtroom procedure. A few moments after the arraignment began, however, I was glad I was there. In open court, the little man standing before the judge blurted out that he had killed a hundred women. If what he said was true, I realized, I was looking at the most prolific killer in modern criminal history.

Only one other newspaper reporter, a woman from the Wichita Falls paper, shared that experience with me. The next morning our stories were on the front pages of our papers, and Henry Lee Lucas had been discovered. By the time I got back to Montague to do a follow-up story later that morning, television station helicopters were swirling over the Montague County courthouse like so many giant dragonflies.

For eight years, on and off, I've been following the Lucas story, first as a reporter and later as a public information officer with the Texas Department of Public Safety. I met Lucas in person during the summer of 1984, while still a reporter, when Williamson County Sheriff Jim Boutwell let me visit Lucas regularly in his jail cell for tape-recorded interviews. That was the beginning of the research for this book.

Since that summer afternoon when Lucas decided to go public with his claims of mass murder, his story has had twists and turns that the most hackneyed screenwriter wouldn't try to get away with.

In this book, I've tried to sort it all out, but there would have been no way to pursue every nuance of the Lucas story. I couldn't look into, or even list, every murder Lucas has claimed. I've had to leave some things out and do some condensing. But thanks to the help of many people, I'm satisfied that this book sheds some light on the alchemy that turned an abused child into a killer.

Most of the names in this book are real. The names

of three of Lucas's relatives were changed. The names
of the two teenage girls Lucas tried to kidnap were
changed, as were the names of the children Lucas
allegedly molested in Maryland. Four other minor
figures in the book also have fictitous names—Larry
Weems, Candy Playford, Bryan Snyder, and Caroline
Talley.

This book is based on a wide assortment of source
material, with numerous personal interviews, including many hours with Lucas as well as sessions with law
enforcement officers, prosecutors, judges, and others
with some knowledge about Lucas. Also used were
case reports, trial transcripts, signed affidavits, police
videos, and published secondary sources. Dialogue is
either from transcripts, published accounts, or recon-
structed from recollections, probability, or other
sources.

I had had pleasant dealings with Sheriff Boutwell on
other news stories long before either of us had ever
heard of Henry Lucas. When, in 1980, the sheriff
proposed a law enforcement conference on unsolved
murders along I-35, he invited me to attend. Later,
Boutwell was the first person to suggest I might want
to do a book on Lucas. In addition to granting me
access to Lucas, he let me read case reports and was
always available, at home or office, to answer my
questions.

I owe an expression of appreciation to many people
with the Texas Department of Public Safety, which
includes the Texas Rangers. DPS Director Col. Joe
Milner readily approved my working on this book (on
my own time, of course).

Capt. H. R. (Lefty) Block, senior captain of the
Texas Rangers, and many of his men were a tremen-
dous help in my research. In particular, Ranger Capt.
Bob Prince of Houston and Ranger Clayton Smith of
Waco, original members of the Lucas Homicide Task

Force, were a great help. Also giving me a lot of time, and access to a lot of material, was former Ranger Phil Ryan of Decatur. Don Overstreet, manager of the DPS Crime Analysis Section, was very helpful, as was analyst Karen Taylor.

In my efforts to learn as much as possible about Lucas's childhood, many people in Virginia aided me, including Montgomery County Sheriff Louis Barbour, who graciously provided a deputy to introduce me to people who had known Lucas and his family and to show me where he had lived. Former police officer Nathaniel L. Bishop of Christiansburg, Virginia, shared a college research paper he had prepared on Lucas's early years that provided much insight into his grim home life.

One of Lucas's sisters, who asked not to be named, readily answered questions for me. She was particularly helpful in providing some details on Lucas's early life and family history.

In Michigan, Tecumseh Police Chief Laurence Van Alstine provided access to the case report on Viola Lucas's 1960 murder. Retired Tecumseh Police officer Donald Rodehaver, who had had dealings with Lucas during his time in Tecumseh, provided useful background and some photographs, and also helped me locate Stella Keith. Keith, who for a time had been Lucas's girlfriend, was a great help in my efforts to learn about Lucas as a young adult and in reconstructing his trial and time in prison. Retired circuit judge Rex B. Martin looked up his original trial notes to answer some of my questions, and William J. Hudson, who was a young counselor at the Michigan State Prison in Jackson and is now chairman of the state parole board, was helpful as well. Finally, Adrian, Michigan, librarian Jeanine K. Wing enthusiastically handled a series of reference questions concerning Lenawee County.

In Jacksonville, Florida, former homicide detective Buddy Terry allowed me to examine his papers and provided excellent information on Lucas and Ottis Toole. In Tallahassee, Florida, Special Agent Joe Mitchell with the Florida Department of Law Enforcement was particularly gracious in his assistance in my research for this book.

In Montague County, Texas, District Attorney Jack McGaughey answered questions and assisted in many ways, including getting me a copy of the transcript of Lucas's 1983 arraignment—when he first publicly said that he had killed a hundred women. In Denton County, Texas, Sheriff's Lieutenant Larry Brearley took me to the field where Lucas said he had killed Becky Powell and answered many questions for me. Donna Fielder, assistant managing editor of the Denton *Record-Chronicle* also was most helpful.

In Williamson County, former district attorney Ed Walsh assisted me in my research on the "Orange Socks" trial. San Angelo *Standard-Times* reporter Bob Becknell also helped out.

In Austin, former assistant U.S. attorney Jan Patterson was very helpful in relating the details of her role in the strange Lucas saga and in answering questions about the workings of the legal system.

In El Paso, former first assistant district attorney Bill Moody, now a district judge, shared his recollections of the Lucas case. Along with El Paso County District Attorney Steve Simmons, he dug through boxes of old records in an El Paso Police storage facility to find Lucas-related material for me. Texas Ranger Buster Collins was extremely helpful. Police detective Benito Perez Jr. and former police sergeant Santiago Apodaca also were a great help.

This list of people who helped me in the research for this book is by no means inclusive. There were many others, and to them, and everyone I did list, my sincere thanks.

Eventually, of course, a writer has to move beyond the research stage and start writing. That's where my wife, Linda, came in. She kept the household running while I concentrated on this book, and generally kept me on track when I would just as soon have gone fishing or dove hunting—or done anything else but sit down and write. When it was necessary that I travel, she was a one-woman travel agency, making all the arrangements. She was always there to offer encouragement and to generally prove that in a world of so much evil, there is still a lot of love.

Any writer with a mother who is a librarian, and former English teacher, is pretty lucky. My mother, Betty Wilke Hudman, answered a lot of reference questions, read this manuscript and, like Linda, was a sounding board for ideas.

Finally, there is the editor of this book at Pocket Books, Leslie Wells. In more than twenty-five years as a writer, I've had many editors, but few have been as enthusiastic and thorough as Leslie.

M. C.
Austin, Texas

CHAPTER ONE

The glass eye hung heavy in its socket, fixed in a dead, slightly downward stare. But the quiet, nervous man driving the beat-up blue-and-white Oldsmobile station wagon had his good brown eye on the dark highway ahead, and that eye, his right eye, did not miss much.

The driver, Henry Lee Lucas, raised the Budweiser to his mouth and sucked down more beer. He glanced at the green Texas highway sign: SAN ANTONIO 78. A straight shot down I-35. He and his buddy, Ottis Toole, could be there in about an hour and a half, but there was no hurry. He liked to take things as they came, and his easygoing friend didn't much care. Most of the time Ottis didn't even seem to know where they were.

They might not stop in San Antonio. Depending on how he felt, they might hit I-10 and go on back down to Houston. They'd driven thousands of miles together, but they always did what Henry wanted. That's just the way it was.

Now, close to midnight, they were on the southern outskirts of Austin. The next sign he saw marked the exit for William Cannon Drive. Just past the city limits sign, he noticed a new black Dodge on the shoulder of the interstate. He peered through the darkness and made out a woman standing in front of the car with its hood raised. He slowed the Oldsmobile and looked closer. Then he pulled off the highway and stopped behind the parked Dodge.

As he approached the woman, he could see she was a good-looking blonde with long wavy hair and blue eyes. Her blue jeans fit snugly over her hips. And she was alone.

"She belongs to me—she's mine," Lucas muttered softly to Toole. Toole smiled, exposing rotting teeth, and shrugged amiably.

Earlier that day, Sandra Mae Dubbs was already feeling fatigue pinch the back of her neck, settling between her shoulder blades. Her hands gripped the wheel tightly. She flexed them, one at a time, and brushed the heavy wave of golden hair back from her eyes. She'd been driving for hours, but she'd be in San Antonio that night.

When she'd left Missouri the day before it was October 2, and the leaves were already turning Halloween colors. But she knew the pleasant crispness of fall wouldn't last. Coming soon were those mornings she hated, times when it was so cold her hands would stick to the car door handle.

Packing to leave Missouri had been wonderful. Gleefully she had culled most of her winter clothes from her wardrobe. The wool suits and heavy coats wouldn't be necessary. In Texas all she'd need would be sweaters and maybe a light coat. She had shed her old clothes, her old life, the bad winters and the bad memories. In the backseat of her new Dodge Diplomat was everything she owned. At thirty-four, she was starting over.

On TV and in magazines she'd seen stories about Texas. They all said the same thing: Texas was booming. There were plenty of jobs and friendly people. She had to agree, Texans had a lot to brag about, particularly San Antonio.

Sandra had seen San Antonio for the first time only three weeks before, when she had flown in to visit her aunt. She'd had a relaxing stroll down the city's winding River Walk, past the outdoor restaurants and nightclubs. Barges and gondolas loaded with tourists slid down the narrow, stone-channeled river beneath a canopy of oaks, banana trees, and palms. The sidewalks were crowded with laughing conventioneers, young men and women in military uniforms and hand-holding lovers of all ages, from teenage couples who could have been on their first date to gray-haired marrieds celebrating their anniversaries. Music from the costumed mariachis made it all seem like a scene out of some romantic movie. Everyone looked relaxed and happy. Sandra had fallen in love with San Antonio.

Though Sandra felt good about her decision to come to Texas, it hadn't been an easy one. But her marriage was over now, the economy in St. Louis was in a slump, and she was ready for a change. She knew she couldn't live with her parents forever. In San Antonio, she'd stay with her aunt until she could find work and get an apartment of her own. Maybe some of the romance of the city would come into her own life.

Sandra smiled when she thought about the last talk with her mother before she left. Her mother seemed to think she was still a little girl. True, the long drive would be her first major automobile trip alone, but, after all, she was thirty-four years old. Before she left St. Charles, a St. Louis suburb, her mother had suggested that if she got into trouble along the way she should tie a white handkerchief to the car's radio antenna.

Her mother was just overdramatizing, Sandra had thought. She had a brand-new car and wasn't going to have any trouble. But when her mother handed her the new handkerchief, Sandra decided to humor her.

She had driven through the rolling hills of Missouri, through the Ozarks, and now sped along the flat country of southern Oklahoma.

The radio was playing, and Sandra was thinking about frozen margaritas and Mexican food at one of the restaurants along the river in San Antonio. It would be too late for that tonight, but she'd go out to eat tomorrow.

The engine stopped without warning and the red speedometer needle slowly arced toward zero. Sandra looked in the rearview mirror, turned on the hazard lights, and guided the sluggish car to the shoulder. Luckily, she had been in the outside lane and no one had been following her too closely.

She almost wanted to laugh. Her mother would love this. She was stranded on the open highway. If she couldn't get the car to restart, the white handkerchief might come in handy after all.

The motor would not turn over. It wouldn't even sputter.

Sandra got out of the car, feeling a little foolish as she tied the white cloth to the antenna. Okay, she said to herself, I surrender.

At first, Sandra thought the handkerchief wasn't going to do any good. But then a black-and-white Oklahoma State Police car glided up behind her Dodge. A smiling trooper ambled toward her, asking what was wrong. He looked under the hood and tried to start it, but the Dodge still wouldn't come to life. The trooper radioed for a wrecker and stood by with her until a mechanic arrived.

The mechanic found that an ignition wire had simply popped loose. Sandra paid for the service call, thanked the trooper, and drove on in to the nearest town, Atoka, Oklahoma. She could hardly wait to phone her mother.

The incident hadn't dulled her happiness. She told her mother what had happened, laughingly reporting that the white handkerchief had done the trick. Yes, she promised, she'd call again when she got to San Antonio. But she'd better get going if she was going to make it that night.

Sandra crossed the Red River into Texas. An hour later, she was on the outskirts of Dallas, pleased she was getting there early enough to beat the rush-hour traffic. Now, outside Dallas, she was only 280 miles from San Antonio, with two major cities left to pass through, Waco and Austin.

This part of the drive was boring. Sandra had seen pictures of some of the scenic parts of Texas, but none of the shots had been taken along this route. The interstate cut through rolling, blackland prairie with small farms and ranches, which disappeared into the early autumn night before she got to Waco. As the sun had gone down, she'd felt a bit of a chill in spite of the temperature. Driving after dark made her a little edgy, but she was on the last leg of the trip now.

In Austin, from the upper deck of I-35, Sandra saw the lights of the airport, the tower of the University of Texas, and the glowing pink dome of the state capitol. She watched for the overhead sign indicating the way for through traffic on the expressway. San Antonio, another sign said, was now only seventy-eight miles away.

With no warning, just south of the city, the Dodge died again. Sandra maneuvered it out of traffic and coasted to the side of the highway. That same wire must have come loose again! Why couldn't the car have died a few miles closer to town, where there were service stations?

Thinking that maybe she could figure out what wire had come loose and reattach it herself, Sandra pulled a flashlight out of the glove compartment and got out of the Dodge. She raised the hood and, shining her light, peered at the engine. As far as she could tell, all the wires appeared to be attached to something. Now she thought of her former husband. While they were married, whenever anything went wrong, she could always call him. Now she was alone, at night, on a busy highway. She looked both ways on the interstate. There were no service station signs visible in either direction. Somehow she had to get to a telephone and call for help—but which direction would that be?

Headlights came up behind her car.

Relief flooded her. For a second, she thought her luck was still with her. Maybe another state trooper had stopped to see what was wrong. But as she looked closer, she saw the lights belonged to a battered old station wagon with—what?—Florida license plates, it looked like.

Two men got out and started walking toward her. Both were smiling. One man was tall, over six feet, and heavyset; the other was shorter and more slender. As they came closer and she could see them more clearly, her feeling of relief drained away. The pair's physical appearances were anything but reassuring. But after all, she chided herself, they had stopped to help her, hadn't they? Sandra could see the taller man had a sweet, gentle smile, but he had bad teeth. The other man's teeth, what there were of them, were not much better looking. The smaller man, who was the older of the two, had a droopy, dead-looking eye that didn't look at her when his other one did. Sandra's nose twitched and she compressed her lips tightly. Both men smelled as if they hadn't bathed in weeks.

"Need some help?" Lucas asked. Sandra noticed his gentle voice, his soft Southern drawl.

"I don't know what's the matter with my car this time," Sandra replied, and explained the earlier trouble with the loose wire.

Both men looked under the hood. While Lucas probed deftly, jiggling wires and checking a hose connection, Sandra caught a glimpse of a naked woman tattooed on his forearm.

"Give 'er a try now, Ottis," he said.

His companion slid behind the wheel and tried to start the car, but when he turned the key the only response was a useless click.

"Your engine's burned up," he told Sandra with a sad smile. His voice was even softer than that of the man with the tattoo.

The engine didn't smell hot, and she hadn't seen a heat indicator on. She glanced toward the other man, who'd seemed so knowledgeable as he checked under the hood. He didn't contradict the diagnosis.

She decided she needed to get a real mechanic out to take a look.

"I need to get to a telephone," she said.

"Yeah, we'll give you a ride—come on and get in," the older man said, motioning toward the station wagon.

Sandra hesitated. "I'm not sure whether I should leave or not," she said.

The older man seemed friendly enough. He assured her everything was all right. Reluctantly, Sandra walked toward the old station wagon, looking over her shoulder, wondering if her car and all her possessions would be there when she got back.

The man with the bad eye got behind the wheel. Sandra got in on the passenger's side, and the tall man got in next to her, crowding her against the driver. She wondered why he hadn't offered to get in the backseat.

The moment the short, dark-haired man pulled into traffic, Sandra realized she had made a terrible mistake. The younger, taller man casually reached under the front seat. In disbelief, Sandra saw his hand emerge with a long knife. Then it was pressing against her pounding throat. The sharp tip felt like a needle pricking her skin.

He hadn't said anything at first, but now he told her

he wanted her purse. Before she could give it to him, he jerked it out of her hands. Both men were smiling.

With the knife still pushed to her neck, the man took the money out of her billfold, tossing the credit cards and other papers out the car window. Then he threw the purse away.

Fighting panic, Sandra asked the older, friendlier man what they were going to do with her.

He looked at her with the one eye. They intended to "have sex with her." He put it that way. No crude language, simply "have sex."

"All right," Sandra said, "but let me do it on my own."

Maybe they would let her go if she cooperated. She could walk to a telephone and call her aunt collect. They would come get her. She would still have her car and her clothes.

The driver pulled off the interstate. He turned east beneath an underpass, then headed north as if intending to drive back into Austin. A few buildings were scattered along the interstate, but they were still on the far outskirts of the city.

They didn't go very far before the man turned into a parking lot in front of a one-story office building. The pavement continued on the back side of the building, where the man stopped the Oldsmobile. Before he cut the headlights off, Sandra saw a plowed field and, in the distance, some trees.

Sandra knew no one was aware of what had happened to her. She was absolutely alone. Still, she might get through this if she handled it right.

The man with the bad eye also had a knife. He was telling her to get out of the station wagon, but the tall man was already pulling on her.

At first, Sandra's fright had been mixed with anger. These men had offered to help her. Instead she had been robbed. Now she was going to be raped. She began crying.

The one-eyed man spoke almost matter-of-factly. Any woman he wanted, he said, he was going to have. He told Sandra to take off her clothes. Still crying, she slowly removed her blue pullover shirt and slipped out of her jeans. The two men watched her, but grew impatient. They grabbed her, tearing at her bra, panty hose, and panties.

Now the taller man held her arms and the shorter man began kissing her, holding the knife to her throat again. She pleaded, then began struggling.

But at four feet eight inches and weighing only 105 pounds, Sandra was powerless in the big man's arms. The little man raised the knife.

"Oh, my God, no!"

The blade slashed into her chest, ripping her heart. Blood pulsing from the wound, Sandra went limp in the big man's arms. He let her fall to the ground. She rolled over and the blade flashed again. Her dream was over—and her nightmare.

The tall man took Sandra's feet, the little man grabbed her arms, and they carried her to a clump of juniper trees across the field from the parking lot behind the building.

Both men then had intercourse with Sandra's bloody body. In the distance, they could hear the traffic on I-35. When they had had enough of it, the short man left to wipe off the blood.

He didn't feel a thing and, as usual, hadn't enjoyed the sex. She was just another woman, he thought— just a whore like his mother.

His friend didn't like women much either. He enjoyed men or boys much better than he did women, but he never had any trouble with sex, no matter if he was using a vacuum cleaner, another man, or a kid. It seemed like that was just about all he ever talked about.

The tall man stayed behind with the body, using his knife to eviscerate her. Before he left the body, he removed Sandra's diamond and ruby ring and her watch. He stuck them in his pants pocket and walked back through the field to the old station wagon.

Back on I-35, headed south toward San Antonio, they drank more beer but didn't talk much about what they had done. Lucas didn't worry about disposing of their knives. He was never without one. Once cleaned, it came in handy for cutting cheese or spreading peanut butter.

Later, at a flea market just north of San Antonio, Toole sold the jewelry for enough money to keep them in beer and gas for a while. Then they were on the highway again. They had no agenda; they were just two killers on the road.

The next day, Wednesday, October 4, 1979, Sandra's relatives in San Antonio were getting increasingly worried. Sandra had not shown up, and her mother had not heard from her since she had called from Oklahoma.

Thinking the Dodge might have caused trouble again and that Sandra might have been forced to spend the night somewhere until it could be repaired, her cousin drove north from San Antonio. Just south of Austin he saw her car parked on the shoulder of the highway. The backseat was packed with her extra clothing, but he didn't see her purse in the locked car. He got back in his car. Maybe she had checked into a motel until a wrecker could come pick up the Dodge. But none of the garages he checked had any pending work orders for a car like Sandra's, and she was not registered at any of the motels along the interstate.

Most worrisome of all was the fact that she had not called anyone. She wouldn't stay out of touch with her family unless something bad had happened. It didn't look right.

Finally, Sandra's cousin contacted the Austin Police

Department. A patrol officer met him where he had called from a pay phone and followed him to Sandra's parked car. After looking over the car, the officer got the information for a missing person's report. The car was locked, and there was no blood or sign of a struggle nearby. But after talking with the cousin, he had to admit it didn't look good. He noted on the report that "foul play was feared."

By Friday, October 6, with still no word from Sandra, an extensive search of the area near where her car had been found was organized. As a Texas Department of Public Safety (DPS) helicopter hovered overhead, police, Travis County sheriff's deputies, and volunteers searched the ground.

Sandra's parents, Frank and Edna Manley, packed and made reservations to fly to Texas.

Later that afternoon, a newspaper reporter talked with Mrs. Manley. She explained her agreement with Sandra that she would call periodically on her way down to San Antonio.

"I can depend on it when she tells me she's going to do something," she said. "She does it. We're just waiting and praying every minute that we find her— and praying she's alive."

But there was still no trace of Sandra on Saturday.

On Sunday, after learning of Dubbs's disappearance through media accounts, a State Highway Department worker turned in a billfold he had found along the interstate earlier that week. It didn't have any money in it, but it did contain identification and papers belonging to Sandra.

The area of the search was expanded on Monday to include side roads off I-35 and two nearby creeks. The DPS helicopter was up again, circling low over the area, its pilot and an Austin police detective, Sgt. Ron Bruce, scanning the fields along the interstate.

Troy Brown heard the whir of the chopper. Brown,

11

chief engineer for MCI Productions, a television production company, had read about Dubbs's disappearance.

Earlier that day he had noticed tire tracks across the garden behind the building. It had made him mad, but he had not connected it with anything out of the ordinary. However, as he reflected on it, it began to seem more suspicious. Certainly it was the first time someone had driven across his garden. He began to wonder why.

Charles Slaughter, one of Brown's co-workers, offered to follow the tracks. He could hear the helicopter as he walked through the field. He followed the depressions made by the wheels, which led to a cedar brake on the edge of the field. Beneath the scent of the cedar he detected a horrible smell.

He caught a glimpse of two bare, discolored legs protruding from behind the trees. He turned from the sight and broke into a run, fighting nausea. A brown-and-tan sheriff's car was passing on the frontage road. Slaughter ran toward it, waving his arms and yelling.

The deputy spoke into his radio mike, then accelerated up the driveway and across the field to the cedar brake. Other officers quickly reached the scene.

Sandra had been missing for six days. It was October, but the days were still warm. The body of a once attractive woman had been ravaged, first by a killer, then by the elements. The officers, accustomed as they were to dealing with death and its aftermath, had to look away.

Sandra's parents had been walking with a search party farther south on I-35. Sergeant Bruce quickly got to them and told them that a body that fit the general description of their daughter had been found, though there could be no positive identification yet. But clothes found in the field near the body matched those Sandra was believed to have been wearing, he told them.

They wanted to go to her. Bruce tried to handle it delicately. Only officers were allowed in the area, he said. He couldn't tell them how bad she looked.

"We want our baby back," Mrs. Manley sobbed as her husband and other relatives tried to comfort her.

Newspaper reporters and television camera crews gathered nearby. They wanted some on-the-record comment. Bruce did not have much to say, but he tried to be cooperative.

"We don't have any suspects, but we have leads to suspects," he said.

Since Sandra's disappearance was first reported, he continued, someone had contacted police to report having seen a woman who looked like Sandra talking with a man near two parked cars on the side of the interstate.

The witness said he saw the woman about 11:45 P.M. on Tuesday, October 2, the day Sandra had disappeared. The headlights of the rear car had been on, but the car in front was dark, the witness said.

Later that Monday, in the basement morgue of Brackenridge Hospital, Travis County Medical Examiner Dr. Robert Bayardo performed an autopsy on the woman. She had been stabbed thirty-five times and cut open. Because of the advanced decomposition of the body, it was impossible to determine if she had had sexual intercourse near the time of her death, but Bayardo said the nudity and the position of the body indicated a sexual attack.

Sandra's parents took their daughter's body back to Missouri for burial and began the struggle to accept the death of a beautiful young woman who had sought nothing more than a chance to start life anew in Texas.

The Dubbs murder was front-page news, but it stayed in the headlines only a few days. Sheriff's investigators, assisted by Austin police, interviewed those who thought they might have seen Sandra and whoever had stopped to help her, but none of the witnesses had seen enough to help identify the man.

The case troubled Captain John Vasquez, head of the Austin Police Department's Crimes Against Persons division. The mutilation of Dubbs's body had been savage. A very dangerous person was out there, and he and the detectives in his department had virtually nothing to go on. If they couldn't make an arrest, the captain thought, they could at least offer some advice that might save someone else's life.

"We need to say something," Vasquez told a reporter. "If you're female, don't hitchhike, and if you have car trouble, don't leave your car."

Vasquez didn't seriously expect his words to do much good. Unfortunately, there were a whole lot of too-trusting people, not only in his city, but everywhere else.

And there were plenty of others, like whoever killed Sandra Dubbs, who preyed on those trusting people. So just in case there was someone living in the Austin area who had decided to start raping and killing stranded women, Vasquez set a trap.

After it was obvious there was not going to be any easy break in the Dubbs case, Vasquez began planning a decoy operation. A woman police officer would pose as a motorist stranded on I-35. In the event the wrong sort of person stopped to offer help, four other undercover officers carrying 12-gauge shotguns would be hidden nearby.

The twenty-eight-year-old officer who volunteered for the duty was married to another officer. When she asked her husband if he thought she should undertake the risky operation, he said it would have to be her decision.

She made up her mind after seeing the color photographs of Dubbs's body and reading the offense reports. She'd do whatever she could, she told

Vasquez, to catch someone who would do what had been done to Dubbs.

The captain coached her on what to say and how to act. This would be her line: "Please help me. My car heated up and I had to stop. The red light came on, and my husband told me never to drive the car when that light is on. Would you please call John and tell him to come get me? Here's his phone number."

"John" was Captain Vasquez, who would be sitting at police headquarters, waiting near a direct-line telephone.

Near the end of the final briefing Vasquez had one last instruction: "If he tries to grab you, hit the ground."

Wearing a brown skirt, blouse, and hightop boots, the woman officer stood near a car, its hood up. Three weeks before, Dubbs had been at the same location on the side of the interstate.

The officer wore a concealed microphone so sensitive that officers hidden nearby could hear her heart beating. In an hour and a half, twenty people stopped to offer help. None made any untoward comments and sixteen actually called "John."

Too much time was lost convincing the genuine Good Samaritans the stranded woman motorist would be all right. A few of the callers even insisted on going back to stay with the woman until her husband arrived. Those persistent citizens had to be clued in on the undercover operation.

After a few more nights, the project was scrapped. The death of Sandra Dubbs apparently had had an impact on Austin area residents. Those who stopped to help the decoy did so out of genuine concern for her safety. No one had attempted to harm her.

The local news media had held back on the decoy story until the police ended the operation. The scheme could have worked, but Vasquez had known all along that it was a long shot. Like a lot of cops, he believed in hunches. In this case, though he still could not rule out the possibility that someone from Austin was behind the brutal sex killing, he had the feeling that whoever killed Dubbs was not a local. He just hoped the killer didn't ever show up again.

The one-eyed man and his soft-voiced friend were on the road. But they would be back.

CHAPTER TWO

"There ain't nobody goin' to find out nothin' 'bout me unless they go investigate where I was born, raised, the kind of people I grew up with. . . . I don't want 'em just takin' my word. . . ."

—Henry Lee Lucas
Williamson County, Texas, Jail
July 17, 1984

Like most box camera images taken by amateurs, the pictures were as plain as the people in them. One deckle-edged snapshot, marred by a diagonal crease across its faded emulsion, showed six people in their Sunday best standing together outdoors, grimly facing the photographer with their hands at their sides or folded formally in front of them. Something about the stern-looking older woman in the baggy dress and little round hat caught the eye first. The others were gathered around her, posing stiffly—distant though close together. The woman wearing the hat clearly had the power.

Another picture was of a dark-haired, broad-shouldered, thick-armed man in white shirt and overalls. It took a moment to realize the perspective was

17

askew. At first glance, it seemed like the man was standing. But the pine trees in the background appeared higher than they should in relation to a man on his feet, and the fair-haired little boy in shorts towered over the man like the trees. Though the picture's bizarre composition betrayed the fact on analysis, it did not show that the man had no legs. His mouth was fixed in a thin, somber line. His brows were furrowed and the lines on his face showed years of rough living. The little boy's head hung downward, like that of a whipped puppy. His small hand rested on the man's wide shoulder, but the touch was light, tentative, as if someone had ordered him to put his hand there even though he hadn't wanted to. The two snapshots had only one thing in common. No one in them—not the women in their finest hats, not the men in their Sunday-go-to-meeting suits, not the dark-haired man or the little boy—looked happy.

Four decades later, after pictures of the man who had been that little boy appeared in newspapers and magazines around the world, when people would have occasion to examine the old photographs, they would stare at the family shown in them and wonder why it had happened. Then, like a print slowly materializing in a darkroom tray, they would realize the answer was there, in those inexpert photographs.

Viola Lucas, half Chippewa Indian, had straight black hair, high cheeks, a dark complexion, and only a few teeth. Mountain living and moonshine had left her with a hard, stern face, a look that went perfectly with her vicious nature. "She was mean as a rattlesnake," one person who knew her later recalled. Another called her "right harsh." She stood a little over five feet three inches and wore long blue or black sack dresses and old shoes. Her two boys and her legless husband were all scared of her, especially when she had a belly full of her own crystal-clear corn mash, which was most of the time. But her mean streak did not discourage the men who came to pay her fifty cents to lift her dress for quick, passionless sex on the old bed in the front room of the Lucas cabin. When the customers showed up, she seldom even bothered to spit out the snuff she chewed most of the time. Nor did she go to the trouble of shooing her kids, or even her husband, out of the cabin when she was turning a trick. In fact, though she was usually indifferent to the bedspring-squeaking, frantic pounding of her male callers, she did seem to enjoy having her boys and husband watch her lying there with her legs spread. But sometimes she was too drunk to notice anyone else was in the room except the man who had just given her four bits.

Folks in the Depression-ravaged backwoods country of Montgomery County, Virginia, knew Viola had men out to her place, but they had trouble understanding why someone would pay for her sexual favors. In her late forties, Viola was no Daisy Mae. She used most of the water they had to haul up from the creek for making moonshine, not bathing. "They didn't know what water was for," someone who knew Viola and her family later recalled. They remembered her as a woman with terrible body odor, who preferred adding a new layer of clothes to washing. While decent people pretty much shunned her, they tended to take pity on her children and her drunken husband, who kept himself up a little better than the woman he lived with. Most folks agreed Viola Lucas would drive any man to drink.

The Lucas place was near Craig Creek, between Brushy and Get mountains on the edge of the vast Jefferson National Forest about nine miles from Blacksburg, Virginia, on the western edge of Appalachia. Their tarpaper-covered cabin, a burned-out schoolhouse on land still owned by the county, stood in a clearing at the end of a dirt road a couple of hundred yards off the unpaved road that went into Blacksburg. No one else lived within two miles of the Lucas cabin.

Nellie Viola Dixon, born in Alderson, West Virginia, had been married before to a footloose coal miner and timber cutter named Warden Waugh. Waugh was a man who seemed to come home only long enough to get her pregnant, and then he would be gone again. After Viola had seven children, four daughters and three boys, she and Waugh split up. The children were farmed out to foster homes and would not see their natural mother again until they were grown. After taking up with Anderson Lucas—some said they were married, some said they just lived together—Viola had a son when she was thirty-five. Then, five years later, on August 23, 1936, she had another son. After-church gossip had it that the second boy, Henry Lee, was not Lucas's child, a rumor supported in Henry's childhood by Viola's open carrying on with a retarded younger man named Bernie Dowdy who lived on nearby Brushy Mountain. Eventually, Viola moved Bernie in with the rest of the family, telling people he had no one else to take care of him. "He wets the bed and everything else, stinks like a hog," Henry later recalled. Bernie was sharing that sometimes wet bed with Henry's mother. One day when he came home from school, Henry walked into the shack to find Bernie in bed with his mother. Viola threatened to beat her son if he didn't stay and watch.

People said that if Anderson Lucas had not lost both legs in the railroad accident, maybe he could have kept his wife in line. He had been a brakeman on a freight train, but an on-the-job accident when he was twenty-one severed one of his legs at the knee, the other just below the knee. With no legs he had no job, and the railroad did not even pay his hospital bill. He managed to make a little money skinning minks or selling pencils in town for a nickel apiece, hopping on his hands from corner to corner like a giant rabbit. Folks started calling him "No Legs" and "Ass and Elbows."

Booze seemed to help the phantom pain he sometimes felt in his nonexistent legs and the deeper torment he suffered from Viola. He yelled at her and did what he could do, but if he made too much of a fuss, she took to him with a board or anything else she could find. Once, in a drunken brawl, he did lash out with one of his powerful arms and stick Bernie in the side with his knife, inflicting a minor wound. Bernie grabbed the knife away from the double amputee and slashed back, nicking off a piece of Anderson Lucas's ear.

The two boys, Andrew Preston and Henry Lee, had it worse than Anderson Lucas. Viola was absolute ruler of the household, a power she used ruthlessly. If one of her boys did something she did not like, she did not take after them with a switch, like most mountain women might. She used a thick limb or, more often, a board.

"They was all the time pounding on me, but I guess I deserved it," her youngest son later recalled.

When it was time for Henry to begin his schooling in 1942, Viola sent him to Mt. Tabor School with long, curly hair. He looked like a little girl. Worse yet, she made him wear a dress. Annie Hall, one of the teachers, took Henry to get a boy's haircut and found him some overalls. When she saw what Henry's teacher had done, Viola stormed to the school and cussed her out for interfering with her son.

When Henry showed up at school battered and bruised, he would tell his teacher he had fallen or gotten in a fight with his brother. His teachers knew better, but there was nothing they could do about it.

About a year after he started school, Viola took her son into Blacksburg one day. She dragged him around town, going from place to place looking for someone. Finally, she pointed to a man Henry had never seen before, and said, "He's your real pa." Sometime later, Henry asked Anderson Lucas if the other man was his father. "That's right, boy."

Anderson Lucas, who could saw out a tolerable breakdown on a fiddle until he got too drunk to work the bow, treated Henry better than his mother did— at least when he was sober. People who knew him remembered him as a gentle person when he wasn't drunk. Sober, he wouldn't beat the boys. Drunk, he once chased Henry around the old Model T truck he'd rigged up with levers to be able to drive. One of the townspeople in Blacksburg saw the father hopping around in pursuit of his son and felt bad for the boy. When Anderson didn't need the money for something to drink, sometimes he'd give Henry and Andrew a few coins so they could go to town and see a movie. "We'd get beat for going, but we'd go," Henry later recalled. Viola Lucas did not want what little money Anderson managed to bring in wasted on the kids.

The one creature that seemed to return Henry's affection was a horse his parents owned. At one point the mare grew heavy with foal, and eventually went into labor. When the horse seemed to be having a hard time of it, Viola Lucas came out of the cabin with a rifle and shot the animal, leaving the colt to die inside its mother. Then Viola whipped the distraught Henry, complaining she was going to have to pay to have the carcass hauled off.

Almost anything could trigger Viola Lucas's explosive temper. Once, when Henry did not fetch some firewood fast enough, Viola swung a board at her son and hit him solidly on the back of his head. Henry crumpled to the ground and was unconscious for three days before someone finally decided the boy ought to go to the hospital. The doctor was told Henry had fallen off a ladder. From then on, Henry periodically suffered dizzy spells, blackouts, and episodes he later described as feeling like he was floating in the air.

Viola Lucas's violence was not always toward her family. One day when Henry was about six, he was sitting behind the car of one of his mother's customers, talking with his older brother, when the man came running out of the cabin. Viola was right behind him, a pistol in hand. Henry heard a shot and saw the man grab his leg. The bullet tore through his limb, kicking up dust at Henry's feet. Blood spewed from the small hole in the fellow's pants. Two buddies who had been outside in the car hustled their wounded friend into the Model A and sped off down the road as Viola cursed them loudly. Henry never knew why his mother had found it necessary to shoot the man.

Another time, Viola had taken out after another of her male visitors with a shotgun, peppering the man's behind with birdshot. If either of the two men ever bothered telling the sheriff about the shootings, the law never came around the Lucas place. They were willing to leave well enough alone.

With Henry going to school, Viola figured he was old enough to help her operate the still that was the family's main source of income, though they did everything from selling pine knots to begging to get by. Henry learned to mix the yeast and sugar into the corn mash, tend the fire, and fill the jugs and jars with the watery-looking white lightning. Viola sold the stuff for four dollars a pint. Before long, Henry acquired a taste for alcohol himself. A few swallows of the moonshine kicked like a mule, but the next effect of the burning liquor was a wonderful sense of well-being. That was a feeling Henry could not get any other way.

Viola prepared meals for herself and Bernie, but usually would not bother to cook for her family. The children had to learn to fend for themselves. Henry got to be a good shot with a .22 and brought home squirrels and rabbits for food. Henry, Andrew, and their father also resorted to stealing food from stores in Blacksburg or rifling through trash cans for table scraps.

At school, Henry's teacher gave him sandwiches, and the parents of some of his classmates sometimes had him over for a meal. When he went into other people's homes and had corn bread and beans off clean plates and bowls, he began to realize that everyone did not live like he did.

One thing he did have in common with the other boys who grew up around Coal Bank Hollow was being handy with a knife, a basic tool of mountain life. A good pocketknife, usually a barlow, was virtually every mountain boy's most prized possession. Both of the Lucas boys depended on their knives, which they prided themselves on keeping sharp. In the Virginia mountains, a knife was a matter both of necessity and pleasure.

In 1943, while trying to make a swing out of a grapevine, Andrew cut at the vine with Henry holding it. The knife slipped, slicing Henry across the nose and eye. The accidental blow left Henry with a puncture wound to his eyeball. When he wiped enough blood off his dirty face to be able to make out anything at all, his vision was shadowy, and he could not see to the side.

Viola told the doctor and others that her son had been climbing around on a grapevine and fell on a pair of scissors, but eventually it came out that Henry's older brother had inflicted the injury. Though Henry was in the Roanoke hospital for weeks, his mother visited him only once.

When Henry was finally able to make it back to school, a sympathetic teacher ordered special large-print books for him. Henry and the other kids played rough, and the teachers had to be tough themselves to maintain a semblance of discipline. One day, when an exasperated teacher struck out at another student with her metal-edged ruler, Henry caught the blow accidentally. To the horror of the teacher, his injured eye ruptured. At the hospital, the doctor had to remove the traumatized eye. As soon as he recovered from that procedure, Henry was fitted for a glass eye. The work was not well done. The prosthesis hung slightly askew in his socket, beneath a droopy eyelid. Henry was embarrassed by the false eye, which he made worse-looking by not keeping it clean.

Viola Lucas could do nothing about her son's lost eye, but some in Coal Bank Hollow whispered that she did have unusual powers.

When they had any money, the Lucas family traded at a service station in town. Once, when the Lucases were getting gasoline for their old truck, Viola noticed a wart on the wrist of A. A. Lafon, the attendant. The wart had appeared on his wrist about a week before and had been bothering him.

Viola grabbed Lafon's hand and rubbed the wart with her fingers.

"Now don't speak to me any more before I leave," she said, getting back in the truck.

Lafon looked down at the wart, shook his head, and watched the Lucases drive away.

About a week later, the wart came off.

Lafon, baffled, told the station owner about the incident.

The owner listened, then shook his head. "You know she ain't nothing but a witch," he said.

If others saw evil in Viola Lucas, she claimed she saw it in her youngest son. Often, when beating him, she told him the pain she was inflicting was for his own good. The devil had to be beaten from him, she said. But she was beginning to worry that it might already be too late. The future she saw for her boy was grim. You will die in prison, she once predicted.

When Henry was young, people who lived along Coal Bank Hollow called him Little Henry and generally felt sorry for the withdrawn, obviously abused child who often was without shoes and always was without socks. But as he grew older, opinions began to change. It began with the stealing: he would go into a store while a partner in crime stayed outside to catch the ball or sack of peanuts Henry would toss outside. Other times, alone, Henry would slip into someone's house and take items of value. "I started stealing, I guess, as soon as I was old enough to run fast," Lucas would later say.

As cruel as his mother could be to him, and despite her own background, sometimes she at least tried to teach him the difference between right and wrong. Once, when she found he had stolen a piece of jewelry, she dragged him to the owner's house and ordered him to return it with an apology. As Henry tearfully did as he was told, Viola said she was going to beat him thoroughly for the theft. No need to do that, they said. His apology is good enough.

On another occasion, when Viola discovered her son had stolen two watches from a store, she went out into the woods and buried them to prevent the crime from being connected to her son.

Henry began roaming the countryside, staying away from home as much as possible. He had no close friends and never passed up a chance to fight. Once a schoolmate beat him up for chunking a rock at his dog for no apparent reason. If he lost a fight, as he did in this case, the beating never seemed to bother him. He was used to getting hit.

At school, when he was in attendance, Henry proved to be of average intelligence and made average grades. But his chaotic home life took its toll. Almost always late to class, he seemed without ambition, willing only to do what it took to get by. His teachers felt he could have done well if he had only applied himself, but at fourteen he was still only in the fifth grade.

Henry was ahead of his class, however, in other areas. He smoked when he could afford cigarettes or succeeded in stealing them, and he drank moonshine and anything else he could get. And he had found something that would, at least temporarily, get his mind off his squalid surroundings and the ever-present threat of physical and mental abuse from his mother: sex.

When he was ten, Bernie Dowdy had told him to follow him up to the top of Brushy Mountain. The twenty-seven-year-old led a bawling calf as they moved through the woods toward the mountaintop. As Lucas looked on, a smiling Bernie stuck his knife in the wide-eyed calf's throat. With the dying animal still quivering, Bernie unbuttoned his overalls and had intercourse with the carcass. Lucas watched as the man thrust himself into the dead animal, oblivious to anything around him, as the blood soaked into the ground. Then it was Lucas's turn with the dead calf. Afterward, the young boy could hardly believe how good it had made him feel.

He began masturbating daily. The solitary sex, in the outhouse or out in the woods somewhere, for a time got his mind off his misery. He liked to slip around at night peeping in windows, hoping for a glimpse of feminine flesh. When he could, he had sex with animals, just like Bernie had shown him. Though Bernie had used a calf that first time, Lucas usually had to settle for a dog. They were easier to handle and not missed as quickly as someone's calf or goat. He found he got as much pleasure out of killing an animal as having sex with it. He could count on little else, but this was a means of making himself feel good.

27

Later, when Lucas was thirteen, Bernie took him to a twenty-year-old woman who agreed to let Lucas have traditional sex for the first time. But it was a setup. Just as Lucas was approaching an orgasm, the woman ordered him to get off of her and pushed him away before he reached a climax. She and Bernie both laughed heartily as Lucas stormed off in frustration. Bernie, who had no sense of commitment to Viola Lucas, then took over where her son left off with the accommodating young mountain woman. Lucas liked sex, but he was beginning to get fed up with women. They all seemed to be whores who could not be trusted.

In 1950, Anderson Lucas died. One winter night, drunk and disgusted with Viola, he crawled out of their cabin into the snow and passed out. No one bothered to drag him back inside. "That's what made him die," Lucas later recalled. "He laid out in the snow and caught pneumonia." That had been the doctor's conclusion as well, but there was talk around the hollow that Anderson Lucas had some bad bruises on his head when he died.

Years later, the man whose wart had disappeared after Viola rubbed it for him recalled a conversation he had had with George Arrington, the sheriff when Anderson Lucas died.

Asked about rumors that Lucas had died from a blow to the head, the sheriff replied: "What am I gonna do? There's no evidence. I can't convict anybody on talk. I reckon I'll just let 'em bury the man."

Anderson Lucas was to be buried in a mountaintop cemetery next to his father. Andrew took his mother and brother to the funeral in the old Plymouth he had. Others at the service noticed that Viola did not seem particularly bereaved. Afterward, Andrew drove them into Blacksburg. Now that the one parent who had even occasionally treated him with kindness was

28

dead, Henry decided he was not going back home. When he told his brother that, Viola overheard and said he wasn't going anywhere. "I just told her I was going. I didn't care what she said," her son would later say.

As soon as she could after the funeral, Viola and Bernie moved to another house. The shack where Henry grew up eventually burned down.

Henry Lucas got a job for a short time as a farmhand. Then he lived for a while with one of his half sisters in Middlebrook, but soon wandered back to the Blacksburg area. He managed to get from place to place by walking or hitchhiking, but he wanted a car. He had learned to drive Andrew's Plymouth, which he had sometimes been able to use around Blacksburg. He liked the power and freedom of being behind the wheel of a fast car. Driving a car recklessly was what put him in jail for the first time.

His second trip to jail was more serious. On March 12, 1952, he was picked up along with his two older half brothers, Harry and Elmer Waugh, for burglary. They had broken into an appliance store and Henry had made off with a battery-powered radio. After a hearing, he was commited to a vocational school for juvenile delinquents in Beaumont, Virginia. But while still in the county jail at Christiansburg, Henry managed to saw out some bars and escape. After a week or so on the dodge, hiding under houses, he decided to turn himself in. On June 12, 1952, he was taken to the Beaumont Training School for Boys.

He did not like the notion of being locked up, but in another sense it seemed to Lucas that crime did indeed pay. For the first time in his life he was someplace with plumbing and electricity. The school even had a television set. Compared with the dirt-floor cabin he grew up in, life at the reform school was luxurious.

Shortly after his arrival at the state institution, the staff began an evaluation of the one-eyed fifteen-year-old from the backwoods of Montgomery County. An employee who took his history noted that Lucas had lived in a small shack of "four rooms, one of which houses two goats that belong to roomer who is a half-witted man who owns half interest in the house." His mother, the worker noted, "drank heavily and admits that she has boot-legged in the past."

Lucas's eye, the report said, drained at times, and his eyelid appeared lightly inflamed. The teenager said he thought he ought to be given a bigger glass eye. Except for enlarged tonsils, he was in pretty good health. His IQ tested out at 76.

The inmates of the school were kept in companies, each with a supervisor. Lucas was assigned to Company B. In August his supervisor reported that the teenager had a "good personality," though he "wants his way quite a bit. . . . One of his major drawbacks is the fact that he needs close supervision for any job that he undertakes. His adjustment is borderline and . . . it is quite difficult to get to know Henry. It seems that he has somewhat of a wall around him and will not verbalize about his problems."

One of Lucas's problems, however, was obvious to school officials: his mother. When Lucas wrote her to demand that she send him assorted personal items to make his stay in the school more comfortable, she replied that she did not have the money to buy him anything. He wrote an angry letter back, telling her to "get out and borrow the money." But nothing came for him, and she did not visit him.

That fall he was transferred to Company K. On October 8 he was fitted for a new artificial eye. Just over a week later, he was reported AWOL. On October 18, however, he was arrested in Bedford, Virginia. The offense cost him thirty whip strokes. He tried to run off one more time and was again lashed after he was caught and returned to the school. After that he quit trying to get away.

A year after his admission, school officials felt they were seeing some signs of improvement in Lucas. He got along well with the other boys in his company, was average in his learning habits, was doing well in his work at the school tailor shop, and observed the rules. His supervisor said Lucas was "rather quiet in school but pleasant when spoken to. He is courteous and polite, cooperative and a willing helper."

Three months away from his seventeenth birthday, on May 29, 1953, Lucas was promoted to the sixth grade. By that summer, after another assessment that found Lucas seemed "to be improving generally and trying hard to do what is right," Lucas was recommended for release in September.

A final report on Lucas concluded he had "reached his maximum adjustment here" and had progressed since his admission. However, the report was qualified: "Although Henry has not taken the initiative to better himself in our program, he has done that which has been required of him. He has not entered into any phases of the program with any enthusiasm. He has, during recent months, abided by the rules and regulations more willingly and it is felt that he has been truthful, but he has not become involved in any more situations where it was necessary for him to alibi his way out."

Lucas's time in the boys' school did not topple the wall the teenager had around him: "He usually appears happy and cheerful but it is difficult to learn this boy's true feelings about anything as he does not relate very well."

After his release from the vocational school, Lucas was in no mood to go back to Blacksburg. He went to Ingalls, North Carolina, where brother Andrew, who had joined the Navy, was stationed.

From North Carolina, Lucas went to Staunton,

Virginia, where he lived with one of his half sisters, Nora Crawford. He got a job as a farmhand, but there were easier ways to get money. On June 28, 1954, Lucas was arrested again for burglary. Viola Lucas did not bother to come to her son's trial. Now eighteen, Henry was convicted and sentenced to four years in the state penitentiary in Richmond.

The lashes laid on him at the vocational school had reminded him of home, but otherwise, Lucas did not find institutional life too unpleasant. He worked in the fields or on road gangs, but he had regular meals, plenty of potato mash alcohol to drink, and, compared with the shack he grew up in, a decent place to stay.

Prison was not pleasant enough to discourage him from escaping. On May 28, 1956, Lucas and a pal managed to slip off from a work crew, stole a car in Kentucky, and headed north. When the car ran out of gas in Troy, Ohio, they abandoned it and hitchhiked to Monroe, Michigan, where they stole another vehicle. From there, they drove west to Lenawee County, where half sister Opal Jennings lived.

Lucas's freedom was short-lived. On June 19, 1956, he was arrested by police in Clinton, Michigan. Convicted in Detroit of violating the federal Dyer Act (transporting a stolen car across state lines), Lucas was committed to the federal reformatory at Chillicothe, Ohio. After serving his eighteen-month sentence, he was transferred to Virginia to finish his burglary sentence.

In prison, Lucas was learning a variety of skills, from carpentry in the chair factory to sewing in the prison tailor shop. At Chillicothe, he had been an elevator operator. According to prison records, he also was enjoying regular sex as the passive partner in fellatio and the active participant in anal intercourse. He was paying for his burglary conviction, but the price did not seem too high.

On August 13, 1959, the rehabilitation supervisor for the Virginia State Penitentiary dictated a letter to Opal Jennings. He wrote that an attempt had been made to work out a parole plan for Lucas, but the effort was unsuccessful. In fact, the parole board had interviewed Lucas on May 26 and voted to deny him parole. At any rate, Lucas would be freed on September 2, the expiration date of his sentence.

The rehabilitation official did not go into why parole had been denied, but Lucas's escape probably had something to do with it.

Even though the parole board wanted Lucas to stay behind bars until he had served every day of his sentence, the rehabilitation officer, doing his job, sought help for the young inmate.

"It is our feeling that Henry should return to a home where he is accepted and where he could receive mature advice and some guidance," the official said in the letter to Lucas's half sister Opal. "At the present time it does not appear we will be able to find a place for him in Virginia."

Lucas, he continued, "is anxious to be helped, but . . . somewhat discouraged by the lack of outside aid he will have. When one studies Henry's background, it is obvious that he is insecure. He needs a home in which he would feel wanted and receive assistance in finding employment. It is hoped that you might be able to accept Henry into your home and provide him with the chance he will need when he is released."

On September 2, 1959, Lucas was discharged from the Virginia prison with $83.09 in his pocket. The prison policy was to provide a released inmate free transportation either to his home or anyplace in Virginia. Lucas requested to go to Alexandria, Virginia, but he only stayed there a day. Then he headed back to Michigan.

News of Lucas's release from prison was of special

interest to the police chief in Blacksburg, who wrote the prison to find out where Lucas had gone after his discharge. Prison superintendent W. F. Smyth, Jr., replied: "As you probably know, he did not have too good a conduct record while in the penitentiary. One of our officers tells me that Lucas planned to go to Michigan when he left here. . . . Whether he ever arrived there or not I am unable to say."

The chief was happy to learn a short time later that Lucas was indeed in Michigan, two states away from Blacksburg and Montgomery County. His half sister Opal had decided to give Lucas the chance his rehabilitation officer believed he needed.

The man who showed up at Tecumseh, Michigan, an industrial town in rural Lenawee County, southwest of Detroit, was no longer merely a troubled youth who had had a miserable home life, a pudgy-faced little boy in oversized hand-me-down clothes whom most folks felt sorry for. At twenty-three, Lucas was a hardened ex-con. The survival skills he had had to develop as a child were even more finely honed by years behind bars. About the only thing that had not changed since he had left home nine years earlier was a burning hatred of his mother. In fact, it was stronger. He stood five feet eight inches, weighed 150 pounds, had long wavy brown hair, and came out of prison covered with tattoos. A battleship rode anchor on his left outside forearm, guarding a naked woman on the other side of the arm. On the upper portion of the same arm was a cluster of cherries bearing the witty legend HERE'S MINE, WHERE'S YOURS? On his right outside forearm a ribbon honored someone named Sylvella. Farther up the arm was another woman, this one clothed. A final tattoo was less visible. Burned into his left thigh was a water pitcher with a curious label—LOVE-MOM.

CHAPTER THREE

William Eldridge lay in bed trying to figure out why he was suddenly awake. Something had thumped heavily against the floor over on the other side of the house. The forty-seven-year-old factory worker guessed the folks next door had carried some more wood in for their stove and maybe dropped a log. It was a cold night. In fact, his landlady's mother had loaned him an extra blanket. He could make out voices through the wall, but he was a little hard of hearing and could not tell for sure if someone was talking in the other apartment or just playing a radio. Since he was awake anyway, he swung out of bed to go to the bathroom. Eldridge flushed the toilet, looked at the clock, saw that it was after 3:00 A.M., and went back to bed. He still had a few hours to sleep before it would be time to get up and head to the plant.

January 11, 1960, had been a fairly quiet night in the small township of Tecumseh, Michigan, but then most nights were. As Police Chief George Kilbourn went through the small stack of reports on his desk, he noted that the only thing that had happened overnight was the burglary of Johnnie & Bill's Cities Service, a garage at 200 East Patterson. Someone had smashed a window and reached through to open the garage door to get at a 1957 Ford on the rack inside. The car had been stolen. Chief Kilbourn and his officers had to contend with the usual problems any small-town police department faced—traffic enforcement, drunks, fights, thefts and burglaries—but violent crime was rare. Most of the rough stuff went on up in Detroit.

But about 12:40 that afternoon, a woman in her mid-forties came running into the police station. Chief Kilbourn recognized her as Opal Jennings. She lived on a farm outside Tecumseh but owned a house in town. He and an FBI agent had arrested her younger half brother, Henry Lucas, a few years back after he escaped from the pen and stole a couple of cars. The chief saw she was breathing hard and had tears in her eyes.

"My mother's dead," she said. "I just found her."

"Has she been ill?" the chief said, standing.

"No, she hasn't," Mrs. Jennings said, her chest heaving. "Somebody needs to go back with me—I don't want go back by myself."

The house was only a few blocks from the station. Chief Kilbourn radioed for one of his officers, George Kempf, to meet him there. The chief arrived moments later with Mrs. Jennings. She unlocked the back door of the house, then opened the front door for the officers, who hurried up the stairs to the bedroom.

An elderly woman, her dress pulled up far enough to expose the tops of her stockings, lay face up on the floor between two double beds. A pair of khaki pants were under her head. Her right arm was crossed over her chest, while the left one lay palm up on the floral carpet.

The chief, a big man, stooped down for a closer look. She was already cold to the touch. He saw what looked to be a slight bruise or cut on the side of her neck. A small amount of blood had dried around her mouth and on her left cheek.

Kilbourn stood and looked around the room. An assortment of clothes were piled up at the foot of one of the beds and other clothing was scattered on the floor. A drinking glass was on the floor, its contents long since soaked into the carpet. A short-handled broom lay within reach of the dead woman on the bed to her left, which was a bare mattress on a boxspring.

Satisfied that there was nothing to be done for the woman, Kilbourn went back downstairs to talk with Mrs. Jennings.

"Do you know if she had had a fight with someone recently?"

Mrs. Jennings looked at the chief in surprise. She had assumed her mother had had a fatal heart attack. Yesterday she had worked out at their farm, shucking corn. Maybe it had been too much for her. Before she could answer, he had another question.

"Did she have a scratch or cut on her neck the last time you saw her?"

"She and Henry were arguin' last night, but they didn't come to blows, least not while I was with them," she said. "I don't remember seeing anything on her neck, either."

Kilbourn hated to question Mrs. Jennings when she was upset, but there were things he needed to know pretty quick. He did not think the woman upstairs had died of natural causes.

"Can you tell me a little more about your mother? I know this is hard," the chief said.

"Her name's Viola Lucas," Mrs. Jennings told the chief. "We don't know exactly how old she is. She's sixty-something, late sixties. She was about twenty when she had me.

"She's been staying with us since right before Thanksgiving," Mrs. Jennings continued. "She was going to take the bus back to Virginia this afternoon and I had come by to help her pack. That's how I came to find her. When I saw her, I walked up to her and touched her with my shoe. I knew she was dead because she was stiff. I was real scared and I ran and got you."

Mrs. Jennings told Chief Kilbourn she had last seen her mother about 9:30 or 10:00 P.M. the night before.

"My husband and I, Mother, and Henry had been over at Bagshaw's," she said. "We were having a few beers and watching that TV show, 'Bourbon Street Beat.' She and Henry had words and she went off to a table by herself and had a beer with a Mexican fellow. But later on she and Henry left to go to the house."

Chief Kilbourn was not surprised to hear that Mrs. Lucas and her son, the fellow he'd arrested back in '56, had been at Bagshaw's. The tavern, one of the town's two popular drinking spots, was across the street from the police station. Considering the number of calls his officers had to answer there, the nearness was convenient, if sometimes annoying.

"Where do you think Henry is now, Mrs. Jennings?"

"Well, last night I helped him fill out an application for a job at the Meyers Aircraft plant," she said. "He was supposed to take that over there this morning. He was hoping to get a metalworking job. Maybe they hired him on the spot."

"If you hear from him, tell him we need to talk to him," Kilbourn said. "I think you'd better call your husband to come get you. We're going to need to look things over a little more before we move your mother."

The chief notified the coroner and as soon as he could called the prosecutor's office. He also telephoned the Michigan State Police, which had a post at nearby Clinton. He was going to need some outside help—he only had six officers in his department with only one or two of those on duty at any given time.

At 4:15 P.M., Dr. J. H. Ahronheim began an autopsy on the body, which had been taken to a local funeral home after the officers photographed the scene inside the bedroom. Rigor mortis had already set in and the body was cold, the pathologist noted. On the right side of the woman's neck, four centimeters below and three centimeters behind the right ear lobe, the doctor found a Y-shaped slitlike stab wound. When he exposed the neck tissues, he found the wound was about 2.5 inches deep and had pierced the innominate artery in two separate places. The doctor also noted superficial bruises on the neck that he believed to be choke marks.

The stab wound, he told the officers present at the post mortem, was the primary cause of death. The wound had brought about hemorrhaging and edema in the neck and possibly had damaged the vagus nerve, which controls the heartbeat. Mrs. Lucas had most likely lived for a time after her wound was inflicted, he added.

While Dr. Ahronheim was completing his autopsy, the man who rented the other side of the Jennings house came to the police station at the request of Chief Kilbourn. William Eldridge said he had rented the east side of the house on Sunday, January 10, from Mrs. Jennings. The following night, she and her husband, along with Mrs. Lucas and her son, visited with him for a while. He gave Lucas an application so he could try for a job at the aircraft plant where he worked, Mrs. Lucas lent him a blanket, and they left, Eldridge said.

"Then I worked for a while and about ten-thirty P.M. I went over to the other side of the house to fix myself some coffee because I did not have the gas turned on in my side of the house yet," Eldridge told officers. "I went to bed about eleven P.M."

He told Kilbourn and the other officers about being awakened by a noise in the early morning hours, something he had thought nothing of at the time.

"I got up about six-thirty . . . and when I went out to fix my coffee and eat I saw the back door was open about six inches and the gas burner was on," Eldridge said.

He went into the room where Henry Lucas had been staying and found it empty. On the floor by the couch was a bowl. Then Eldridge noticed the job application Lucas was supposed to turn in at the plant that day. Wondering why Lucas had left the application in the apartment, Eldridge ate his breakfast and went to work.

Kilbourn and Michigan State Police detective Sgt. C. H. Southworth were taking a statement from Mrs. Jennings when a man came to the station and asked to see the chief. The owner of Bagshaw's Tavern had found in a trash can a letter that someone had torn into small pieces.

"I don't know if it amounts to anything, but I think this letter was to Henry from Stella Curtis," the bar owner said. "I've seen 'em in there together before."

Using Scotch tape, Kilbourn painstakingly put the four-page handwritten letter back together. "Read all before you get mad" was written at the top of the letter, which was addressed to "Henry" and dated September 14.

Kilbourn and the other officers read the letter.

Henry,

I don't know just how to say this, but it just has to be said. There are so many things that have to be straightened out. First I'm gonna stop going out till things are cooled off. If you or Randy get into trouble it's gonna be my fault. Second, Randy doesn't even know where you live, so how can he shoot at you? Third, if you keep carrying those knives around then you are really gonna get into trouble. So wise up and live right. . . . Don't blame Randy. Cause I'm not going with him either.

I'm gonna return your ring so I will be free to make any decision. When I'm with you I have a good time. But, I'm not sure if it's just the good times I'm after or what. So I have to find out. If you can, please go out so you can have a chance to find out what I mean. You have never gone with anyone but me for so long that you don't know what love really is. Don't feel bad or hate me but I've got to live the way I find best. . . .

Don't come over for a while. I'll let you know when I've reached a decision. . . .

On the following day, Chief Kilbourn, Sgt. Southworth, and detective Leslie Wykes met with the twenty-two-year-old woman who wrote the "Dear John" letter to Lucas. The redheaded divorcee said she had met Lucas at a Stanley home products party at Mrs. Jennings's house in the late spring of 1956, when Lucas was briefly free after escaping from prison. She only saw him a couple of times before he was arrested and returned to prison, she added, and did not see him again until his release that September.

Lucas and an ex-boyfriend of hers—the Randy mentioned in her letter—had had words, she said, which was why she had quit dating both of them.

"Henry came to my house one night . . . and said that Randy had been at his house and took a shot at him and if he did not watch out that he had a knife and he knew how to use it," she said.

She told the officers she had seen Lucas with a small pearl-handled pocketknife and a butcher knife at various times. He always seemed to be sharpening them, honing them to a razor's edge.

"I . . . told him that he had better give me the butcher knife before he got into trouble," she continued. "Henry said that even if I got that one, he had others."

Stella also told the officers that Lucas blamed his mother for the fact he had been in prison and that he "did not like the idea of his mother being here [in Tecumseh] for fear of her interfering with him."

Kilbourn thanked her for her information. She had clearly been frightened by Lucas's fondness for knives. Her letter to him had probably saved her some trouble.

"If you hear from him, give me a call," the chief said.

Since Lucas apparently had been the last person to see his mother alive, Chief Kilbourn had the state police put out a broadcast to pick him up for questioning. He had not shown up at the aircraft plant and no one had seen him since he and his mother left Bagshaw's Tavern. The chief figured there was a good chance it was Lucas who had broken into the garage and stolen the 1957 Ford. The broadcast had gone out over the Michigan and Ohio state police radio channels the same afternoon Viola Lucas's body was discovered.

About 1:30 P.M. on Sunday, January 16, Ohio Highway Patrol trooper H. W. Lowe was driving just west of Toledo, Ohio, when a hitchhiker caught his eye. The young man had no baggage and was shabbily dressed. The officer decided to find out who he was and where he was headed.

Lowe made a U-turn, flipped on his flashing red light, and pulled his patrol car off the roadway.

"State Police," he said as he stepped out of his car. "Where you headed?"

"Michigan," the man replied.

"Can I see some identification, please?"

Alternating between watching the traffic and keeping an eye on the young man, Trooper Lowe waited patiently while the hitchhiker dug a driver's license and draft card from his pants.

When the trooper read the name on the license, his casual attitude toward the hitchhiker changed. The Michigan license the man produced had been issued to Henry Lee Lucas of Tecumseh, Michigan. The hitchhiker, who Lowe noted had only one eye, matched the description given on the license. The trooper knew that Lucas was wanted in Michigan as a suspect in the murder of his mother.

"You're under arrest for first-degree murder," Lowe said, watching the hitchhiker's hands. "Slowly turn around and put your hands up."

Lowe patted the young man down, finding a pocket-knife in his overcoat. The trooper snapped the handcuffs on and helped him into the patrol car.

En route to the highway patrol post, Lowe checked by radio to see if Lucas was still wanted by Michigan authorities. Michigan State Police radio replied that he was and that the Tecumseh Police would be notified of Lucas's arrest.

"I ain't wanted in Michigan," Lucas told Lowe. "I just got out of prison in Virginia. This is a mistake."

"If there's been a mistake, we'll get it taken care of at the post," the trooper said.

Fifteen minutes later, the Michigan State Police arrived to question Lucas. At first, he denied harming his mother. At 4:30 P.M., however, Lucas agreed to give a statement to the officers.

"Will you tell us in your own words just what took place on the night of January eleventh, at about the time you left the Bagshaw Tavern?" detective Sergeant Southworth asked.

"When we left Bagshaw's my mother started to

43

argue with me, and it just kept getting worse, until we got into a fight," Lucas said. "I slapped her two or three times, in back of the fire department, and then we went on from there and she kept on arguing all the way down to the house. I went in the house and went upstairs to get some bedclothes, and she came up and started all over again, and I hit her again. And I reached in my pocket, or I had the knife in my hand, I don't know which. And I hit her with the knife and she fell on the floor and I ran."

Lucas said he walked to a nearby garage, where he tried to start a car he found parked behind it. The engine would not turn over, so he broke out a window, opened the back door, and took another car, leaving the overhead door open.

"I drove away then and went toward Ohio," he said. "I left this car in Cincinnati, Ohio, about nine A.M. and hitched the rest of the way for two days to Blacksburg, Virginia. I stayed at Mother's house one night . . . and then started back [to Michigan]. I hitched for one more night and part of another day before I was picked up."

The officers had every reason to believe Lucas's story about his travels since the killing. After he signed his statement, they took him to a hospital for treatment of a bad blister on his heel and a swollen ankle. He said he had probably walked at least two hundred miles.

Lucas agreed to waive extradition and was returned to Michigan, where he was ordered held without bail. The Michigan officers then began developing the corroborative evidence needed to back up Lucas's confession. Though the Michigan Department of Health laboratory was unable to find blood traces on the pocketknife Lucas had been carrying, an examiner reported that a stain on the shirt Lucas wore the night of the murder could have been human blood. A hair found by the pathologist caught in a ring on Mrs.

Lucas's left hand was compared with a sample of Lucas's hair and a hair sample taken from the pillow Lucas had been using at his sister's house. The examiner concluded the hair found on Mrs. Lucas's body was similar "and could have come from the same individual."

The car stolen from the Tecumseh garage was located in Cincinnati, abandoned on a side street. A polygraph examination on January 20 indicated some deception on Lucas's part in discussing whether he remembered putting his hands around his mother's neck and opening his knife before he struck her with it.

Lucas's trial was set for March 22.

One of the most popular shows on television that winter was "Perry Mason," an hour-long courtroom drama based on the enduring characters from the fiction of Earle Stanley Gardner. Now, as prosecutor Kenneth Glaser, Jr., began his opening remarks to the jury in the case of the *People of the State of Michigan* versus *Henry Lee Lucas*, he realized that one of the first things he was going to have to do was convince the jury that all murder trials do not have the drama and unexpected twists of a television play. But the courtroom on the second floor of the red brick Lenawee County courthouse would have suited Hollywood fine. The old-style, high-ceilinged courtroom with paneled walls and decorative molded figures was a stately setting for the processes of justice.

"At the outset I would like to say that we do not claim that this was a well-planned and well-executed murder," Glaser began. "Fortunately, in our courtrooms we seldom see crime executed with the careful calculation and the masterful planning that you sometimes see on your TV sets. . . . We want you to realize that we are not here . . . to entertain anybody. This is the real thing."

Glaser proceeded with a broad overview of his case—a homicide that even he doubted could be seen as a first-degree murder.

"Unless the evidence turns out differently than what we expect, we probably will not press you for a verdict of first-degree murder because we feel that the long planning, the premeditation which as we understand it is the distinction [between first- and second-degree murder] probably is not present, in all fairness to the defendant."

Still, Glaser concluded, Lucas's actions on the night in question "when he stabbed that knife into his mother's neck" would prove him guilty of murder.

In his opening remarks, the court-appointed defense attorney suggested it would take a mind reader to fathom what was going on in the defendant's head the night of Viola Lucas's death.

The defense strategy was obvious. Lucas had more than likely killed his mother. But was it murder or the lesser crime of manslaughter—causing the death of another without any intent? That depended upon what Lucas had been thinking at the time, something that a long string of witnesses put on by the people was not likely to show. His only witness, the defense attorney said, would be the defendant.

"Nobody else can actually say definitely what was in Henry Lucas's mind," he continued.

Glaser presented his case through the testimony of eleven witnesses, beginning with Mrs. Jennings. The prosecutor then questioned the officers who investigated the case, the pathologist, the factory worker who had heard the loud noise in the house where the murder occurred, the state trooper who arrested Lucas, the detectives who took statements from him (the statements were successfully admitted into evidence and read to the jury), and the forensic specialist who examined the hair strands found on the body and compared them to Lucas's hair.

The prosecutor used testimony from Opal Jennings, her husband, and one of their sons to establish Lucas's possession of a knife immediately prior to the murder and to develop his general preoccupation with knives. Glaser had also subpoenaed Stella Curtis, Opal Jennings's two other children, and another police officer, but he felt he had proven the people's case well enough without them having to take the stand.

Though the defense attorney had said he intended his sole witness to be Lucas, he modified his strategy and called one of the prosecution witnesses—the defendant's half sister. He used Mrs. Jennings's testimony to show the jury that society had lost no saint with the death of Viola Lucas, whose daughter reluctantly portrayed as a mean-tempered woman who had supported herself over the years by receiving "help" from "men which she knew," men who were not her husband. Under cross-examination, Glaser got Jennings to be more specific.

"Are you claiming that your mother was a prostitute?"

"I hate to say it, but that's the way she always talked to me," Opal Jennings replied.

"All right. Are you claiming she was when she was up here in Michigan?"

"No . . . I will not say that. I did not see my mother with anybody here, only just to sit down and drink a beer."

"So if there were anything like that in her past, this was all back a long ways, wasn't it?"

"Quite a few years back," she replied.

Following the noon recess, the defense put on its star witness, the soft-spoken defendant. Lucas tracked his signed statements, though he was less specific on one significant point.

"I hit her with my fist as far as I know. After that I don't know whether I hit her with a knife or not, to be honest with you," Lucas testified.

The defense attorney asked Lucas if he remembered reaching into his pocket for a knife. He said he did not.

"Now, you told the officers at one time in this statement you gave them, Henry, that you do remember reaching in your pocket."

"I know it, but I don't. I wouldn't say I didn't reach in there because I probably did, but I just don't remember."

"Do you remember when your mother fell down?"

"Yes, sir."

"Pardon?"

"I remember that."

"Did you have your knife in your hand then?"

"Yes, sir."

"What?"

"I had it in there then."

Glaser could not have been more pleased if he had been asking the questions. Lucas's attorney quickly changed the subject. He led him through his life story, eliciting testimony that showed how the defendant grew up amid abuse and poverty. And then he returned to the night in question.

"After your mother fell to the floor, Henry, did you check to see whether or not she was dead then?"

"Not right then I didn't."

"What did you do?"

"Turned out the light is what I done. After that I went downstairs."

"What did you do downstairs?"

"I sat on the davenport awhile, tried to smoke a cigarette but I couldn't. Sat down for a while. Just went all to pieces."

"What do you mean, you went all to pieces?"

"Just nerves, I guess. Cried for a while. After that I don't know. I just got where I couldn't stay no more."

The defense attorney could think of only one more question.

"Did you love your mother, Henry?"

"Not in particular I didn't."

In his cross-examination, Glaser concentrated on Lucas's recollection of whether he had a knife in his hand when he hit his mother, contrasting his testimony against his written statements.

"Did you tell them you hit her with a knife but you didn't know whether it was open or not?" Glaser asked.

"I think I did. I'm not sure."

A few questions later:

"Did you tell the detectives that you had practiced and learned to draw the knife from your pocket and open it on the way out of your pocket?"

"I did."

Glaser then held up the pocketknife taken from Lucas when he was arrested in Ohio.

"Do you identify this, Henry, as the knife that you struck your mother with?"

"I did."

"You demonstrated to Detective Southworth as he testified here, is that right?"

"I tried to, the best I could."

The defense attorney asked four more questions on redirect and then rested his case.

In his charge to the jury Judge Rex B. Martin summarized the case of the people and the defense, discussed the term "reasonable doubt" and other procedural matters, and then laid out their options: They could find Lucas guilty of either first- or second-degree murder, they could find him guilty of manslaughter, or they could find him not guilty.

The jury retired at 3:37 P.M. and was back at 4:20 P.M., after only forty-three minutes of deliberation. The six-man, six-woman jury had opted for second-degree murder. Lucas showed no emotion when the jury foreman announced the verdict, but Opal broke into tears. As he was led from the courtroom by a deputy, Lucas fixed his good eye on Stella Curtis, who had sat through the entire trial. Then a little emotion showed through.

"Good-bye," he said, his one eye blurred by tears.

"Bye, Hank," Stella replied.

On May 25, Lucas stood before Judge Martin for sentencing. The testimony had shown that Viola Lucas had not been much of a mother, but she had been a human being and she had been killed by her own son. After watching him for two days in the courtroom and listening to his testimony, Martin did not feel Lucas was without some redeeming aspects. Maybe, in this case, the system would work and Henry Lee Lucas could be rehabilitated.

"I would like the record to show that, despite the fact that you have been in prison before, I don't think everything that appears in your record should necessarily indicate that there aren't some saving qualities in your character," the judge said.

Martin paused a moment. He had been on the bench for seven years. Prior to that he had spent nine years in the county prosecutor's office, three as an assistant and six as the chief prosecutor. First elected to the bench in 1953, he had been returned each term after that without opposition. In symbol and theory, justice is blind. In reality, justice is subjective. He could sentence Lucas to any number of years he chose, up to life. But with a life sentence, though it sounded harsh, Lucas could be free in twelve years.

"I don't like what you've done in the past and I'm sure you don't either, but I do think that there have been things in your environment and background that have kept you from going as straight as maybe you yourself would want to," Martin said. He then sentenced Lucas to a minimum of twenty years to a maximum of forty years in prison.

"I wanted to set a minimum that would let you out

while you're still in your early thirties, if you behave yourself," Martin said. If he caused no trouble in prison, "Certainly the Parole Board won't hear any objection from me when it comes time for your parole."

The judge urged Lucas to get some education and learn a skill that would help him get a job when he was out of prison. After an initial quarantine, Martin continued, he would have an opportunity to have visitors and write letters.

"Keep track of your family, your sisters especially —keep writing them letters," Martin said. "If you want to you can write me and I'll be glad to hear from you and glad to answer those letters."

The judge, as he always did with those he sentenced, wished Lucas good luck and then watched as the twenty-four-year-old was led out of his courtroom. With the kind of background he had, Martin knew, Lucas was going to need all the luck he could get.

The State Prison of Southern Michigan at Jackson, completed in 1934 after ten years of construction, was the largest walled prison in the world. Lucas was now one of nearly five thousand inmates.

"I don't know why I committed this crime," Lucas told a social worker at the prison's reception center. "My mother and I got into a fight and it just turned out that way."

Lucas said his mother had been pressuring him to return to Virginia with her, but that he felt he could make a better living in Michigan. "She kept arguing and she called me just about every dirty name that she knew," he continued. "I also called her a few dirty names, too, but finally she started saying that I was having sexual relations with my sister, Opal, and that really made me mad."

The social worker offered this evaluation in his report: "Lucas appears to be a very inadequate individual who has feelings of insecurity and inferiority. The man has recidivistic tendencies and seems to have very little insight into his problem. He seems to have a tendency to act impulsively without giving due consideration to his actions. The man appears to be a rather passive and inoffensive individual; however, it is indicated that he has a rather explosive temper and is unable to curb his actions during one of his fits of temper."

Lucas told the interviewer he had been stabbed three times during his previous incarcerations. Though the wounds had not been life-threatening, they had persuaded him that he would never be without a knife "for protection." The interviewer noted, "The records indicate he has carried, and in many reported instances, has boastingly displayed 'his protection.'"

Lucas said he wanted to attend school while in prison and desired vocational training as an automobile mechanic. When he was released, he said, he planned to move back to Tecumseh to live with his half sister "if she will have me."

The social worker recommended that Lucas's wish for educational opportunities be granted and suggested "frequent contacts with the counselor and participation in the social education classes."

While noting that Lucas was "quite cooperative and apparently truthful during the interview," the social worker was mixed in his feelings about Lucas. He wrote: "He should be able to make a satisfactory adjustment while incarcerated, however, the prognosis for future adjustment in the free community is doubtful."

Despite his previous time behind bars, Lucas was having a hard enough time just adjusting to prison life. That summer, in prison less than two months, Lucas scrawled a letter to Opal that his counselor intercepted. In it Lucas hinted he might kill himself. On July 21, 1960, because of the letter, he was admitted to the prison psychiatric clinic for evaluation.

Kenneth Davis, a psychiatric social worker, looked at the chain-smoking young man in prison whites sitting across from him. He seemed acutely depressed.

"What's wrong, Henry?"

"I've been blacking out," he answered.

"Do you have any idea what's causing that? Have you ever had any kind of head injury?" Davis asked, looking through Lucas's file for any clue.

"It's the thinking I have done about my crime."

Lucas told Davis about his final confrontation with his mother, adding something he had not mentioned in his confessions or in court. "I was drunk and I had sex with her after she was dead."

The guilt was really eating at him, he told Davis.

"I don't have nothing to live for. I've thought about killing myself but I ain't been able to do it."

Davis asked him if he had been seeing things or thinking about things that hadn't really happened.

"No, they checked me at the hospital. I ain't sick. It's the thinking I've been doing."

Davis studied the young inmate before him. Lucas's responses to his questions were slow. Davis couldn't decide for the moment whether that was attributable to Lucas's fairly low IQ or his depression. And he had not always seemed depressed. In fact, Davis at times had seen the inmate remarkably free of any anxiety.

The social worker wondered if Lucas was trying to con him or was indeed profoundly depressed.

Davis looked again at Lucas's record. He had not received any medication since his admission to the prison and Davis thought it a good idea to keep him off any prescription until his condition could be further evaluated. The social worker reached a preliminary conclusion that Lucas's problem was "an acute situational upset in a person of borderline intelligence." But he was not absolutely sure. Davis recommended an indefinite stay in the psychiatric clinic for additional testing and evaluation.

Meanwhile, Lucas continued writing Opal and threatening suicide. He also threatened her if she did not visit.

Lucas remained in the prison's psychiatric unit, where he was evaluated again nine months later, in March 1961. In his report a staff psychologist reviewed Lucas's history, noting the conflict he had had with his mother. He concluded that Lucas's difficult childhood had left him "fixated on a level in which his involvement in satisfaction of very basic needs has never allowed the development of faculties for receiving and offering the multitude of more subtle qualities which make up relationships." But Lucas had not, the psychologist felt, surrendered to "regressive and autistic pathological moods . . . and is not psychotic." His threats of suicide and violence to others amounted only to drama, he felt. "He would like to be a 'mad dog,' but is a whipped puppy." The psychologist had another observation. "He considers himself an island; he habitually has fantasies of driving a car, but with no destination in mind."

Diagnosing Lucas as a "passive-agressive personality, dependent type," the psychologist recommended Lucas be returned to the general prison population. "He can be expected to continue to make pleas and threats but will very likely give quite adequate and dramatic warning stopping short of drastic extremes of behavior."

That summer, however, after twice slashing himself with a razor blade in apparent suicide attempts, Lucas was transferred from Jackson to a state hospital with a diagnosis of "schizophrenic reaction, simple type."

Lucas remained at the state hospital for almost five

years, until April 28, 1966, when he was transferred back to the maximum-security prison at Jackson. In recommending that Lucas be returned to the prison, the hospital's medical superintendent wrote: "This patient has received intensive psychiatric treatment by which he has improved and has been given a responsible assignment in terms of his treatment program and his hospital adjustment seems to be satisfactory. He recently appeared in staff conference for re-evaluation of his mental condition and it is the consensus of the psychiatric staff that he has received maximum benefit from treatment and hospitalization, there is no evidence of psychosis, and he could adjust in the general population in prison."

By late 1967, nearly eight years into his sentence, prison personnel were beginning to feel Lucas had made some progress. Noting that Lucas had "had a great deal of difficulty with mental problems" during his first six years in prison, associate counselor William J. Hudson felt after talking with the inmate that he was "doing much better at the present time than he did on the earlier part of his sentence. . . ."

One thing did worry Hudson, however. Lucas had had only one visitor since his imprisonment, and that had been shortly after his arrival in Jackson in the late spring of 1960. Since then he had had no contact with his family. His only correspondence, aside from the early letters to his older half sister, had been with a former inmate he had made friends with while a patient in the state hospital.

On January 3, 1968, the Michigan Parole Board considered Lucas's case. After the interview, one board member concluded that the prisoner was "not of good mental health today." Another board member said Lucas seemed to him "on the brink" during the interview. They concluded that he needed to serve his minimum sentence.

But that summer, approaching his thirty-second

birthday, Lucas seemed to be improving. The supervisor of the prison vocational school, where Lucas worked, recommended that the Special Consideration Committee take a look at his case. That committee could recommend him for another parole hearing, which it did.

In Lucas's parole eligibility report, Hudson said he had worked with Lucas for two years and that "he seemingly has made an excellent adjustment." For one thing, Hudson noted, Lucas had "kindled an association with a young divorcee. . . ." Hudson said he had talked with her several times and had been impressed with her attitude. She intended to "do everything in her power to help Mr. Lucas when he re-enters the community," he wrote.

Actually, though Hudson did not mention it in his report, Lucas's association with the young woman was a rekindling, not something new. The woman was Stella Curtis, whose letter breaking off their relationship had been found in Bagshaw's Tavern the day Viola Lucas's body was discovered. She had not seen Lucas or thought much about him since his conviction. Then one day a letter came from him. Lucas said he was lonely. "If you don't hate me too much, will you come see me?"

Stella had broken off with Lucas because she sensed trouble between him and Randy and because of his family, particularly his mother. "He was a nice kid," Stella later recalled, "real bashful and quiet. But I didn't want to get mixed up in that family. His mother was a class A terror. The only time I ever saw him mad was when his mother picked on him."

But Stella liked to "fight for the underdog," and when she got Lucas's letter, she decided to reply. Before long, she drove to Jackson for a visit.

After an eight-year hiatus, Lucas and Opal also were back in touch. "These people [Opal and her husband] have indicated an interest in the subject and would provide home placement for him if paroled," Hudson wrote.

In two years Hudson had watched Lucas change dramatically. When Hudson first saw Lucas, the inmate handled his frustrations in "an almost infantile manner." Now, Hudson felt, Lucas was dealing with life as an adult. Still, the associate counselor hedged his bet a little: "Realistically, because of Mr. Lucas's past mental difficulties . . . prognosis could properly be placed as guarded."

In September 1968 the parole board agreed with Hudson that Lucas had shown marked improvement. But, "in view of the offense and prior history," the members felt Lucas needed a bit more time behind bars to further demonstrate that improvement.

Lucas was made a trusty and got a job as a porter in the front house, the prison administration building. Working from 6:30 A.M. to 4 P.M. seven days a week, he was putting $6.50 a month into his prison account. He was happy with the work, and his supervisor had no complaints about his performance. In his spare time he watched television and did artwork in the prison hobby shop. "He has a good attitude and minds his own business," a new counselor reported.

The visits from Stella continued, but he stopped hearing from Opal again. "He states that his [half sisters] refuse to have anything to do with him because of the crime," the report said.

A year later, in September 1969, Lucas had a new job, this time as a clerk in the prison stationery store. Lucas's new supervisor was almost effusive in his praise of the inmate's work habits and conduct. Lucas, his counselor wrote, "gets along well with others and I do believe, from my conversation with him, that he knows what he has to do to make it on the outside." Concluding the evaluation, his counselor said that if Lucas continued with the kind of progress he had been making, "he will be a very good candidate for parole upon his minimum, which is only approximately a year away."

On March 13, 1970, a decade after Lucas's admission to prison, Melvin Harris, his new counselor, felt the thirty-three-year-old inmate was ready for parole. In ten years Lucas had never been a disciplinary problem. With the exception of his early suicide threats and attempts, he had "performed well in every way." Harris pointed again to the transformation of Lucas.

"I feel that Lucas had made a great deal of progress and should be given an opportunity for a parole release," Harris wrote. "Lucas himself states that he feels he is cured. He attributes the crime to the fact that he was the kind of person that was easily excited and could not control his behavior."

That cold night he struck his mother down, Lucas came close to losing two mothers: the old whore who had given him birth and his half sister Opal. Twenty-two years older than Lucas, she had met her little brother for the first time when he was nine. Viola brought her boys to New York State, where Opal and her first husband were living at the time. She, like others who saw how Viola Lucas treated the little boy, had felt sorry for him. Once, when she visited Virginia, she found Henry and his older brother wearing little more than rags. She bought them some new clothes. After Henry left home and got in trouble with the law, Opal had still tried to do what she could for him, a kindness that usually only meant trouble for her.

And then he had gone and killed their mother, though sometimes Opal and other members of the family tried to rationalize that the lack of blood on her body meant she had had a fatal heart attack during the fight with Henry. But the doctor said during the trial that her death had been caused by the knife Henry stuck in her neck. For some reason, it had not come up in the trial, but Opal later recalled that a silver medallion and chain was missing from her mother's neck when she found her body. After his trial, Henry sent her the medallion and chain. That was why she had pretty well left Lucas alone while he was in prison. He'd sent her some letters threatening to kill himself —or her—if she did not come to visit him. She finally did come—once—but she did not feel the same toward him as she had before that night in Tecumseh.

"After the killing, there was a whole lot of hurt in the family," Opal would recall. "We couldn't believe he would do that."

It was Stella, not Opal, who was there to meet Lucas after a decade in prison.

At 11:00 A.M. on June 3, 1970, Lucas was led into the lobby of the prison by Harris, his counselor. He had $30 in cash, a new pair of slacks, shirt, and jacket, and a bus ticket from Toledo, Ohio, to Maryland. He had been paroled to another of his half sisters, Nora Crawford, who lived in Elkton, Maryland.

Stella greeted him with a hug. Harris filled her in on the terms of Lucas's parole and she promised to have him in Toledo in time to catch the bus to Maryland.

"I hope you straighten your life out, Hank," Harris told him, extending his hand. "Good luck."

Stella drove him back to Ridgeway, a few miles outside Tecumseh, where she lived with her parents and nine-year-old daughter, a child from a short-lived relationship in Baltimore, Maryland, not long after Lucas had gone to prison. They had dinner with her family that evening, and then she drove Lucas to Toledo for an eight o'clock bus.

Before Viola Lucas's murder, Stella's interest in him had been romantic. But the letters and prison visits had been in the name of friendship—nothing more. They never saw each other again.

* * *

Lucas stayed in Elkton for two months, then moved to Port Deposit, Maryland, where Wanda Weaver, his third and youngest half sister, lived with her husband and three daughters.

In August 1971, Opal and her husband took a vacation and drove to Maryland for a visit with Wanda and her family and a somewhat reluctant reunion with Lucas. Opal was not there long before Wanda pulled her aside for a private talk, sister to sister. Henry and Eugene, her husband, were just not getting along. She did not want Lucas living with them any longer.

Opal and Kenneth stayed for a couple of weeks. When they headed back to Michigan, Lucas went with them. He had gotten approval to have parole transferred from Maryland to Michigan.

Even though he had killed her mother, Opal felt an obligation to give her troubled half brother another chance. Taking him back into her home would not be easy, but then neither had his life been easy.

"The day before mom died she said she wanted me to take care of Henry," Opal later recalled. "She told me he's going to spend his whole life in prison."

Opal hoped her mother had been wrong.

CHAPTER FOUR

Fifteen-year-old Leslie Warrne left home for school about seven that morning, taking her usual route to the bus stop in Palmyra, Michigan. As she walked along the edge of the highway, a blue car drove past her slowly. Leslie noticed that the dark-haired man behind the wheel gave her a long look, but she was thinking about school and dismissed it from her mind when the car went on by. Then the car drove by her a second time.

The man drove down the highway, but as the car neared the railroad tracks that crossed the roadway, Leslie saw its brake lights come on. Suddenly, the car turned and headed back toward her. Now frightened, Leslie ran to the corner, hoping her bus would get there soon.

The car pulled up next to her, so close she had to move back to keep from being hit.

"Get in or I'll shoot you," the man said. Leslie could see his right hand, apparently holding a gun, crossed over his left side.

"No," she said, backing away. "I'm not getting in your car."

The man got out of the car and moved toward her, one hand behind his back.

61

"Your boyfriend told me to shoot you because you're going out on him," the man said, standing near the car door.

Leslie moved farther back, nervously looking up the road for the yellow school bus. Not believing that Doug could have anything to do with what was happening, she asked the stranger her boyfriend's name.

"Joe," the man said. "He lives in Adrian, doesn't he?"

"No, he doesn't," she stammered. "And his name's not Joe."

If I try to run, he might shoot me, Leslie thought to herself. She was so scared, it was hard to even think. Then the school bus pulled into view.

"I'll see you later," the dark-haired man said as soon as he saw the approaching bus. "You're lucky this time."

He got back in his car and drove off as the bus stopped for the shaken teenager.

At school, Leslie told two of her best friends what had happened that morning. They told a teacher, who in turn contacted the young student's parents.

By 9:30 A.M., detective Howard Esterline was talking with Leslie about the early-morning incident. She described the man in the car as being about five feet seven inches tall, weighing 150 pounds, with wavy, dark brown hair. It did not look like he had shaved in several days. He had been wearing a dirty blue shirt and beige pants. Leslie had even tried to make a mental note of the car's license plate number, and she told the detective two numbers she thought might be close.

The teenager remembered one other thing—the same car had followed the school bus the morning before.

* * *

Shortly before 2 P.M. on the same day Leslie Warrne had been approached by the man in the car, seventeen-year-old Marcie Goodwyn left her house in Tecumseh to visit some friends. As she drove along the highway, she passed a car parked on the roadside. The guy in the car waved, as if asking for assistance. Thinking the man had car trouble and might need a ride, Marcie pulled her car over behind the parked car.

The other driver put his vehicle in reverse and backed up parallel to Marcie, who was still in her car.

Suddenly, the seventeen-year-old realized the man was pointing a gun at her.

"Take your hands from the steering wheel and put them in the air," the man ordered.

Marcie screamed at the sight of the gun, but instead of following his instructions, she hit the gas, leaving the gunman behind in a shower of gravel and dust. She told police a short time later she had been too shaken to note the license plate on the vehicle, but the description of the driver and the car matched the one given by the younger girl that morning.

Investigators had already run the two plate numbers provided by Leslie. The first came back to a Kenneth Jennings of Route 2, Britton. The car was a dark blue 1965 Mercury. The other car was a Pontiac. Since both Leslie and Marcie had said the car was a Mercury, detectives decided to check out Jennings first.

Officers drove to Jennings's residence and found him at home.

"Do you own a 1965 Mercury?" one of the officers asked.

"That's my car," Jennings said, "but I haven't been driving it today. About six o'clock this morning my wife's brother asked if he could use it. Said he'd be back about six or six-thirty this evening."

"Who's your brother-in-law and what does he look like?" Detective Esterline asked.

"His name's Henry Lucas," Jennings said. "He got out of prison about a year ago."

When Jennings described his thirty-five-year-old brother-in-law, the officers realized he matched the description given that day by both girls.

"Is Henry in trouble again?"

"Could be," Esterline replied.

"Is it about animals?" Jennings asked.

"What do you mean?" The question caught the officer by surprise. "What about animals?"

"Well, we had a dog and a goat when Henry moved in with us. About a month ago they turned up missing. We found the dog hanging with a rope around its neck back in a shed. Then we found the goat all butchered up. Opal's real torn up about it. She thinks he killed 'em. She said it's not the first time animals have disappeared when he's been around."

The detective went back to the sheriff's office and pulled an old mug shot of Lucas taken on February 8, 1960, when he was in custody for the murder of his mother, an offense many of the officers in the county well remembered. Lucas, Esterline learned, had served ten years in prison before being paroled on June 3, 1970. His brother-in-law said Lucas had been staying with them, working at a local dairy.

Detective Esterline's next call was to the district attorney's office. He filled the prosecutor in on the two cases and the fact that Lucas, a paroled murderer, looked like a good suspect.

"If you can get one of the girls to identify him from a mug shot, go ahead and pick him up," the prosecutor told Esterline.

Later that evening, the detective went to Marcie's residence and showed her the old black-and-white mug shot. As her parents looked on, she studied the picture for a moment.

"That looks like him," she said. "He had a bad-looking eye."

Based on that identification, Lucas was arrested at his half sister's house that evening and booked into jail.

Lucas readily admitted to the offense, though he left out some incriminating details.

"Is it true that you did try to pick this girl up and have her get into the car with you?" Detective Esterline asked.

"I stopped and talked to her and asked her to go with me," Lucas answered.

Later, when Esterline asked Lucas why he had tried to abduct the girl, he said, "For sex."

After asking Lucas about the second abduction attempt, Esterline went back to the matter of sex.

"Do you have a sex problem?" he asked.

"I do."

"What kind of a sex problem?"

"I just crave women all of the time."

The following day, Lucas was charged with two counts of attempted kidnapping and then taken before a circuit court judge for arraignment. Jurist and the accused recognized each other immediately: the judge was Rex Martin.

Martin looked down on the disheveled one-eyed man standing before him. He was sad, but not surprised, to see Lucas in trouble again. Finding that Lucas was financially unable to hire a lawyer, Judge Martin appointed a local attorney to represent him.

By 3:30 P.M. an identification lineup had been arranged. As the two victims watched from the darkness of the lineup room viewing area, Lucas and five other persons of roughly the same size and appearance were walked out for the girls to take a look at under the glare of harsh lights that kept the men from seeing the witnesses. Leslie immediately identified suspect number three—Lucas—as the man who had tried to get her in his car. The older girl said she could not be sure, but that number three looked the most like the man who had pointed a gun at her the day before.

With Lucas's statement, in which Lucas denied having a gun but admitted trying to get the girls into his brother-in-law's car, and with the positive identifications made by both victims, the people had a strong case. In an examining trial on October 20, the prosecutor's office put Leslie Warrne on the stand to relate the details of her close call the month before. After her testimony, Lucas was bound over for trial in circuit court. At the arraignment, a plea of not guilty was entered. After the brief hearing, Lucas was returned to jail, where he was held in lieu of $15,000 bail.

Several days later, Lucas's attorney filed a motion that his client was mentally incompetent to stand trial. The petition pointed out that Lucas had "a long history of mental disorder dating back to childhood," had spent more than four years under psychiatric care in a state hospital, and had attempted suicide several times while in prison. In response to the motion, Judge Martin entered an order committing Lucas to the state's center for forensic psychiatry for evaluation.

Lucas appeared again before Judge Martin in December. The judge had not yet seen a written report based on Lucas's psychiatric evaluation, but both the defense and the prosecutor had been told that Lucas was mentally competent to stand trial. As soon as he heard that the mental incompetency route was not going to work, the defense attorney recommended to Lucas that he go ahead and plead guilty. The people's case against him was too strong.

Judge Martin asked the defense attorney if he had any objection to moving along with the hearing without waiting for the formal written psychiatric report. The attorney agreed to go ahead.

"All right. Now, Henry, your attorney came in to talk to me this morning about this particular matter, and he advises me that you wish to change your plea. Is that right?"

"Yes, sir."

The judge asked Lucas to move closer to the bench so they could talk without having to shout. He explained to Lucas that he was entitled to a trial at which he could confront any witnesses against him and made sure he understood the nature of the charge against him.

"And how do you plead to it?"

"I plead guilty," Lucas replied.

After he was satisfied that Lucas understood what he was doing, and that no promises had been made to him in exchange for a guilty plea, Martin used a transcript of the examining trial to move through the various points of Leslie Warrne's account of what had happened to her that morning in September.

"She said that when you pulled up alongside of her, that you told her to get in the car and that you would shoot her because you had a gun. Do you remember saying that?"

"Yes, sir, I do," Lucas replied.

"You did say that to her?"

"Yes."

Lucas said he had not had a gun, but that he held his hand behind his back. He demonstrated for the judge.

"And did you tell her you were supposed to shoot her because her boyfriend asked you to and because she was going out with somebody else?"

"Yes."

Lucas confirmed that he had told the girl her boyfriend's name was Joe. "I think that's the name I give her."

Suddenly, it seemed as if Lucas was back at the intersection of the two roads, trying to get the teenager into his car.

"And then . . . the school bus came along, and you took off then, right?" the judge asked.

"It's coming down the other road," Lucas said, slipping into the present tense as if he were seeing the bus there in court.

"And she testified she was afraid," Martin asked, looking at his notes. "Did she look afraid to you?"

"She was afraid," Lucas replied.

In this case, motivation had no strong bearing on the offense, but the judge was curious about what had been on Lucas's mind that September morning.

"Henry, can you tell me what made you do a thing like this?"

After a moment, Lucas replied, "Just the urge I get sometimes to scare people and . . . ."

The judge interrupted. "You scared her, didn't you?"

"Yes."

Martin did not explore Lucas's motivation any further.

Checking once more with Lucas's attorney to make sure his client's plea was being made with his approval, Judge Martin accepted the plea and found Lucas guilty.

Back in open court, the judge asked Lucas if he had anything to say before he passed sentence. Lucas simply replied, "No, sir."

Martin looked down from the bench at the greasy-haired, one-eyed man standing before him and suddenly felt a sense of dread sweep over him. Something about this man set off his internal alarm system.

The judge studied him for a minute more.

"Henry, as you know, when we originally sentenced you here sometime ago, I was real concerned about you and concerned about what might happen to you in free society."

"Yes, sir."

"I think you still realize that this type of activity

worries the court because I not only represent the people as a whole, but I am really an agent of all the people in the county, and with this type of activity, I'm always afraid that someday something serious is going to happen. Something serious has happened once in your life, and certainly you don't want it to happen again, and I don't want it to happen again, and it really concerns me that we have had this type of activity so soon after you've been out on parole."

Martin warned Lucas that his parole on his murder conviction likely would be revoked in light of his new conviction.

"On this particular charge, I think the sentence should be such that they'll realize that I think it was a serious offense and I think it might have serious consequences," Martin said.

Earlier in the hearing, responding to a letter he had received from Lucas, the judge told him that he had talked with his attorney, who had assured him that Lucas's concerns about getting the proper dosage of the Thorazine prescribed for him had been taken care of. The attorney told Judge Martin he had discussed the situation with the sheriff and was satisfied his client would be provided the medication he needed.

Then Martin returned to the matter of Lucas's medication.

"You say that when you take your medication, that you get along much better than you do normally," he asked Lucas.

"Yes."

"Certainly, you talk very rationally, and you act very rationally when you are with me and after you have had your medication. Whether this might save you from getting into this type of assaultive action again, I don't know. I think maybe that would be something for doctors to tell more than I can."

Martin thought for a moment. Here was a man who had killed his own mother, a man suspected by his own family of killing helpless animals, a man who freely admitted trying to kidnap two teenage girls.

"It will be the sentence of the court that you be confined in the prison at Jackson, under the supervision, direction, and control of the Michigan Department of Corrections for a minimum period of four years to a maximum period of five years," the judge intoned formally.

Then, again more personally, he continued: "I'm going to suggest in the sentencing, Henry, that you again be examined by psychiatrists so that they can make a determination of whether this medicine is going to do you any actual good or whether . . . with the use of it, you can be able to restrain yourself from some of these proclivities that you have had."

Lucas said he understood, but showed no emotion, staring at the judge with his one good eye, an eye betraying no more feeling than its glass companion.

For the record, the judge mentioned that Lucas had written him from prison at various times in the past. Sometimes he had answered the letters, sometimes, when he could not figure out what Lucas was trying to say, he had not.

"I think at those times you were in a mental condition where there was a lot of confusion, because maybe a week later I'd get a letter from you and it was perfectly even and level and sane, and I could answer it. I'll be glad to answer your letters again if I can. All right, Henry. Good luck to you."

The thirty-five-year-old defendant was led out of the courtroom, looking far less bothered by the prospect of up to five years in prison than the man who had just handed him the sentence.

Lucas had not even been in prison a month before he began to have second thoughts about his guilty plea. Taking Judge Martin up on his offer to stay in touch, Lucas wrote the court asking for a new "tryal."

Martin notified him that a hearing had been set on the matter, and on January 26, 1972, Lucas wrote with a request that he be allowed to be on hand for it because "I will haft to be present to present my Case, if not, any thing could happen and their fore, I want to be their." He also wanted a new lawyer appointed to represent him at the hearing. Then he went on to brief his case for the judge: "Under the Constutition gartnes [guarantees] this right that no procedings are to be held with out the Defendant. That and such procedings is in violation of this Constutition." Martin pondered the letter. Lucas was not much of a speller, but he was a quick study when it came to practicing jailhouse law.

The judge appointed another attorney to take Lucas's case. In short order, the lawyer filed a motion to withdraw his new client's guilty plea and have a new trial along with a motion to quash the indictment against Lucas and discharge him from prison.

In his motion, Lucas's new attorney argued that the facts in the case did not meet the requirements set out in Michigan's kidnapping law: that the victim be seized and moved or that the victim be secretly confined at the location where he was originally seized.

Martin denied both of the attorney's motions on March 14, writing in his order that Lucas had been charged with attempting to kidnap the victim, not with kidnapping.

"The Court has known the defendant in the past and sentenced him on one occasion for matricide," Martin wrote in his order. "There was no question in the Court's mind he would have driven off with the girl if she had succumbed to his threats and gotten into the car. The Court would not be able to say what he would have later done to or with the girl, with or without her consent. The Court does know he meant to get her into the car, drive away from the public spot, and do so by the threat of using a gun. The defendant did not want to attempt any more activities there in broad daylight, in open country, not too far from the complaining witness' home and with the school bus supposedly due in the near future. Any movement from that place with the defendant would have resulted in an increased risk to the victim."

Martin concluded that the transcript of Lucas's testimony showed he had intended to "willfully, maliciously, and without lawful authority confine her against her will. He took some affirmative, overt action to carry out his intent. He was frustrated by the appearance of the school bus. His attempt failed. It was an attempt to kidnap under the statute. The motion will be denied."

On June 20, 1972, Lucas's attorney filed an appeal of the case with the Michigan Court of Appeals. In May 1973, the appeals court, retaining no jurisdiction, remanded the case to the county circuit court. In July, the attorney filed a petition for a review of Lucas's guilty plea, alleging the plea had not been made voluntarily, and, among other points, that Lucas was "under the influence of the drug Thorazine" when he made his guilty plea. After a hearing on July 10, Judge Martin found that Lucas had been competent to stand trial on December 2, 1971, and denied the motion for a review of Lucas's guilty plea. On July 19, the lawyer made one more effort in behalf of Lucas, a motion for a reduction of his sentence; it was denied.

Lucas applied for parole in 1974, but the parole board reported that "we do not have the assurance necessary to grant a parole." In fact, one member of the board wrote, "The sexual overtones of the present offense coupled with the previous behavior and lack of meaningful treatment programs call for extreme caution."

In March of 1973, the prison psychiatric clinic sent

inmate No. 102860 (Lucas) a memo outlining something called called SONAR—a sex offender treatment program. The unsigned four-paragraph communication said the staff had found that "by placing [sex offenders] in a therapy group, they are able to relate many similar feelings, as well as experiences, and as a result, develop insights for themselves about why they became involved in their particular deviant sexual behavior as well as learn more appropriate methods of coping with life's many problems." The memo writer invited Lucas to fill out an attached questionnaire. Lucas would then be placed on a waiting list and notified as soon as there was an opening in the group.

The reference to "sexual overtones" in the parole board action touched off a flurry of writ writing by Lucas.

"I Henry L. Lucas does protest the charge which this Court and County Jail places against me. The charge being a sex charge. I wish and prays that this Court will set forth an act upon this charge of sex because that there were not, no sex overtones with in my case," Lucas raged in his homemade petition, written in bold hand lettering. He wanted the statement made the day of his arrest, in which he said his motive had been sex, to be removed from his prison record since "these sex charges . . . have not been proved or made by law or brought on by a tryal." Failure to remove the record would amount to an act of "Dubble Jeperty," he argued.

After learning that Judge Martin had set a hearing in response to his letter motion, Lucas mailed another two-page document further pleading his case. He added, "I . . . wishes to inform said court that while being confined I have got a good trade and can be a part of susidie [society] without further wrong doings and said defendant wishes to state that he will not be a burden to this State or County after his release. Because he will not remain in this state."

On September 4, 1974, in response to a letter from Lucas, the parole board wrote that its action in his case "remains unchanged." The board had not said he committed a sexual offense, "merely that the offense had sexual overtones. A careful review of the file still indicates that to be the case." A month later, Judge Martin denied Lucas's motion for "deletion of charge," noting that neither Lucas nor his attorney had shown up for the hearing.

On October 8, 1974, Lucas sent Judge Martin a letter that came dangerously near being a threat. The prisoner was clearly angry that the judge had denied his motion that the "sex charge" be removed from his prison record and proceeded to lecture the jurist:

> Failure to comply with laws which you have been chozen to uphold is a criminal oficence and such charges can be sent to the State Supreme Court also can result in removal from office.
>
> I do not wish this. But it seems that little choice is being left open to people but have those who faill to comply with laws which has been set down by Courts and senators allover the United States. Then those must be pusished [punished] like Prescndent Nixon was removed for not upholding his oath. What ever you deside will be a desision of law. If my past record makes up your mind for the laws of Michigan then they should put up walls around Michigan because ever body has a past record. . . .

Lucas wrote that even though his sentence was almost completed, "I am going to cont. to fight this charge after my release from prison. That all can depend upon. I sure want [won't] be here in Mich. but where at least I will be safe from the kind of law which Lenawee County has been noted."

On August 22, 1975, Lucas was released from

prison, having served three and a half years. This time, as he had written Judge Martin, he did not intend to stay in Michigan. He would go to Maryland, where half sisters Nora and Wanda lived. He figured he had just about worn out his welcome with Opal and Kenneth Jennings.

After walking out of prison, Lucas spent only one night in Michigan before he was on his way to Perryville, Maryland, where his half sister Wanda lived. Later Lucas would say he had begged prison officials not to release him, that he would be a danger to society. In fact, he had done just about everything he could to shorten his sentence, other than trying to escape. And despite his claim that he would continue to press for suppression of the "sex charge" on his record, Judge Martin never again heard from the one-eyed man who had tripped his internal alarm system. But the man who had put him in prison twice would not get a chance to forget Henry Lee Lucas.

CHAPTER FIVE

The big man pedaled his bicycle past the used-car lots, pawn shops, and taverns that litter Jacksonville's long Main Street. Main is part of old U.S. Highway 1, which stretched all the way up the East Coast. But he wasn't going anywhere near that far. Sweat beaded his balding head, trickled down his thick neck, soaked the T-shirt across his broad back. Tall—an inch over six feet—he hunched over the handlebars, maneuvering absently through the light late-night traffic. His powerful legs, encased in worn and faded jeans, pumped furiously.

He had to get to Mama. That was all that mattered. Not that there was any real hurry. Mama wasn't going anywhere.

He'd tried to sleep after finishing with the gay guy he'd picked up earlier in the evening, but the peaceful blackness wouldn't come. The sex hadn't even made him drowsy, he hadn't been able to drink himself to sleep, and the pills didn't work. All he could think of was Mama. He was hearing those voices again, the voices that told him he should just go ahead and kill himself so he could go to rest. But Mama would make it all better.

Forty blocks from the cheap dump he rented he climbed off his bike. He rolled it behind shrubbery, hiding it from sight. A practiced thief himself, he knew the risks in this part of town. The high black iron gate was locked at sundown, but it was no big deal for a man his height to climb over the red brick wall. He dropped lightly to the springy turf below. Shafts of pale moonlight filtered through drapes of Spanish moss, turning the hovering angel statues an eerie silver. He didn't need much light. He knew the way. With his long-legged lope he ran to Mama.

Mama had been here since May. They'd cut open her heart in the hospital. Not long after that she went to sleep and never woke up. They'd brought her out here to Evergreen Cemetery and put her in the ground.

He stopped running and stood for a moment, adjusting to the darkness, staring down at the familiar grave. His breath came fast, tearing at his lungs. He fell to his knees and threw his body over the mound of sod marked by the simple tombstone.

He waited, but nothing happened. He was afraid maybe she didn't know he'd come to her, seeking her comfort, just like when he was a kid. Then he felt the ground under him grow warm, the same as the last time. The earth beneath him started moving, rocking, soothing. Now he knew she was aware of him, his body stretched out on top of hers. He felt the unbearable tension drain away. Safe with Mama, he closed his eyes and drifted off to sleep.

With a drunk for a husband, Sarah Toole figured she had a sorry excuse for a marriage. The one thing he provided her with was plenty of babies. On March 5, 1947, she was back in the hospital again in labor with her eighth child, a boy she named Ottis Elwood. Sarah and William Henry Toole, who was a painter when he was sober enough to work, would have one more baby. But by the time Ottis was seven, Sarah had had enough of her husband's drinking and breeding. In

1954 she ran him off for good. She told her nine children she never wanted to hear them even speak their father's name. Ever.

Sarah and her children lived in Springfield, a neighborhood of roughly twenty square blocks just north of downtown Jacksonville. In its day it had been one of the most elegant sections of the city, with fine old Victorian homes lining tree-canopied streets. But upper-class families moved out as poor people, minorities, and crime moved in. A few old folks on fixed incomes remained behind, bewildered by the change in their once-familiar neighborhood, feeling like prisoners in their own homes.

As real estate came on the market, much of it was snapped up by absentee landlords and turned into rental property. Along Main Street in the Springfield area, mom-and-pop businesses gave way to seedy bars.

Springfield was getting to be a rough place to raise kids, but Sarah didn't have any choice. With her worthless husband long gone and good riddance, she worked hard to keep food on the table for all the kids. She had a job at the Goodwill store downtown and at times she accepted welfare assistance. Later in her life she was reduced to pushing a shopping cart around the rough neighborhood, collecting aluminum cans and scrap metal to sell by the pound.

She never touched hard liquor and wondered how she'd tolerated her husband's drinking as long as she had.

She'd suffered more hurts than the physical abuse from a drunken man. A God-fearing woman never far from her Bible, she believed God must have a special reason for trying her so sorely. The twin girls of her first pregnancy died before their second birthday. And little Albert, her last child, died in infancy of spinal meningitis.

Ottis grew up as the baby of her brood. God tested

her with Ottis, too. He was born simpleminded. And he was shy, clinging to her legs and peeping fearfully from behind her skirts. He always needed more of Mama's attention than the others. Sarah was only too glad to give it, but she knew she wouldn't be around forever.

Still, when one of her babies came down with croup or colic or something worse, Sarah Toole took good care of them. Her cures were a mix of Christian prayers and ancient Indian remedies she'd learned from her Cherokee mother. When one of her children came crying with a cut, Sarah read a Bible verse out loud three times to stop the bleeding and applied a spiderweb to close the wound. With God's help, she could even banish her children's bad dreams. Sarah believed that tucking a Bible under the pillow warded off nightmares.

Sarah was troubled that Ottis, of all her children, seemed to need so much of her time. She couldn't be with him every minute, but she tried to protect him as best she could. Not everyone was so kind. After Ottis started school, other kids sensed his slowness and teased him without mercy. They taunted him with "retard" and other less kindly names. Once a kid chunked a rock at him, hitting him hard in the head. After that Ottis experienced periodic seizures. When those fits came on him, the humiliation was even worse.

Ottis got along better playing with his older brothers and sisters. One of the games he liked best was invented by the oldest of his five sisters, Drusilla. She enjoyed dressing her baby brother up like a girl. His other sisters thought it was fun. Ottis reveled in the attention. He lost some of his shyness as he played like a pretty lady.

Sarah Toole couldn't see any harm in it.

Ottis failed the first grade. The following year he was placed in special education classes. After that, he was "socially" promoted from grade to grade by sympathetic teachers. He was learning very little, at least in the traditional sense. He was, however, getting an early and explicit education in sex. As Ottis matured physically, Drusilla tired of the game of dressing him like a girl and decided to use him like a man.

Drusilla never got to the age of ten as a virgin. She'd had sex with grown men and figured it couldn't be much different with baby brother Ottis. Up to the time they were caught, Drusilla seemed to get a bigger kick out of it than Ottis.

Dressing up and acting ladylike had brought him the attention he craved—but this thing with his sister was done furtively and with much giggling and whispering on her part. His shyness returned. He was pretty sure Mama wouldn't like it if she knew. Before long, Drusilla got in trouble with the police and was sent off to the Florida School for Girls.

Ottis was slow in many ways, but when it came to sex he was ahead of his seventh-grade classmates. By the time they began to speculate about girls, Ottis had already had private lessons from his sister. When they began to joke nervously about masturbation, this too was old news to Ottis.

The man next door had shown him how to do things that made them both feel good—things that seemed *right*. Ottis enjoyed the things he and the man did. The things he'd done with Drusilla made him feel bad.

When Ottis couldn't be with his male friend or when he felt a little tense, he gripped himself and pumped with abandon. But unlike his classmates, he didn't conjure up images of girls; his fantasy world was the shower in the boy's locker room.

Other boys got turned on as they pored over girlie magazines. Ottis couldn't for the life of him figure out what they could see in those pictures, but he sure did enjoy studying all those bulging male crotches. Ottis found other ways to bring about his own sexual excitement. Muscled male flesh was a turn-on, but he soon found something else that drove him into a sexual frenzy.

Maybe the excitement it generated in others was contagious. Neighbors ringed the sidewalk and craned to see the firemen in their shiny coats struggling to control the powerful hoses, the policemen pushing back the curious bystanders. Ottis loved the wailing sirens, the flashing lights, the shooting flames and exploding sparks, the hiss and hum from the pumper trucks, the smoke that ate at the back of his throat, the dark lake of water at his feet that reflected the blaze.

Night fires were the best.

The second Ottis heard sirens he slammed out the door like a shot, running or pedaling his bicycle as fast as he could. Ottis wasn't bright, but inevitably it came to him that he didn't have to wait for a fire to just happen. *He could make them happen.*

Perhaps it was the tremendous sense of power, spiced with the fear of getting caught, that gave him such a thrill when he started a fire himself. Whatever it was, and Ottis did not have the intellect to ponder it, he did love a good fire. The higher the flames, the more demanding his erection. Hiding in the dark with a good view of the licking flames, he masturbated with a joyful fervor, his climax so powerful he could hardly stand when he was spent.

Sex was an obsession with Ottis Toole. Sex tapped and released some internal reservoir of fear and tension in him. Sex was the one thing that made him feel better than anything else in the world. The form it took didn't matter a whole lot—a crackling good night fire and masturbation or oral sex with a drunk so bombed out he thought he was getting it from a woman.

Ottis didn't need much of anything else in his life to

be completely happy—except maybe booze, pot, pills, and king-sized Kools.

Ottis was a month shy of his thirteenth birthday before he got into trouble with the police the first time. He pedaled off on somebody else's bicycle. The police called it theft and arrested him. Mama cried, and that made him feel bad. The juvenile court placed him under supervision, but it didn't help. Ottis's problems were too complex and ran too deep. Eight months later he was busted for breaking and entering and was committed to the Florida State School for Boys on October 30, 1960.

When he came home from the detention school, his teenage hormones were running wild. He didn't want to be in school anymore, and despite his love for his mother, he didn't want to be home, either. He skipped school and ran away frequently. He finally dropped out in the eighth grade, but his education continued on the streets. He would always be mentally immature, but physically he could almost pass for a grown man. With his sturdy build, he had no trouble getting a job. He had little to fear from strangers, and people didn't tease him like they used to, either. When someone ran their mouth too much around him, they paid a price.

But all the teasing he had endured because of his slowness had soured him on people, even if it was easy to beat up anyone who gave him any lip. He tended to keep pretty much to himself, except when he wanted sex. One of his favorite places for that was Confederate Park, down at Main and Hubbard, the southern boundary of Springfield. Men looking for dates came to the public restroom at the old municipal park. Transients sprawled on the grass in the shade of the live oaks, palms, cedars, and magnolias. Empty wine bottles overflowed from the trash cans. Eventually, Ottis's homosexual behavior landed him in jail. When Ottis was seventeen, in the summer of 1964, a policemen arrested him for loitering in the park, looking for tricks. That bust got him ninety days at the city work farm north of town, a stay that gave him plenty of opportunity to enjoy men.

He was on the streets again by November, but an arrest later that winter for stealing a battery and some gasoline sent him back to the farm for another ninety days.

His next arrest, for interstate transportation of a stolen motor vehicle—he briefly led a Georgia state trooper on a high-speed chase—got him two years of hard time in the Federal Correctional Institute in Ashland, Kentucky. After his release from prison in 1967, Toole managed to make it only nineteen days before he was behind bars again, this time on a misdemeanor malicious mischief rap that was dismissed.

Between stints in jail, he stayed with his mother and stepfather, Bob Harley. Later Sarah rented an apartment for her son so he could have his own place. But her nurturing efforts did not seem to be helping her youngest.

Daughter Drusilla was not having much more luck with her life. Like her long-gone father and little brother Ottis, Drusilla drank too much. Eventually she turned to other drugs. She went from man to man faster than her homosexual younger brother, and, like her mother, she was fertile. She gave birth to three children by two fathers, the oldest being a daughter she named Sarah, after her mother. Next came two children by a man named Frank Powell, Sr.—Frieda Lorraine, who would come to be nicknamed Becky, born February 27, 1967, and finally, a son, Frank, Jr., born September 18, 1968.

By the mid 1970's, Toole had thirteen arrests on his record, ranging from lewd and lascivious behavior to carrying a concealed weapon. He was well known by the local police, but there were too many for him to know all of them. Once, he went to jail after propositioning an undercover cop in a porno theater. Despite that case of mistaken identity on Toole's part, most of the time he had no trouble connecting with a man. When dressed in drag, he made a striking woman.

On the streets, Toole could get any kind of pill he wanted, including estrogen, which he took for a time to enlarge his breasts. He kept his legs shaved smooth. Wearing a wig, makeup, a flashy dress, and sheer stockings, he fooled many a man into thinking he was a woman. He had lost a few teeth after years on the street, but by the time he got around to opening his mouth, the men he had picked up either did not notice or did not care.

Toole found that dressing up like a woman was handy for other than sexual reasons. As a pretty "woman," he seemed to be able to get away with more. In a bar, he might start a fight and then blend into the background when the police arrived, playing the role of the defenseless damsel. Once, when he fancied some flowers on the porch of a nearby boardinghouse, he waited until he was in drag before he spirited them away.

Ottis made no attempt to hide his homosexuality, but he wondered sometimes if he was missing out on something by not being married. Barely past his teens, he had decided to give married life a try. Four days later, when one of his sisters volunteered to his new wife that Toole was gay, she promptly left him. On January 14, 1977, nearly thirty, he married again, this time to a woman who was fifty-one. They had sex occasionally, but he just did not enjoy it. When he wanted real pleasure, he went looking for a man. His wife put up with it because the men he brought home never stayed around long.

The kind of man he liked most was one who went

both ways. He enjoyed taking a bisexual home, having sex with him, and then letting him have sex with his oldest niece. Toole liked to watch, and Drusilla's young Sarah didn't seem to mind.

During the day, Ottis was almost a different person. He had the reputation of being a hard worker. He spent time in a variety of jobs, the longest as a cleanup man for a roofing company. He also did maintenance chores for the owner of several boardinghouses in the area. If someone needed a couch moved, he was so strong he could carry it himself. Others saw him as a big, childlike man, not very bright, but generally personable, except when he got mad. Sometimes running out of drugs would throw him into a mood; sometimes it was something someone had said.

Once, when a renter at one of the cheap apartment houses he helped maintain called him a "fag," Toole chased the man down the street, firing a couple of shots in his direction with a .22.

At night, sometimes in drag, he set out looking for men, booze, drugs, and thrills. The Jacksonville Fire Department put out a lot of suspicious fires in Springfield, most of them rundown structures no one was particularly sorry to see go.

Toole continued to turn tricks for money or drugs and for love. When he wanted someone to take home for the night, one of the places he had the best luck in finding temporary male companionship was the city rescue mission in the heart of Springfield.

Lucas didn't know what he was looking for. He was just looking, sitting on the steps of the rescue mission, a block over from Main Street. With his one good eye he watched the people going by. Mostly they were rough people in a rough part of town. Blacks and white trash—local winos, drifters like himself, whores, pimps, dealers. Just across the street, though, was a church. And on this Sunday, well-dressed people came to worship. They, and their church, seemed out of place in the rundown neighborhood.

He hadn't decided if he was going to stay in Florida or move on somewhere else. The only thing he knew for sure was that he wasn't going back to Maryland anytime soon. He had had it with his sisters and Betty, though as far as he knew he and she were still married. It seemed like women were always trying to tell him what to do or accusing him of something. On top of all that, the police were probably after him for stealing his nephew's pickup truck.

He'd been out of prison for three and a half years, and he was in no hurry to get back. The day after he'd been paroled, with a plane ticket provided by the prison, he'd flown to Baltimore, Maryland, where he'd caught a bus.

His half sister Wanda and her daughter, Lavern, met him at the bus station and drove him to Port Deposit, where Wanda and her husband, Eugene, lived. Half sister Nora lived nearby. Eugene and Lucas had never gotten along very well, and after only a day or two, Wanda called Lavern. "He's driving Eugene crazy," she said of her half brother. "Can he stay with you and Doug?" she asked.

Lavern and Doug, who lived in Pennsylvania, took him in and helped him find a job as a truck driver at a mushroom farm. A week later he got another job on another mushroom farm, but was soon fired. Since Doug had dropped him off at work at 6:30 A.M. that day and wouldn't be back by until quitting time, he'd walked more than five miles back to Lavern's. In October, Eugene agreed to sell him an old car cheap and let him pay it off a bit at a time when he had work.

At thirty-nine, Lucas had spent most of his adult life in prison. Other than his brief fling with Stella, he'd never had anything like a traditional relationship with a woman, though he had had sex with a few others.

Most of his sex had either been with animals or, in prison, with other inmates. But barely two months after he'd been released from prison, he was applying for a marriage license.

He had met Betty Crawford back in 1970 at his sister Nora's house, shortly after he'd gotten out of prison. At the time, Betty was married to his sister's son, Charles Crawford. Charles was out of work and the couple was living hand-to-mouth. Not long after he finally got a job, Charles was killed in an on-the-job accident. Betty was left with three little girls.

When he came back to Maryland in August 1975, Wanda told him that Betty had wanted to see him when he got out of prison. He found her living in a small, dirty apartment in Port Deposit. She cooked him dinner that night.

Betty was a heavyset woman ten years his junior. She had a good personality and Lucas liked the kids. Before long, he asked Betty to marry him. She said yes. She wasn't having much luck on her own, and Lucas did really seem to like the children.

Just how much Lucas liked the children was something Betty would not learn for some time. After their small wedding, they moved from Betty's rundown apartment to a double-decker trailer house in a mobile home park. The sexual abuse had started even before Lucas married Betty.

One night, when they were staying with one of her aunts, eight-year-old Cindy was bedded down in a sleeping bag. She awakened to find that Lucas had slipped in next to her and had his hand between her legs. She pushed him away, zipped the bag up to her neck, and he silently left.

During the winter, since the upstairs bedrooms of their trailer were not heated, everyone slept downstairs. Lucas insisted Cindy sleep with him and Betty so she could stay warm. But when Betty went to sleep, Lucas turned his attention to the little girl. The sexual abuse quickly moved beyond fondling.

Lucas always seemed willing to take care of the girls when Betty went shopping or for some other reason left the trailer. Often, when she was gone, he would order both girls upstairs. Once, repeating what he had been subjected to as a child, he had intercourse with nine-year-old Kathy, the oldest girl, and made Cindy watch. Later he tried to have sex with Cindy, but she resisted and he gave up.

Lucas seemed to want them daily. If he could not get to them while Betty was gone, he waited until she was asleep. In January 1977, the girls later recalled, Lucas took them to help him gather corn cobs from a field. Cindy was sick at the time, but he insisted she go. After they worked in the field for a while, Lucas told them to get in his car, which he backed into the corn stalks. Hidden from view, Lucas had intercourse with Kathy in the backseat, again ordering Cindy to look at them. Soon after finishing with the nine-year-old, Lucas told Cindy to take her clothes off. Again, she later told police, she succeeded in fending him off and finally talked him into taking them home.

Cindy's reluctance to do what Lucas told her was costly. Once, she later claimed, he beat her "black and blue." Lucas did eventually succeed in having sex with her, she said, but only once. Both little girls were terrified of their stepfather. They later told their mother, and police, that Lucas enforced his sexual abuse with repeated threats to kill them if they did not do what he said or if they told anyone what he did to them.

Cindy later told police she nearly got revenge on Lucas. She was doing the dishes, she said, when Lucas came up from behind and began touching her. Washing a butcher knife at the time, she told him to stop or she would stab him.

"You wouldn't stab your dad," she quoted Lucas as saying.

But when he did not stop, she whirled and slashed at him with the soapy blade. The knife made only a superficial wound, but Lucas left her alone, Cindy said.

Betty had noticed that the girls never wanted to be around Lucas and seemed fearful of being alone with him, but she mistakenly believed that since their father had died when they were very young, they just were not used to being around a man.

Betty's mother, however, believed there was more than a paternal instinct behind Lucas's interest in the children. Before long, she even had Lucas's sisters convinced he was having sex with the children.

When Betty's mother found blood on one of the little girls' panties, she accused Lucas. He vigorously denied it, but she said she didn't believe him. His sister had accused him of making the little girls stay home from school when Betty wasn't around and of sometimes taking them out to a gravel pit behind the trailer where they lived.

In June 1977 they made a trip to Texas. Betty's mother had been staying with another daughter in Hurst, a bedroom community near Fort Worth. Lucas had driven Betty, the girls, and a couple he and Betty were friends with down to Texas to pick up her mother and take her back to Maryland. En route, they slept in the car.

Not long after they were back in Maryland, Lucas decided he had had enough of Betty and her mother, though he would miss the girls. Little girls always did what they were told.

Lucas and his wife still had their trailer in Port Deposit, but on the night of July 6, 1977, they'd stayed at his sister's house, sleeping upstairs. About 5:00 A.M. the next morning, he got out of bed, leaving Betty still asleep. He gathered the clothes he had with him, got in his car, and drove away. He didn't even bother going by their trailer to get the rest of his things.

To be closer to her other two sisters, Opal Jennings had moved from Michigan to Maryland. For a few weeks after leaving Betty, Lucas stayed with Opal and her husband. He helped Opal with the summer canning and drank with her husband. They lived in a trailer, but Lucas slept in his car on their property.

Later that month, Lucas and Wanda's husband left Maryland for a family reunion in West Virginia. At Harper's Ferry, they got stuck in traffic at a bridge construction site. The two men started talking with another motorist, a man headed for Shreveport, Louisiana, and Lucas decided to join him. On the way, they stopped at Lindhurst, Virginia, where Lucas visited his half brother, Harry Waugh. They then continued on to Shreveport, where Lucas stayed for a few days. The other man drove on to California.

Lucas's family did not hear from him again until he called Wanda collect from Knoxville, Tennessee. He said he was hitchhiking back toward Maryland. He called again from Baltimore, saying he'd been arrested for hitchhiking and asking if Wanda could come pick him up. She did, and he stayed with her again for a while.

A job with a carpet-laying firm took him to Wilmington, Delaware. Later he went with two of his nephews to Hinton, West Virginia to work for a carpet company there.

In early 1978, Lucas met Rhonda Knuckles, a hotel maid. They lived together for about three months, most of the time in a rented mobile home. One of his nephews co-signed a note so Lucas could buy bedroom furniture and carpeting for the trailer.

Rhonda thought Lucas was willing to do anything for her and believed they were headed toward marriage. Whenever she brought up the subject with

Lucas, however, he had an excuse for why they should not marry. He was divorced from a woman in Maryland, he said, and had been to prison for killing a man in a bar. Only later did she learn Lucas was lying on both counts.

Lucas came home one day saying he'd been laid off. He didn't strain himself looking for another job. Rhonda, who had a sick son, was not working either. Around each other twenty-four hours a day, their relationship deteriorated rapidly. So did their sex life. Rhonda watched him become more and more withdrawn, not wanting to be touched. Often he sat and simply stared into space, smoking and drinking coffee incessantly. Then Lucas accused her of seeing another man.

"If I can't have you, nobody can have you," Lucas said.

"What are you going to do, kill me?"

"Yeah, I'd rather do that than let any other man have you."

Rhonda tried to reassure Lucas there was no one else in her life. Though she was scared of him, she did everything she could to help him. Finally, she realized he needed professional help. As she later recalled, "It was too deep for me in there."

In early March, they broke up. Rhonda gave Lucas money for a bus ticket to Maryland.

Back in Maryland, he stayed again with Opal for a while and then moved in with Wanda and Eugene. Since getting out of prison, he had stayed off and on with all three sisters and one of his nieces. Even when he was staying somewhere on his own, he often dropped by for a visit at mealtime. He couldn't seem to get along with anyone in his family for very long, though they almost always came to his rescue when he asked for help.

In February 1979, Wanda confronted the man she had known since he was a little boy. She did not want to believe it, but she suspected Lucas was abusing her granddaughter.

Lucas denied it, vehemently.

"Do you want me to leave?" he asked.

"Only if you did it," she said.

The next day Lucas was gone. So was Wanda's son's pickup truck.

He had headed south on I-95. He didn't know for sure where he'd go, but he knew one thing: he wasn't going to go back to his family again. He had had it with all of them.

He drove down to Miami, then decided to turn back north to Jacksonville. The truck broke down and he didn't have the money to get it fixed. He fenced the tools that had been in the bed of the truck and abandoned it.

Now he was at the mission near skid row, watching the people go by and waiting for the soup line to open. A big man with a jack-o'-lantern smile sauntered up the stairs toward him. He recognized Ottis Toole. They'd met in a tavern in Pennsylvania when he was working at the mushroom farm. They'd had a few beers together before Ottis went back to Florida.

"What are you doing sitting here, Henry?" His voice was sweet, Southern.

"I just come over here to sit down," Lucas smiled, lighting up a Pall Mall.

"Come on, let's go home," Ottis said. "I'll let you meet Mama and Dad and my sister's kids."

Lucas followed Toole to his mother's rented house, about seven blocks away. As soon as he got there, he felt at home.

Sarah Toole Harley was washing clothes when her son showed up and introduced Lucas. Ottis went to get them some beer and Lucas struck up a conversation with Sarah. When she was ready to hang up the clothes, Lucas went over and grabbed an armful and started helping.

"What are you doing that for?" she asked, surprised.

"I'm just helping you hang clothes up." Lucas smiled as he answered.

"Well, nobody ever did that before," she said.

"As long as I'm here and I can help you, let me know," he said.

They sat in the backyard that afternoon, drinking beer and talking. He'd been there several hours when he noticed a pretty girl in shorts peeking at him from around the corner of the house. She looked about twelve years old. When she realized he had seen her, she disappeared. A few minutes later, she came back out in a pair of long pants.

Ottis beamed as she walked toward him.

"How do you like my brother?" he said, pointing to Lucas.

"I don't know him," she replied solemnly. "I didn't know you had another brother." Abruptly, she ran back into the house.

Ottis said her name was Becky. She was his sister Drusilla Powell's daughter. Drusilla also had a little boy named Frank and another daughter named Sarah, he said. Sarah was the oldest and already off on her own, though she sometimes stayed with the grandmother for whom she'd been named.

Lucas took a deep drag on his beer. He'd lost count of how many cans he and Ottis had gone through. Ottis's sister's kids were cute, but Becky was already his favorite. Like Ottis, she seemed a little slow, but she had pretty long, dark hair.

"Henry, I don't want you going off to that mission tonight. Somebody'd shoot the shit out of you or rob you before you got there. You stay here with us," Ottis said.

"Well, I ain't got any money," Lucas said. "I guess I'll stay."

Ottis and his wife, Novella, lived in a small apartment behind the larger house his mother and stepfather rented. That night Lucas bedded down in the front room and Ottis and his wife went back to their bedroom. Before long, Lucas could hear them arguing. He knew what was eating on her: she was jealous. Ottis was queer and she knew her husband would rather have him back there than her. He couldn't figure why Ottis would have married her in the first place. But that was his problem. He took one last swig of beer and settled back to get some sleep. He drifted off thinking about Ottis's niece.

The next day he found out more about her. As it turned out, her mother was a dopehead, divorced from the children's father. Drusilla lived downtown with her boyfriend. She wasn't fit to be mothering the two kids at home, and Sarah Harley had gone to court to get custody of them. Soon Lucas found himself pretty attached to them, especially Becky.

Ottis was working for a roofing company, and on Ottis's recommendation they hired Lucas. The men made a little more than $100 a week. That wasn't a lot of money, but then Henry had never had much, and he'd always managed to get by. What he didn't have the money to buy he could always steal. The work wasn't all that steady, so he and Ottis had plenty of time to get out on their own.

Ottis felt good around Henry. Henry took care of him. He knew how to do things Ottis never could figure out. Best of all, Henry had managed to buy a car. Ottis sometimes borrowed or stole a car, but he had never had a driver's license and had been busted twice for driving without one. Each time the police had told him to get a license, but he knew he couldn't have passed the written test. He had trouble even understanding the road signs, but Henry always knew where to go.

Before long Ottis and Novella were spending less and less time together. But a new family unit was developing.

Lucas and Ottis spent an increasing amount of time with Becky and Frank. The kids liked to ride in the backseat as their uncle and the one-eyed man they came to regard as their other uncle drove around Jacksonville. They took other trips, too, heading north up I-95 or west on I-10. In a way, Jacksonville was at the elbow of the nation—the upper arm stretched all the way up the East Coast to Maine; the lower half, bent horizontally, extended all the way to California. For someone who liked to travel by car, Jacksonville made a fine hometown.

For all of his life, Toole had had only one person he could always count on—his mother. Now sixty-three, her struggle to raise eight children and make a modest living was catching up with her. At a time when most people could look forward to taking it easy and enjoying their grandchildren, her burdens seemed greater than ever. Drusilla, struggling with her drug addiction, was in no shape to raise Becky and Frank, so the kids were with her most of the time. She saw that they had food, clothing, went to school, and went to church. Granddaughter Sarah, Drusilla's oldest child, had already gone out on her own, headed into life's basement down the same dreary steps her mother had taken.

Now, it seemed, Sarah Harley had a ninth child—Henry Lee Lucas. He had become part of the family. He helped her take care of Becky and Frank, and she and Henry often made the rounds together when Henry was out looking for junk to sell.

For too many years, Sarah Harley had been the tent pole for the entire family, especially for her troubled son Ottis. She paid the bills and handled his money, often picking up his checks at the roofing company. The strain on her heart, emotionally and physically, was finally too much. She had to have heart surgery, but it didn't help much. In May 1981, she died of a heart attack in the bedroom of her rented house. Three days later, she was buried in Evergreen Cemetery.

Ottis was devastated by his mother's death. She had only gone to sleep, he told Henry. At nights, he haunted the cemetery, visiting her grave. She knew he was coming to her, he believed.

A month later, on June 17, a worried Howell Toole, Ottis's older brother, called the police and asked to talk to an officer. It was Howell's birthday, but he didn't feel like celebrating. Howell Toole told the officer about his mother's death. No decisions had been made yet about her estate, but Ottis and a friend of his, Henry Lucas, had been staying at the house she rented, apparently helping themselves to her things.

"A lot of her stuff is missing," the brother told the officer. "Now I can't find Ottis and Henry. My niece and nephew are gone, too."

The officer filled out a report and suggested that Howell contact the state prosecutor's office. What happened next would be their call, the officer said.

A month later Howell Toole telephoned the police again. Ottis and Henry had shown up, briefly. But now his pickup truck was missing and the two were gone again.

"Ottis stole my truck," Howell told the officer.

This time the officer noted in his report that the state prosecutor's office had been informed of Howell's complaint but had declined to handle the case.

A couple of weeks later, on August 1, police were called to a convenience store on Main Street in

Springfield. The first officer on the scene found an agitated Ottis rubbing a red spot on his face.

"He said he was going to kill my ass," Ottis told the officer, shaking his head to clear his mind.

"Who?" the patrolman asked.

"Howell, my brother. He busted me with his fist. Pulled a pistol on my ass."

The officer cruised the area, finding Howell a few blocks away. He had a pistol, all right, but it was an antique. It wouldn't fire.

"If you want to file charges, you need to go see the state's attorney," the officer told Ottis after filling out his report.

The old two-story Victorian house, framed by huge oaks festooned with hanging moss, had once been as fine an address as there was anywhere in Jacksonville. But the splendor was gone now. The bedrooms of the old house at 117 East Second Street had all been converted into apartments that rented for about $100 a week.

George Sonenberg remembered when Springfield had been just about the best part of town in Jacksonville. But with each decade after World War Two it had become more and more rundown. Now it was just a place to stay. At least it was dry and reasonably warm, better than being outside in the cold rain. On this night, shortly before ten o'clock, Sonenberg already was in bed in his downstairs apartment, number five.

Upstairs in apartment three, Bryan Snyder thought he smelled smoke. When he opened his door, the hall was so full of smoke he couldn't see. His first impulse was to run for the stairs, but the smoke was too thick. Coughing, trying to feel his way back to his room, where maybe he could get out the window, his hands burned when he touched the wall.

In apartment two, Candy Playford also realized that flames and smoke blocked her escape downstairs. She pushed open her window and jumped. When she hit the ground, her leg bent in the wrong direction and she screamed in pain. Caroline Talley also jumped from the second floor. When she got to her feet after the fall, her neck and back hurt.

Flames were already shooting from windows when the first fire engines pulled up outside the burning boardinghouse. Moments later, police cars and city rescue units screeched to a stop in front of the old house.

"I think Mr. Sonenberg's still inside," one of the boardinghouse residents shouted.

The firefighters knocked the blaze down in a hurry. Within minutes firefighters in air masks began checking the rooms one by one. Sonenberg was found unconscious on the charred floor next to his bed, his smoke-filled lungs laboring for air. He was badly burned.

When the rescue crew members burst through the emergency room doors at Baptist Hospital the patient on the gurney was still unconscious. As soon as he was stablized and cleaned up, he was wheeled to the intensive care unit.

Not quite a week after the January 4, 1982, fire, the sixty-five-year-old burn victim died. Later that day, a pathologist with the medical examiner's office viewed the body. In the doctor's opinion, no autopsy was necessary. He noted the location and extent of the burns, the marks left by the various IV's that had been stuck in the patient to keep him hydrated and nourished, and ruled the death due to "conflagration by accident." The body was then released for burial.

Meanwhile, investigators with the Fire Prevention Bureau had determined that the fire had started on a foam rubber mattress in a vacant apartment on the first floor, next door to Sonenberg's apartment. The fire had spread from the empty room down the hall to the stairs.

In checking with the manager of the rooming house, a fire department captain learned that a man had moved out of the apartment where the fire had started the day before. Since the weather had been bad that night, it appeared someone had slipped into the boardinghouse in hopes of getting a dry night's sleep and apparently was careless with a cigarette. The person must have run off when the fire started.

Case number 5501 was labeled an accidental death and listed as cleared.

Howell Toole was worried about his niece and nephew now that their grandmother was dead. He had tried to get custody of them, but for the time being they were staying with their mother and her latest husband in Auburndale. But on December 16, Drusilla was found dead of a drug overdose. The next day, Becky and Frank were placed in the custody of the Florida Department of Health and Rehabilitation Services at nearby Bartow. Two weeks later, Becky was listed as a runaway from the emergency shelter. Lucas had driven to the shelter, found her outside, and picked her up. On January 9, 1982, Lucas got rid of one clunker, bought another, transferred the insurance, and hit the road with Becky, headed west. Ottis, still hearing those voices that said he should kill himself and go to rest, was bewildered that Lucas had left him behind and taken his favorite niece. He prowled Springfield all night looking for them.

CHAPTER SIX

For a second, Kevin Key did not realize what was wrong when he felt the car's slight hesitation, a subtle change that was hardly noticeable. The nineteen-year-old and his date, Rita Salazar, eighteen, were still talking about the movie they had just seen back in Austin, *Midnight Express*. Based on the story of a young American's imprisonment in Turkey for trying to smuggle two kilos of hashish, the movie had been a downer. The brutality and degradation had been uncomfortably realistic, and for Kevin maybe a little too close to home. He knew what it was like to be on the inside of a jail, though his treatment after his arrest on a burglary charge had never been anything like he had just seen on the big screen. Walking out of the movie had almost been like waking up from a bad dream—you knew what you had just experienced was not reality, at least not your reality. This was America. A person still could feel fairly safe on this side of the ocean. Over in the Middle East everything was crazy. Life did not seem to mean much to those people.

Kevin put a little more pressure on the accelerator, but the car began losing speed. Then it hit him. He looked down at the gas gauge and saw the needle way below the empty mark.

"We're out of gas! Steve told me to get some more, and I just blew it off."

"Hey, that's okay," Rita said. "No big deal."

Kevin stayed on the highway as long as he could, then eased over onto the shoulder, letting his brother's car coast as far as possible. Finally, the Ford Torino came to a halt. He tried to get it going again, but realized that was only going to make it harder to restart once he poured some gas in the tank. Each crank drained the carburetor even more.

They were about eleven miles north of Austin on Interstate 35. Even though it was nearly midnight on a Sunday, Kevin figured they could hitch a ride to an all-night service station so he could get a starter can of gas.

Cars and big trucks whizzed by the couple as they walked north on the shoulder of the highway. A steady drizzle was falling, adding to the irritation and the lonely feeling of being stranded late at night. Surely someone will stop anytime now, Kevin thought, embarrassed at the way an otherwise nice night with a pretty girl had been screwed up. But he had no one to blame but himself. His brother Steve had warned him the car was just about out of gas. He should have taken the time to stop and buy a few dollars' worth, which was about all he could have afforded. In fact, now he might even have to borrow a few bucks from Rita to pay for the gas. And the service station would probably want a deposit on the can, he thought.

They had not walked too far when a car finally pulled up behind them, bathing them in its headlights. Turning and squinting into the bright lights, Kevin and Rita could not see who was in the car, but they were thankful someone had finally stopped.

If anyone had been riding in the backseat of the car headed north on the interstate that night, they would have been fighting the urge to gag from the stench. The two men in the front seat did not pay much attention to personal hygiene. Body odor, beer breath, and cigarette smoke combined with long-unbrushed teeth mixed together to form a smell that would send a normal person reeling. But the two men in the car knocking down beer after beer did not find it bothersome.

As usual, they did not know where they were headed. The driver took pleasure from just being behind the wheel. His passenger was not smart enough to figure out where he was, but he would not care if he did know.

Suddenly the headlights of their car lit up a couple walking along the edge of the highway. Lucas hit his brakes. He could see that the girl had long dark hair and a nice figure. Ottis was more interested in the young man who was with her.

"We ran out of gas," Kevin told the smiling driver, who had rolled down his window. "Could you give us a ride into town?"

Lucas invited the couple to get in.

Rita had hung back during the short conversation, but she felt relieved as Kevin opened the back door for her and let her slide first into the backseat.

As soon as the door shut and the car started moving, the big man on the passenger's side of the front seat swung around with a pistol pointed at the boy's smooth face.

Rita screamed.

"Shut up!" the driver yelled.

"Hey, I've got a few bucks," Kevin stammered. "You can have everything I've got. Just let us out of the car and we'll walk on into town ourselves."

In the dark Kevin slipped his father's ring off his finger and dropped it into his boottop. The joke would be on them in this robbery. They could have the few dollars he had in his pocket, but they wouldn't know about his gold ring.

As the big man held the pistol on them, the driver turned off the interstate and headed down a narrow paved road.

"Please, just take us to Round Rock," Rita begged as she began to cry.

The driver went only a short distance off the interstate before stopping.

The big man got out and came around to Kevin's side of the car. He opened the door and with a strong hand pulled the young man from the backseat. The driver stayed in the car, looking back at Rita with a smile.

"Okay, man, you can have my money," Kevin said, reaching for his wallet.

But Toole decided to help himself. He casually shot the boy.

For a moment, Kevin did not realize he had been hit. Instinctively, he turned and tried to run. He made it a few feet, but then it seemed as if he had no legs. His mind told him to keep running, but there was nothing under him and suddenly he was falling.

Toole walked closer and pointed the .22 at the prone form. He smiled in pleasure as he kept pulling the trigger, his ears beginning to ring from the pop of the semiautomatic. When he was satisfied there was no way the boy could still be alive, he bent down and pulled his billfold from his pants.

Once Toole was back in the car, Lucas turned around and headed back to the interstate as the girl in the back sobbed hysterically.

"Why'd you shoot him?" she screamed. "Where are you taking me? Please let me out!"

Lucas knew the answer only to the first question. The young man had been shot because his friend was finished with him. He was not needed anymore. The pretty girl would be nice to have around a little longer. He had no idea, though, where they were going.

As the car headed back toward the interstate, Toole went through Kevin's wallet. After removing the cash, he tossed the billfold out the window.

Both men were enjoying the girl's frantic pleadings, alternated by racking sobs. But when she started trying to open the back door, apparently figuring on jumping out, Lucas had had enough.

Taking his friend's pistol, which he was at least smart enough to know how to reload, Lucas started shooting the noisy girl. Like all women, he thought, she was too much trouble.

Lucas stopped the car, pulled her out onto the roadway, and shot her a few more times just to make sure she was through raising so much hell.

And then they sped north, their adrenaline pumping from the excitement of it all. However, Lucas was frustrated in having to get rid of the girl so soon. As he often did, Toole leaned over and took care of him.

Most of the time, it was quiet out in the country north of Georgetown, where Williamson County sheriff Jim Boutwell lived. That was the main reason he had moved out there. Sometimes, if the weather was right, the traffic noise from I-35, a couple of miles away, drifted to the sheriff's house. And occasionally, Boutwell and his wife, Louise, could hear the distant drone of a small plane taking off or landing at the county airport a few miles to the south. But being a pilot himself, Boutwell never found it bothersome. He was so used to it, most of the time he did not even notice the sound.

Tall and as thin as a cedar post on a barbed-wire fence, Boutwell had been sheriff less than a year. But his law enforcement career went way back. He was first commissioned as a peace officer in 1949, when he got a deputy sheriff's badge in El Paso County, in far

West Texas. Though he held a commission from the sheriff there, he was on the payroll of the Texas Department of Public Safety as a pilot.

Boutwell eventually transferred into the department's internal security section, the forerunner of its Criminal Intelligence Service. He was given a Texas Ranger commission, though he reported through a different chain of command. He stayed with the state law enforcement agency until 1954, when he quit to run a flying school in Austin.

In 1966, when former Eagle Scout Charles J. Whitman mounted the University of Texas tower in the heart of one of the largest college campuses in the nation and began firing down on students and passersby below, the Austin Police Department asked Boutwell if he would fly an officer around the tower as an observer. The police officer rushed to the small airport where Boutwell had his plane, and the aircraft was soon circling the tower. The sniper realized what police were doing and fired several high-powered rifle shots toward the plane, leaving a few neat round holes in the thin fuselage. The rampage ended ninety minutes after it began when police stormed Whitman's perch and killed him in a blast of buckshot and pistol rounds. Boutwell landed his plane without incident.

Boutwell was working as a deputy in the Williamson County Sheriff's Department when the sheriff died. County commissioners appointed A. O. Schier to fill the vacancy, and Schier in turn named Boutwell as his chief deputy. When election time came, Schier said he did not want the job. In May 1978, Boutwell ran and won. A week after the primary, Schier resigned and the commissioners appointed Boutwell to fill the brief unexpired term. In the general election that fall he was elected to a full four-year term as sheriff.

The lanky lawman enjoyed his new job, but he also appreciated coming home in the evening. After work and before dinner, he liked to pull his boots off, shuck the ornate hand-tooled gun belt holding the .45 semi-automatic and take it to the bedroom, and fix himself a big glass of water and ice—and then splash in a jigger of bourbon for flavoring. Then he would talk with Louise, who worked at one of the high schools in north Austin, about her day and his. They enjoyed an easygoing, modern country lifestyle, a way of living in Texas that had drawn more and more people to the so-called shiny buckle of the Sunbelt.

Boutwell's county had grown from a population of 30,000 in 1970 to nearly 100,000 by 1978. What had not changed was the size of his area of responsibility. The county just north of Austin covered 1,104 square miles.

But he was managing to cope with the problems of growth, a backwash from the booming capital city thirty miles to the south. His two biggest headaches were burglaries and drugs, law enforcement problems aggravated by his county's proximity to a big city. Williamson County had its share of violent crime, but no homicides had gone unsolved in more than a half century. Adroitly dealing with county commissioners, Boutwell had already been able to get money for more deputies—never enough, of course—and improvements for his jail, a century-old limestone building just north of the courthouse square. He was a popular law enforcement officer, able to get along well with other agencies, prosecutors, and the press.

He knew being a sheriff was seldom just a forty-hour-a-week job. The late-night telephone calls at home, the ones that meant he had to get out of bed, dress, and strap his .45 back on to go somewhere as the symbol of order and authority in his county, were all part of the job.

At 8:55 A.M. on Monday, November 6, 1978, Larry Weems went to the courthouse office of Texas Parks and Wildlife Department game warden Burt Williams. Weems, a passerby, told Williams he had found a billfold in a ditch about four miles north of town.

Though Texas game wardens are fully commissioned peace officers, they generally have their hands full investigating hunting and fishing law violations. Williams asked Weems to drop the wallet by the sheriff's office.

A few minutes later, Weems turned the damp leather billfold over to a secretary in the sheriff's office, who thanked him and handed it over to deputy Arma Harper.

Harper fished a laminated Texas driver's license from the billfold and looked at the small color photograph of its owner, Frank Kevin Key of 5602 Mapleleaf in Austin. The wallet also contained a Social Security card, a department store credit card, a photograph of a soldier wearing a beret, a photograph of an attractive blonde, and a business card. The card caught Harper's interest: it bore the name of a Travis County adult probation officer.

The deputy dialed the number.

The probation officer said Key was one of his cases, a young man on probation for burglary. He had been living up to the terms of probation and had kept all his appointments. The probation officer gave the deputy Key's home phone number.

"Let me know if there's been some kind of trouble," he added.

Deputy Harper then called Key's residence. Geraldine Key, Kevin's mother, answered the phone. Kevin had not come home Sunday night after going out on a date with a young girl from Georgetown, she said, and he had not shown up for work that morning. She was already worried, more so after hearing from the deputy that her son's billfold had been found off the side of a county road. Mrs. Key described the car her son had been driving: a 1974 Ford Torino, dark blue vinyl over light blue. She even knew the license plate number, DYE-687. Harper thanked her for the information, said he would keep her posted, and hung up.

The deputy's next step was to check the department's radio log to see if any deputies had stopped the vehicle the night before, or checked its registration. The sheet showed no activity involving the vehicle. Next Harper checked with the local office of the Texas Department of Public Safety. A Highway Patrol trooper there said he did not recall having seen the vehicle either. Neither had the car been involved in a traffic accident—at least, not in the Georgetown area.

"I'll give you a holler if I see the car," the trooper said.

Harper knew there were a number of possibilities as to why Key's billfold had been lost, ranging from routine to troublesome. But for the time being, not having any other leads, he turned his attention to other matters.

Later that afternoon, the Highway Patrol trooper noticed a car parked on the side of the interstate. He was on his way to another call, but after reconfirming the description of Key's car, he used his intercity radio frequency to ask that a Round Rock police officer check out the car.

A few moments later, the Round Rock city officer radioed that the license plate on the parked car was DYE-687. The car was locked, he said, and nothing appeared out of order inside other than the rearview mirror, which was down on the floorboard.

After learning the car had been found, deputy Harper telephoned Mrs. Key again. She still had not heard from Kevin, she said.

"We've found your son's car out on the interstate," he told her. "You might want to make arrangements to have it picked up before somebody comes along and strips it."

About 6 P.M. Mrs. Key called the sheriff's department from a pay phone. She and her other son, Steve, had driven from Austin to pick up the car, but they were having trouble finding it.

The radio operator handed the phone to Deputy Charles Maxey.

"Is Kevin with you?" he asked.

"No, I still haven't heard from him," she said. "I'm worried. This isn't like him."

"Will you hold the phone for a minute, Mrs. Key?"

Maxey put the line on hold and dialed Chief Criminal Investigator Ray Hardison's line. After listening to a quick rundown on the discovery of the wallet and the car, Hardison said he wanted to talk to Mrs. Key.

The deputy got the number of the pay phone, gave it to Hardison, and he called her back.

"I know one of our deputies suggested you pick up the car," Hardison said, "but since Kevin still hasn't turned up, I'd like to check things out a little more first. We'll stay in touch, and please let us know if you hear anything from Kevin, okay?"

After he got off the telephone from talking with Mrs. Key, Hardison told deputies Maxey and Red Watson to go take another look at the car.

"When you get through, have it towed on in," he said.

The car was parked about a foot off of the interstate and about seven yards west of a fence line. On the other side of the fence, about twenty yards away, were a dilapidated old farmhouse and barn. The ground and grass around the car did not appear to have been walked on since the rain had stopped earlier that morning. The officers noted that the car's ashtray had been pulled out and was on top of the dash. As the Round Rock officer had reported earlier, nothing seemed particularly out of order in the car. The deputies climbed under the fence and checked the abandoned buildings but found nothing unusual. About 8 P.M., satisfied there was nothing else to be learned at the scene, the officers had the car picked up by a wrecker.

Maxey called Hardison and filled him in on his investigation around the car. After he had reported in, Maxey drove to where the wallet had been found earlier that morning. Deputy Watson went back on routine patrol.

Deputy Maxey slowly cruised east on the county road near where the wallet had been found, playing his spotlight along the ditch on the north side of the pavement. He then turned around and drove about a hundred yards to the west, parked the car, and started walking back east, this time checking the south side of the roadway.

The deputy swept his flashlight beam back and forth along the ditch as he walked east. About two hundred yards off the interstate, he stopped abruptly. Just ahead of him, sprawled face down, was the body of a young man dressed in a black shirt and tan pants. Maxey stooped to confirm what he already knew. The man was dead, cold to the touch.

Maxey went back to his patrol car and picked up his radio microphone.

"Twenty-two to Georgetown."

"Go ahead, twenty-two."

"I've got a DOS out here," he said, reporting the location. "Contact unit one and a judge."

In fifteen minutes Sheriff Boutwell, who had been at home, pulled up to the scene. A few minutes later, Hardison arrived and briefed Boutwell on the earlier discovery of the wallet and car.

"I imagine this is Kevin Key," Hardison said, pointing to the dead man.

The tall sheriff squatted down and moved the body enough to shine his light on the bloody face. The youth appeared to have been shot several times in the head. His wallet was missing, but he had a set of car keys in his pocket. Boutwell was not surprised to see the keys were to a Ford.

Within a few minutes, the officers had found three .22-caliber hulls in the general vicinity of the body, but nothing else that would offer any clue as to what had happened to the young man.

Though nothing was certain until they had a positive identification, Boutwell and Hardison had little doubt that the dead youth was the missing Kevin Key. And, assuming that was correct, where was the young Georgetown girl who was supposed to have been with him?

At 10:14 P.M. Sheriff Boutwell radioed his dispatcher to telephone Texas Ranger Joe Davis, who lived in Round Rock.

Boutwell knew some law enforcement officers who were reluctant to call on the Texas Rangers for help. For egotistical or political reasons, sometimes both, some sheriffs chose to go it alone on an investigation and leave the state out of it. But Boutwell didn't think that way. He'd worked closely with the Ranger service for years.

In one form or another, the Rangers had been around since 1823, when Stephen F. Austin first colonized Texas. The modern Rangers were part of the Texas Department of Public Safety. Highly trained and motivated, they had jurisdiction anywhere in the state. Boutwell never hesitated to call on the Rangers when he needed help. And as he looked down at a young man more than likely killed by someone merely passing through his county, he knew he needed some help.

When Ranger Davis reached the scene, Boutwell filled him in on what he had so far. A short time later, Justice of the Peace Bill Hill, acting as coroner, went through the legal formality of pronouncing the body dead and ordering an autopsy.

After the body had been removed, Boutwell assigned a deputy to stand guard at the crime scene overnight to prevent damage to any evidence they might have overlooked in the darkness.

Forty minutes into Tuesday, November 7, Mrs. Consuelo Salazar of Georgetown called the sheriff's office. Her daughter, Rita, had left on a date about 7:10 P.M. on Sunday, she said, and never came home.

On a hunch, Boutwell called the McLennan County Sheriff's Office in Waco, a city of 100,000 about seventy miles north of Georgetown on I-35. Earlier, on Monday, that department had put out a teletype requesting assistance in identifying a young woman found shot to death just off the interstate near the community of Hewitt, in McLennan County. After talking with Deputy Wendall Crunk, who was investigating the murder of the woman, Boutwell was pretty sure he had found Rita Salazar. Then he went home for a few hours' sleep.

By 7:30 A.M. Tuesday, Boutwell and Ranger Davis were back where the body of the young man had been found the night before. They took photographs of the scene, found three more spent .22 shells, and prepared a sketch marking the location of each shell found so far.

From the crime scene Boutwell drove to Austin, where Travis County Medical Examiner Dr. Robert Bayardo performed an autopsy on the body found in the ditch the night before. A photo comparison confirmed the young man was definitely Kevin Key. The pathologist found ten gunshot wounds in Key's head, neck, back, left upper arm, and right flank. Seven .22-caliber bullets and two lead fragments were recovered from the body. Samples of the victim's blood and urine were taken to be tested for alcohol or other drugs.

Back in Georgetown, the sheriff met with Ranger Davis, Hardison, McLennan County Deputy Crunk and another Texas Ranger, James Wright of Waco.

At 2:20 A.M. that Monday, Deputy Crunk related, a man who lived in the small McLennan County community of Hewitt had telephoned the DPS regional headquarters in Waco to report he had heard gunshots and had seen a suspicious vehicle.

The DPS communications operator who took the call relayed the information to the Hewitt police chief, who went to the area where the shots had been reported.

"He checked both sides of the interstate and found a girl's body," the deputy said. "She was lying facedown in the ditch just off the east service road. Her right foot was just touching the pavement."

The girl's head was turned a little to the right, he continued. She was clutching a bloody white sweater in her right hand. Several blood stains were around the body. Nearby was an empty .22 shell. Four more hulls were scattered about thirty feet from the body.

After the body was turned over, the deputy said, officers found a .22 slug on the woman's right breast, the spent projectile lying on her bra. While photographs were being taken of the victim, a broken gold necklace was found and placed into an evidence bag.

As Boutwell listened to the details of the McLennan County case, his mind raced over various points of his case. He was beginning to picture what must have happened to the couple.

"I checked Kevin's car," Boutwell told the other officers. "It was out of gas. It looks to me like they were headed to Georgetown to drop off Rita when the car stalled out on him. He locked the car, put the keys in his pocket, and they started walking north, probably trying to hitch a ride. Looks like the wrong kind of person stopped."

Boutwell related something interesting he had learned at the autopsy: the ME's office had found a gold ring in one of Key's boots.

"Looks like they were robbed," Boutwell said. "Kevin must have had a chance to drop that ring in his boot. Someone shot him and left him in the ditch. Then they headed north with Rita, shot her in McLennan County, and then dumped her. Does it look like she was raped?"

Crunk swallowed some coffee.

"We don't have the autopsy report yet, but she was fully clothed," he said.

The deputy said the man who had reported the shots had gotten a pretty good look at the car the killers were probably in. The vehicle was full-sized, dark, and probably a four-door. It had an amber side light on the front and a red side light on the rear. The witness had been too far off to make out any facial features of the car's occupants, however.

Over the next several days, the Williamson County officers and Texas Rangers substantiated the events of the young couple's final hours of life. They documented how much money they had had, the period of time they had been in the theater, the extent of the couple's relationship (three weeks), and their backgrounds, neither of which suggested anything likely to have had a bearing on their deaths. Key had been convicted of burglary in Austin, but he seemed to have been doing well on probation. No suggestion of any additional criminal activities on his part had come to light. It looked like he had made a youthful mistake, realized it, and was trying to do right. Boutwell wished every probation case worked out that well. His department would sure have a lot less work to do.

The officers explored all the standard possibilities in looking for suspects—disgruntled former lovers, family members, co-workers, local characters—but nothing panned out.

Appeals through the news media for information from anyone who might have seen the stranded couple the night of their deaths netted the officers a few calls, but again no meaningful leads came to light.

The autopsy of Salazar indicated she had not been sexually assaulted prior to her death. Since she had been kept alive after her date was shot, the officers had considered it likely that a sexual motive was behind that. But vaginal, oral, and anal swabs to check for spermatozoa had all been negative.

The pathologist found ten bullet wounds in Salazar, six entrance wounds and four exit wounds. Death had come from a shot that penetrated her heart.

A synopsis of the case, with a detailed description of the .22 hulls found at the two crime scenes, was published in the DPS's Crime Analysis Bulletin on December 7, 1978, with a plea that any agency having a similar robbery-homicide involving a .22-caliber weapon contact Sheriff Boutwell or the Texas Rangers. The bulletin brought a couple of responses from other agencies with open cases, but ballistic comparisons did not produce any matches.

By October of 1979, almost a year later, Williamson County Sheriff's Office Offense No. 78-11-12 remained unsolved.

That Halloween, Boutwell and his deputies were hoping for a quiet night. Shortly after sundown, they knew, the numerous subdivisions out in the county would be swarming with pint-sized ghosts and ghouls, young trick-or-treaters in a variety of grisly and bizarre costumes out for an early evening of traditional fun. Boutwell wanted it to be a safe evening—no auto-pedestrian accidents, no tampered-with candy, no criminal mischief in the name of "tricks."

At 4:28 P.M., barely an hour before sundown, radio dispatcher Linda Rumbaugh called the sheriff on his extension.

"Sheriff, we just got a call from Bill Stuewe," she said. "He says he and R. V. Barker found the body of a nude female off the west frontage road, just past the Walburg overpass."

Boutwell did not know Stuewe but he did know Barker. There was no chance the call was a Halloween prank.

"I'll get Judge Hill and be on my way," Boutwell told Rumbaugh.

Boutwell swung by the office of Bill Hill, the justice of the peace, and then drove to a service station on I-35, where Stuewe was waiting to lead officers to the body. Criminal Investigator Hardison also was on his way, as was Chief Deputy Jim Wilson.

Barker had his four-year-old grandson with him when he saw something in the culvert and backed up to take a second look. Barker saw Stuewe driving by and signaled him to stop. When they were sure they had found a body, Stuewe had gone to call the sheriff's office.

"She's right down there in the culvert," Stuewe pointed.

The two officers, Stuewe, and the JP climbed over the guardrail and walked through knee-high dead grass to the edge of the culvert.

The first thing that struck the sheriff was how pale the nude body looked and how out of place, sprawled on the concrete like some piece of roadside litter. The next thing that hit him was the socks she had on—bright orange. She was lying on her right side, almost facedown, just beyond the edge of the culvert. One arm was beneath her, the other bent at the elbow and angled down at her side. Medium-length reddish-brown hair fanned out on the concrete above her head.

116

"Looks like somebody dragged her off the roadway and tossed her off the edge of the culvert," Boutwell said as the men walked down into the weed-cluttered ditch.

As Hardison and Chief Deputy Wilson began looking for evidence, Boutwell got his camera out of his car and began photographing the victim from various angles.

The officers noted some abrasions on the woman's back and buttocks, possibly caused when she was dragged to the drop-off. A small amount of blood had collected beneath her mouth, but there were no obvious signs of injury. The body had already begun to stiffen and discolor.

Boutwell and the other officers found very little in the way of physical evidence. No items of clothing other than the socks, no purse, no possible murder weapon. The officers did pick up a couple of matchbook covers and a stained piece of paper towel found near the victim. It appeared the young woman had been using the towel as a makeshift sanitary napkin.

As little as he had to go on, Boutwell wanted everything done right. He had a deputy drive District Attorney Ed Walsh, his assistant, and an investigator to the scene. If Boutwell ever found who killed this girl, it would be up to Walsh and his staff to get him convicted. The sheriff wanted the prosecution in on the case from the start.

After all the measurements had been taken, Boutwell and the other officers pulled on surgical gloves before they lifted the body into a black rubber crash bag. A local funeral home took the body to the morgue at Austin's Brackenridge Hospital for an autopsy.

Back at his office, Boutwell called the medical examiner's office in Austin with instructions not to handle the body without gloves.

"The DPS has a new technique for lifting prints off

of smooth skin," Boutwell explained. "They're going to send somebody over to give it a try on this girl."

Since no identification had been found near the body, and since Boutwell had no missing person's reports in his county that matched the girl, he also asked the ME's office to do a dental chart and check for any unusual characteristics about the victim that might help in her identification.

The sheriff then contacted Harold Hoffmeister, chief of the Latent Prints Section for the DPS in Austin. Hoffmeister agreed to make arrangements with the ME's office to check the body for prints.

While Boutwell was on the telephone, Hardison prepared a teletype describing the victim and what little was known about her death for distribution to all Texas law enforcement agencies. The officers hoped some department would be able to connect the victim to a missing person in their jurisdiction.

The first response to the message came from an FBI agent in Houston. His office was investigating the disappearance of a woman wanted in connection with the theft of $70,000 from a Houston bank. The woman, who fit the general description of the victim found in Williamson County, had been missing since the day before, the FBI agent said.

Ten minutes later, an Austin Police Department detective called the sheriff's office. An eighteen-year-old white female with red hair had been injured in a traffic accident in Austin on October 25. She had been released from the hospital on the following day and had telephoned her father in South Dakota on October 27. She might have been trying to get home, and a likely route would have been I-35. Maybe she had thumbed a ride from the wrong person.

The only possibility that Boutwell had turned up in his own jurisdiction was a report by one of his deputies. At 2:47 A.M., the deputy had seen a gray 1976 model van parked off the roadway on I-35, not far from where the body was found later that day. The deputy had noted the plate number, but the vehicle was legally parked and he had had no reason to check it further at the time. Later, it was gone. The registration came back to a man in Irving, a city 170 miles north of Georgetown.

Boutwell sent a teletype to the Irving Police Department requesting any information it might have on the van and its registered owner.

Then he called it a night.

Travis County Medical Examiner Dr. Robert Bayardo started the autopsy at 8:30 A.M. The dead woman was tall—five feet nine inches—and a little heavyset at 158 pounds. She had brown hair with a reddish tint, hazel eyes, pierced ears, bushy eyebrows, and something of a pug nose. She had never had any dental work. Total body X-rays showed no old bone injuries.

The only visible marks on her body were the abrasions noted the day before and bruises around her neck. Aside from the orange socks, the only man-made object found on her body was a silver ring with an abalone shell. The ring was on the dead girl's left index finger. To Hardison, it looked like Zuñi Indian handcrafting, a piece of jewelry that could be purchased in just about any pawn shop for $15 or $20.

The pathologist concluded that the victim was in her early twenties, had never given birth, and had died from manual strangulation. Judging from her stomach contents, her last meal had been chicken, french fries, and a leafy vegetable, probably lettuce. The doctor had another observation: she had not been a particularly well-kept person. She had hair under her arms and on her legs, infected insect bites on her ankles, long toenails, and a genital inflammation possibly indicating venereal disease.

Despite a careful check, a DPS technician had been

unable to lift any prints from the body. With the time of death estimated at twelve to fourteen hours before the body was found, the victim had been exposed to the elements too long for any prints to have survived.

Head and pubic hair samples, fingernail scrapings, two small wood chips, and a small piece of black thread found on her left wrist were handed by Bayardo over to Hardison for submission to the DPS Crime Lab for further analysis. Blood tests revealed no alcohol or drugs had been in her system at the time of death.

The examination provided another puzzling piece of information. Though the woman was nude, vaginal, anal, and oral smears were negative for any trace of spermatozoa.

Hardison thanked the doctor for his verbal report and left to deliver the evidence to the DPS headquarters in north Austin.

As Boutwell and his investigators checked every possibility in their effort to identify the woman found dumped in the culvert, the first anniversary of the Kevin Key–Rita Salazar murders passed. Extensive publicity, including publication of an artist's drawing of the latest Williamson County homicide victim, brought some two hundred responses from across the nation, but none of the leads panned out. The victim's fingerprints could not be found in the more than three million print cards kept by the DPS or in the FBI's extensive fingerprint records in Washington.

A Texas Ranger stationed in the next county furnished Boutwell with a copy of his report on an aggravated rape case that had occurred on October 17. A young woman, nude, had been found wandering on a rural road. She had been raped and badly beaten, suffering multiple skull fractures, a broken jaw, a broken nose, and possible internal injuries. Military authorities had arrested a Fort Hood soldier in the case.

On the surface, the Bell County case looked promising, but when the Williamson County officers and the Ranger delved into it further, they were satisfied the soldier had no involvement in their murder.

Ten days after the discovery of the young woman's body in the culvert, she was given a pauper's burial in Georgetown City Cemetery. A local funeral home donated a casket and Boutwell and several of his deputies took up a collection to get a small spray of flowers for her grave. Boutwell, District Attorney Walsh, and a few deputies went to the cemetery for a short graveside service. It was a sunny, cool morning. Birds were singing as a minister from one of Georgetown's churches read from the Book of Matthew: "Are not two sparrows sold for a farthing? and one of them shall not fall on the ground without your Father. . . . Fear ye not therefore, ye are of more value than many sparrows."

Officially, the victim went on the books as a Jane Doe. But Boutwell and other officers gave her another name: Orange Socks.

The sheriff, frustrated at the lack of success in all three of the unsolved deaths along I-35 in less than a year, described his situation in aeronautical terms when he talked about the cases with other officers. "I feel like the pilot who ran out of airspeed, altitude, and ideas all at the same time."

In the late summer of 1980, both of the murder cases under his jurisdiction still unsolved, Sheriff Boutwell did have another idea. From other officers and through the news media he had heard of several other unsolved homicides that appeared to have only one thing in common—all had happened near I-35, the interstate highway that stretched from Laredo,

Texas, all the way to Duluth, Minnesota. The super-highway bisected the nation, an asphalt river that carried far more commerce than the Mississippi.

Boutwell called Floyd Hacker, chief of the DPS Criminal Law Enforcement Division.

"Floyd, Joe and I've been working a couple of murders we haven't been able to get anywhere with," Boutwell said. "Both of my two were found near I-35. The girl that was with the victim I've got in Williamson County was found shot to death off I-35 in McLennan County, so I know the killer went on north from here. I've been hearing about some other murders along the interstate. I'm beginning to wonder if we've got some old boy who's traveling I-35 killing people."

Though it seemed to Boutwell that an unusual number of murders were happening along the interstate, no single agency was looking for any connections.

"I think what we have here is the old story of the left hand not knowing what the right hand is doing," Boutwell said. "Do you think we could put together a conference so that all the different agencies with unsolved cases along I-35 could get together and talk this thing over? If we compare notes, we just might come up with something. I damn sure don't have anything as it stands."

Hacker asked Boutwell to write him a letter outlining what he had just gone over. A conference sounded like a good idea to him, too.

Boutwell followed through with a letter on August 29: "We have a killer (or killers) still on the loose, traveling I-35. We know that the M.O. is not the same in all murders. Guns, knives, and strangulation have been utilized in killing these victims. Some may have been raped; some haven't."

The sheriff repeated his suggestion that the DPS organize a one- or two-day seminar at the state headquarters in Austin for an exchange of information between the various agencies with unsolved murders along I-35. A comparison of all the cases might reveal some other common denominator and perhaps a profile of a suspect could be developed, he wrote. Officers attending the conference could explore further options, including setting up a program with trucking companies and truck stops in the hope of developing information on possible suspects and establishing a uniform system for storage of missing-person reports and checking them against unidentified homicide victims.

"Floyd, we know that I-35 is a common denominator in these cases," Boutwell concluded. "I believe that a pooling and integration of existing knowledge might narrow the search (for a suspect) considerably, and it seems to me that the resources and abilities of the DPS might tie all the various leads developed by the different agencies into an encyclopedia of information which might lead to the arrest and successful prosecution of the I-35 killer(s)."

Hacker thought Boutwell had a good idea. A conference was set for October 28–30, 1980. Twenty-nine officers representing eighteen different law enforcement agencies with jurisdiction along I-35 registered for the meeting.

At the conference, the officers discussed more than twenty unsolved homicides during the three-day gathering. Some of the victims in the cases had been shot, some stabbed, some strangled, and one smothered with a pillowcase. The victims varied in age and background. The only thing they had in common was that their bodies had been found either on or near I-35 between 1976 and 1980. All but two of the cases, which were in cities ranging from Laredo on the south to Oklahoma City on the north, had occurred within the last two years.

Officers distributed photocopied summaries of

their unsolved cases to other officers at the conference, then, when their turn at the head of the classroom came, they sketched in other details. An outside observer would have thought the conference seemed peculiarly low key, considering the long list of unsolved murders, but Boutwell was getting exactly what he wanted: an exchange of information. He wanted every police officer in the Southwest to know about Orange Socks, Kevin Key, Rita Salazar, and other victims.

A reporter covering the conference, having agreed in advance not to go into too much detail on the various cases, asked some of the officers why they thought there had been so many murders along I-35.

"An awful lot of sin goes up and down that highway," Texas Ranger Ed Gooding offered.

The media attention had been another goal Boutwell had had in suggesting the homicide conference. Perhaps some additional publicity on the unsolved cases would tickle someone's memory—or trouble someone's conscience. One of the people who would eventually hear about the I-35 homicide conference was a sheriff in north Texas, a man with a good memory.

CHAPTER SEVEN

Lucas, wearing insulated overalls, walked unseen in the cold, moonless night through the pasture toward the roadway. He had the shovel up on his shoulder, the way a squirrel hunter might carry his .22. When he got to the bridge, he made his way down the incline into the ditch.

The metal pipe was right where he had left it. Using that and a long piece of two-by-four lumber he found nearby, he probed inside the corrugated metal drainage pipe until he felt something soft. Then he pushed until it protruded from the other side.

She was so mushy and smelly, he was pleasantly surprised she held together as he stuffed her into the two plastic garbage bags he had with him. That finished, he went fifteen or twenty feet beyond the bridge and used the shovel to dig a hole for the dress and panties, which he pulled from under the bridge after he got her out. Shucking his overalls, he tied the arms and legs of the garment together to make a sling strong enough to carry her.

Struggling under the odoriferous bundle, Lucas managed to get her back to his place. Setting his heavy load down on the floor, he busied himself in getting a good fire started in his rusty wood-burning stove. When he was satisfied he had a fire that would last, he stuffed the garbage bags into the stove. It smelled pretty bad as it burned, but it put out nice heat, which felt good after the long, cold walk. He settled back by the stove to make sure it kept burning and popped open a beer.

Except for his silver badge and his ornate nickel-plated .45 semiautomatic, just about the most important piece of equipment Texas Ranger Phil Ryan carried was a red hardback daybook. The book told the thirty-seven-year-old Ranger where he had been and where he needed to go next. As one of only ninety-four Rangers in a state with 254 counties populated by more than sixteen million people, Ryan stayed busy. But he was doing what he had dreamed of for years. In the fifth grade he had belonged to a club called the Rangers. From that time on he had wanted to become a real Texas Ranger, a goal he had finally reached on August 1, 1980, after fourteen years as a Highway Patrol trooper.

On Monday, September 20, 1982, the day he first heard that an elderly woman was missing in Montague County, Ryan was working an oil field theft case and looking into a series of tractor thefts. His red book told him most of the rest of the week would be spent in court. He could drop anything in an emergency, but for the time being, he had more work than he could say grace over. For a Ranger, that wasn't unusual.

The following Monday, September 27, Montague County Sheriff W. F. Conway called Ryan. The woman was still missing.

"It doesn't look right," the sheriff told the Ranger, who was stuck at the Wise County courthouse in Decatur for a pretrial hearing.

Ryan trusted Conway's judgment. Sheriff Conway, better known in his county as "Hound Dog," had been a lawman for twenty-six of his sixty-one years.

The "Hound Dog" nickname came from his reputation as a tenacious investigator, though some officers kidded the sheriff that the monicker had more to do with the size of his ears. A peace officer of the old school, Conway stood six feet two inches and wore a double gun belt, the buckle hidden by an ample belly. When he didn't have his gun on, he was likely to be found in overalls, tending to some farming chore on his place near the small community of Forestburg. He was a sheriff who did not hesitate to say what was on his mind, and some officers, younger and more formally educated, had trouble getting along with him. But Ryan, who got a kick out of seeing the sheriff do and say things that would have kept him tied up in Internal Affairs for days, had had no problems with him since moving to north Texas after making the Rangers. He knew Conway liked to take care of his own business and that when he called on the Rangers for assistance he knew he needed help.

Ryan covered three counties and part of a fourth from his home base of Decatur, thirty miles north of Fort Worth. The least populated was Montague County, 928 square miles of rolling grassland just south of the Red River from Oklahoma. With a population of only 18,000, a major crime was rare. The county seat, Montague, had only four hundred residents. The white-pillared, red-brick courthouse stood in a square framed by an assortment of old business buildings that looked like they had been built as a set for a Western movie. The few commercial establishments in town struggled to stay open, and some had long since given up. The roof had already caved in— literally—on one business right across from the courthouse. The town's only movie house had been closed so long no one even remembered what it had been called. If a person wanted a cup of coffee in Montague, they had better have a friend who had a pot brewed. There was no café, though the general store sold soft drinks. The streets in town did not even have names. Since everyone knew where everyone else lived, it would have been a waste of tax dollars to put up signs.

Montague was less than a ninety-minute drive from Dallas–Fort Worth, but the distance between the glassy glitter of the big cities and the Montague area could more accurately be measured in decades. Visitors—the few there were—saw Montague as a rural area frozen in the 1930s. But to local residents, it was a peaceful place where no one had to worry about locking their doors.

On Wednesday, September 29, Ryan pulled his unmarked state car outside the only new building in town, the sheriff's office and jail. County officials gladly would have kept the old jail in use for years to come, but new, strict jail standards enforced by the state had made it obsolete, forcing the recent construction of the modern law enforcement facility.

Over coffee, Sheriff Conway filled Ryan in on what he had. As the Ranger listened to the sheriff, he marveled again at the man's memory. His "computer" was the one in his head, his "records section" in his shirt pocket. Conway kept what he needed in that pocket, transferring the accumulation to a clean shirt each day. After a couple of weeks, his wife, Jennie, collected the pocket's contents and put the assorted notes in a plastic bag. Another bag held the sheriff's telephone messages. She placed the bags in a carefully dated cardboard box or paper bag. If the sheriff could remember the date something happened, Jennie Conway could find what passed for the official paperwork.

So far, most of the information on the disappearance of eighty-year-old Kate Pearl Rich was in the sheriff's mental "files." Conway laid out what he had for Ryan. On Sunday, September 18, one of Mrs. Rich's daughters had called him, clearly worried. Her mother was missing. The elderly woman lived by herself in an old frame house in the small community of Ringgold, a fading railroad and cotton gin town not far from the Oklahoma border.

Since Mrs. Rich had nine children, it had taken the family a while to determine that their mother had not just gone to visit one of them. Each child had called another until they realized none of them knew her whereabouts. Just about everyone in the county knew Mrs. Rich, or at least knew who she was. She had come to Ringgold in 1940 with her husband, Hiram, who supported their family by doing odd jobs. Widowed since 1948, for years she had offered county residents her services as a midwife. To scores of area people she was a second mother. As mother of her own sizable brood, Mrs. Rich had thirty-one grandchildren and twenty-seven great-grandchildren.

Sheriff Conway had driven right out to the well-known woman's house after receiving the call. The white paint was peeling off the clapboard walls of the modest four-room house; its wide front porch was cluttered with an assortment of mismatched chairs and various odds and ends. Mrs. Rich's dog and some of her fifteen cats had been locked inside, leaving the place smelly and the floors littered with drying feces. A half-completed quilt was draped over a chair, as if Mrs. Rich had put it there intending to come right back to it. But Conway found no trace of the elderly woman. Two of her daughters came to the house and, after looking around, told the sheriff they couldn't find their mother's purse. They didn't think anything else was missing.

The sheriff went over the house carefully. Nothing appeared out of order, though it was hard to tell for sure. Like many elderly people, Mrs. Rich was not the most tidy of housekeepers. But Conway was not concerned with the neatness of her house. What bothered him was something else he knew about Mrs. Rich: she trusted everyone. Her family had told him she would "take to" a stranger as if she'd known him forever and would accept a ride with anyone just to get out of her house for a while. Still recovering from a broken hip, however, she would have needed help getting in a car.

After listening to Conway's rundown, Ryan agreed with the sheriff that the disappearance looked suspicious. Mrs. Rich's sizable family and many of their friends already had checked all around her house and elsewhere in the Ringgold vicinity. Ryan felt they needed some help.

"I'll call Garland and see if we can get the chopper over here for a search," Ryan said.

After the briefing by Conway, Ranger Ryan contacted the DPS regional headquarters in Garland, near Dallas, and requested the use of one of the department's helicopters. Ryan, the sheriff, District Attorney Investigator Paul Smith, and DPS Pilot-Investigator Paul Creech covered the Ringgold area thoroughly. For a time, the pilot was on the verge of having to break off the search to join in on a high-speed pursuit of a shooting suspect in a nearby county, but a short time later the gunman wrecked his car and the chase ended. The officers returned their full concentration to the search, but the effort was fruitless.

Sheriff Conway had done a lot of legwork on the case before contacting Ryan. From another of the missing woman's daughters, Mrs. Obera Smart of Hemet, California, the sheriff had learned that a handyman and his wife had stayed with Mrs. Rich for a while in the late spring. Mrs. Smart told the sheriff that her husband had picked up the man and his young wife as hitchhikers on a foggy morning in January 1982 near Beaumont, California. The couple told Smart they did not have ten cents between them and had spent the night before in a ditch, sharing one dirty blanket. Her husband had felt sorry for them, she said. For several months, Smart paid the man to help him in his antique furniture-refinishing business. Then, in May, worried about the aging Mrs. Rich living alone in Texas, the Smarts offered the man a job as the woman's handyman. When he accepted, they bought the couple one-way bus tickets to Ringgold. The job was short-lived.

A telephone call to another of Mrs. Rich's daughters from the couple who ran a small store in Ringgold was the first thing to concern the family about the new handyman. Though Mrs. Rich received only $250 a month to live on, the handyman and his wife had spent $50 of her money at the nearby store in only four days. The store owners, who were used to trading directly with Mrs. Rich, said the elderly woman had written two $25 checks, which the handyman had taken to the store on separate occasions and spent primarily on cigarettes, junk food, and soft drinks. The store owners knew Mrs. Rich did not smoke or eat the type of food they were buying with her checks.

The daughter who got the call ran a café in a small community just across the river in Oklahoma. She got in touch with her sister in Wichita Falls and they decided to meet in Ringgold to check into the situation firsthand.

They went to the store first. The proprietors showed the daughters a list of the items purchased with their mother's money. From the store the daughters went to their mother's house, where they found the handyman and his wife still in bed. Their mother was up and eating breakfast. Neither daughter could see any sign that any work had been done around the place. In fact, the house was filthy, especially the room occupied by the hired man and his wife, a plump girl with long brown hair who looked too young to be with a man his age. Their extra clothing, still gray from ground-in dirt and full of holes, had been washed and was hanging outside.

The daughters politely told the man that his staying in the house might jeopardize their mother's Social Security payments and asked him to leave. The man, who seemed affable enough to the daughters, said he understood. After the couple had gathered up their few belongings, one of the daughters gave them a ride to the highway, where the now jobless man and his wife could hitch a ride to Wichita Falls. That had been the last they had heard of him, they told Sheriff Conway.

Conway soon learned that the man who had stayed with Mrs. Rich was named Henry Lee Lucas and that he had not made it to Wichita Falls. After leaving Mrs. Rich's place, he and his wife, Becky, had been picked up by Ruben Moore, a roofing contractor and minister of a small religious commune in Stoneburg called the House of Prayer.

After the unsuccessful aerial search for Mrs. Rich, Ryan entered her name and description into NCIC—the National Crime Information Center—as a missing person. The computer entry also included a description of the car Lucas was driving when last seen in Montague County, a 1966 Ford Galaxy that had been hand-painted blue.

Steve Gibbert, who had sold the junker to Lucas, contacted Sheriff Conway on October 4.

"I found this letter in my grandmother's mailbox," he told the sheriff. "When she passed away, I got her car, the one I sold to Lucas."

The letter was from the California Highway Patrol. Since a computer check of the car's license plate number showed Gibbert's grandmother as the registered owner of the vehicle, the letter had come to her address. The car, the letter said, had been found abandoned on September 21 and was stored at a wrecking yard in Needles, California.

Sheriff Conway called the CHP and spoke with an officer who agreed to go take a look at the car. A short time later, the officer called Conway back. He had found what appeared to be bloodstains in the front seat and floorboard of the vehicle. A quilt had been covering the stains, the officer said.

The CHP officer said a detective with the sheriff's office there would check the car more closely and assist in any way he could.

On October 9, Ryan, Conway, and D.A.'s Investigator Smith went to Stoneburg to talk to anyone at the House of Prayer who had known Lucas and his young wife.

Rueben Moore, the fifty-two-year-old minister who had offered Lucas a ride and a job, had come to Montague County three years earlier, seeking his personal Zion. For $55,000 he bought a failed poultry operation on fifteen acres between Stoneburg and Ringgold that locals called "the chicken ranch." He raised a plywood steeple atop one of the long tin-roofed chicken barns and built a chapel inside. In another chicken barn, he built an apartment for himself and one for his elderly father.

Soon a dozen or so Pentecostals were living at the converted chicken ranch, supporting themselves with sales from a thrift shop stocked with donated items and supplementing their diet with produce from the communal garden they tended. Their lives revolved around the four-times-a-week worship services, at which they spoke in tongues, handled snakes, annointed the sick with holy oil, and confessed their sins in the fervent hope of salvation. In addition to watching over his flock, Moore, a big, powerful man with a ruddy face and hazel eyes, worked as a roofing contractor when jobs came up. Despite his size, he was a gentle sort, always ready to give a second chance to someone down on his luck. The House of Prayer was his promised land, and he was willing to share it with others less fortunate.

When Moore saw Lucas and Becky trying to thumb a ride on the side of the highway about ten miles north of Stoneburg, he knew they needed help. He stopped his truck, which was loaded down with roofing tools and materials, and asked where they were headed.

Lucas said he needed to get to Wichita Falls to pick up some money at the Western Union office. Moore told the couple to get in his truck and he drove them into town. The money order hadn't arrived, so Moore volunteered to take the couple to the House of Prayer for the night and drive them back to the Western Union office the next day. If they wanted to stay for a while there, Moore said, Lucas could have a job.

"I liked the guy," Moore would recall. "He was my type of guy in that he didn't run his mouth all the time and tried to help people. He was the best worker I ever hired."

Moore told Ryan and the officers he thought it was May 26, 1982, when he had picked up the couple. They stayed at the House of Prayer for most of the rest of that summer, he said, living in a small makeshift apartment inside the long former chicken barn. The down-and-out drifter proved to be a pretty fair "fixer upper," repairing appliances for the church's thrift shop and occasionally helping out on a roofing job, Moore told the Ranger. Lucas donated most of his money to the church. After he got a car from Gibbert, he spent a lot of time under its hood, Moore said.

Since Moore respected the fact that Lucas didn't talk much, he hadn't learned a whole lot about the slight dark-haired man. He figured Lucas had probably done time, but he firmly believed the biblical injunction "Judge not lest ye be judged."

Moore knew even less about the young woman everyone had assumed was Lucas's wife. She'd said she had family in Florida.

Faye Munnerlyn, who also lived at the House of Prayer, told Ryan that Becky had been as unkempt as Lucas. Large for her age, her brown hair was long and stringy. She usually wore an untucked workshirt and men's shoes that were too big for her. Faye gave her a dress so she'd have something a little more feminine for church services.

Becky, Moore said, looked like she was nineteen but acted like she was twelve—or younger. She seemed slightly retarded. One of her greatest pleasures was driving a riding lawn mower around the property like it was a go-cart. Later, after Lucas had a car, he let her drive it on the church property. Faye said Becky also liked to bang the keys of an old piano they had in the church, offering to give lessons to anyone who happened by, even though she couldn't play a note.

Though everyone assumed Lucas and Becky were married, when she was around Lucas she seemed more like a little girl with her father. Sometimes, working intently on his car or some appliance, Lucas would yell for a tool and Becky would fetch it like an obedient servant.

In their small room at night, Lucas evidently made other demands of the young girl. Faye told the officers that Becky had once confided to her that she was pregnant but that she never got any bigger and had not mentioned it again.

Moore said Lucas seemed to care for Becky, but Faye said the teenager had once told her, "Henry cusses me until one o'clock in the morning. No woman should have to put up with what I do."

That August Becky apparently decided she had had

enough of Lucas, or at least the House of Prayer. She said she wanted to go back to Florida. Moore told Ryan that Lucas had not wanted to leave the House of Prayer but finally gave in, saying they would get a ride east with a trucker.

"About a month ago, me and Gilbert Beagle took Becky and Henry to the truck stop in Alvord," recalled Moore's father, eighty-five-year-old John Moore. "Before we left, I gave Henry a hundred ten dollars.

"Henry came back the next evening," the elder Moore continued. "He told me that Becky had run off with a trucker and took all their money. I gave him another fifty dollars."

Rueben Moore, who had heard the same story from Lucas, said he, too, saw Lucas the day after he had left with Becky.

"He was walking by himself along the highway from Bowie," Moore told the officers. "When I stopped to talk with him, he started crying. Becky had left him, he said."

Lucas told Moore that with the help of a trucker who had a citizen's band radio, he had finally found out that Becky was staying at a motel in San Antonio, more than three hundred miles to the south of Montague County. He had gotten a ride there in an attempt to get his wife back and had a fight with the truck driver, he had told Moore. But Becky, he said, had decided to stay with the trucker. He had returned alone to Montague County, shattered by the rejection of his young wife.

Moore told the officers he felt sorry for the drifter, who seemed devastated at the turn of events. After Becky left, both Moores told Ryan and the other officers, Lucas stayed in the room he had shared with his young wife, though he would periodically leave for a few days, announcing he was going to look for Becky. Then, in September, Lucas left for what everyone thought would be for good, though he had said he would be back.

Beagle told Ryan he had last seen Lucas when the two of them had driven in Lucas's car to Bowie, the largest city in the county, to buy some clothes. Lucas had dropped him off after the shopping trip and said he was going to visit Mrs. Rich, whom he called Granny. Beagle said Lucas returned about 7:00 P.M. that evening, September 16. Around 5:00 A.M. the next day, Beagle told the officers, Lucas drove off from the House of Prayer, telling him he would be back the following day. He had not returned, however. When they checked his room, his clothes were gone.

Conway and Ryan appreciated the cooperation they were getting from Moore and other House of Prayer residents, but the officers had learned some things about Lucas that the minister and his followers at the House of Prayer did not know. An NCIC check showed that Lucas had been arrested numerous times. That a drifter like Lucas had a record was not surprising, but he also was a convicted murderer. The nature of the murder made Lucas's background of even more concern: Lucas had gone to prison for killing his elderly mother.

The officers also were learning more about Becky. During Henry and Becky's stay with the Smarts, several long-distance telephone calls had been billed to their number. One of the places called was Jacksonville, Florida. When Ryan called the number, he talked with a man who said he was a friend of Becky's family. Becky was only fifteen years old, he told the Ranger. As far as he knew, she and Lucas were not married. They had met while Lucas was staying at her grandmother's house in Jacksonville. After the grandmother died, he said, she had lived with her mother. But when the mother died, she was placed in a juvenile care facility. In January she had run off with Lucas. Then, in late April or early May, she had called him from California and said she was coming home soon. But he had not heard from her since then, he said.

The family friend agreed to send the Texas officers the most recent photograph he had of Becky, a two-year-old color school picture. He also said he would let the officers know if he heard from her again.

Given Lucas's background and the strange-sounding story Lucas had told when he returned to the House of Prayer without Becky, Ryan was beginning to get an uneasy feeling about the runaway. His concern for Mrs. Rich had grown even stronger. Though she had not been reported missing until September 18, the last time anyone remembered having seen her was September 16, the day Lucas had said he was going to her place for a visit.

Ryan got a Ranger in San Antonio to check the motel where Lucas said he had confronted the truck driver who took Becky away from him. No one at the motel remembered any fights or having seen anyone who resembled Lucas or Becky.

Another development, though still not nearly enough to make an arrest possible in the case, added to the growing suspicion of Lucas. The blood found in the abandoned car in California, the one Lucas was seen in when he left Montague County, was determined to have been human, type unknown.

At the House of Prayer, no one had seen Lucas or heard anything from him until Tuesday, October 5, when he had called Moore collect from Indiana. He was still looking for Becky, he said. And he needed some money.

At 11 P.M. on October 17, Sheriff Conway telephoned Ryan at home.

"Guess whose house burned tonight?" the sheriff began. "And guess who's back in town?"

Conway said Mrs. Rich's house had been gutted by a fire that appeared to have been intentionally set. And Lucas was back at the House of Prayer.

"I'm in a murder trial," the Ranger told the sheriff. "Let's go out real early in the morning and talk to him. I'll meet you at your office and we'll go on out to Stoneburg."

Ryan went to sleep wondering what would make a murder suspect come back to the place he was under suspicion. Did he think he was smarter than the officers? Was he really clean? Was he just stupid? Or did he want to get caught?

Early on the morning of October 18, Ryan, Conway, and Investigator Smith parked outside the House of Prayer.

Lucas, unshaven and smelly, met the officers at the door of his room with a steaming cup of coffee in his hand. He looked worse than he did in the police mug shots Ryan had seen before.

"I'm Phil Ryan, Texas Rangers," the officer began. "A lady named Kate Rich is missing and we need to talk to you about it."

Lucas could not have been more cooperative.

"I really liked her," he said.

Ryan knew he had to handle his interview with Lucas very carefully. He had no warrant to hold him on and only circumstantial evidence to link him to Mrs. Rich's disappearance.

"Will you meet us over at the sheriff's office?" Ryan asked.

"No, I can't. I don't have a car," Lucas said.

The Ranger said they would be happy to give Lucas a ride and then bring him back after they had talked. Lucas said that was fine.

At the sheriff's office, Ryan and Lucas settled down on either side of a desk. Lucas had a cup of coffee and smoked one cigarette after another.

Gently, Ryan eased into conversation with the drifter. Now that they were inside, the body odor was worse, but Ryan did not show that it bothered him.

"Henry, would you mind signing a waiver so we could make copies of anything you have in your billfold? I'd also like to get a blood sample from you and maybe have you take a polygraph test."

Lucas readily agreed.

Both the Ranger and Lucas were congenial, but an hour into their conversation Ryan knew Lucas was lying. He answered questions quickly, with seeming candor and often with a big smile that exposed a mouthful of bad teeth, but the answers did not always add up.

He had met Becky Powell three years before in Florida. He loved her. They had traveled together across the country. Earlier that year, in California, Jack Smart had given them a ride and him a job. In the spring, he and Becky took a bus to Ringgold to work for Mrs. Rich, Smart's mother-in-law. But three days after they arrived, another of Mrs. Rich's daughters told them to leave. That's when Ruben Moore stopped to pick him and Becky up and offered to let them stay at the House of Prayer, Lucas said.

On August 23, his forty-sixth birthday, they got a ride to a truck stop to hitch a ride back to Florida. Then Becky ran off with the trucker, Lucas told the Ranger.

"I guess you know about the warrant I got on me," Lucas offered, exposing his broken teeth in a grin that was friendly, almost disarming.

Ryan nodded, acting like he knew all about it. "That's the one out of Florida?" he probed.

"No, out of Maryland," Lucas corrected.

"Yeah, that's right," Ryan said.

"It was for stealing a pickup while I was on probation," Lucas continued.

"What was the name of that probation officer

again?" Ryan asked, pretending the name was right on the tip of his tongue.

Lucas told him.

They talked until noon. Conway and Smith took Lucas to Bowie for his blood test. Ryan had to be in court back in Decatur at 1 P.M., but as soon as he was away from Lucas, he got on the telephone to Port Deposit, Maryland. A short time later, he had the warrant number from the sheriff's office there. The office there did not know if Maryland would want to extradite Lucas, but Ryan had enough information to hold Lucas for a while. Later that afternoon, Sheriff Conway got a warrant so Lucas could be booked into his jail as a fugitive from justice.

A half day of talking to Lucas had not netted Ryan much information other than finding out about the warrant, which would at least buy some time. Lucas had been most cooperative, but had stuck to his story, cockeyed as it was. Ryan did not want to toss in his cards in his mental poker game with Lucas, but he had to be in court on another case. For the time being, he would call it a draw.

That afternoon Conway took Lucas to the Dallas County Sheriff's Office for a polygraph examination.

"Did you plan with anyone to kidnap Kate Rich?" the examiner asked, after hooking Lucas up to the polygraph and explaining the procedure to him.

"No."

"Did you take Kate Rich away from her home against her will?"

"No."

"Did you do anything to Kate Rich that would cause her to die?"

Lucas began coughing heavily. "No," he finally managed.

After Lucas's coughing stopped and he had had time to compose himself, the examiner asked three more questions.

"The last time you saw Kate Rich, was she alive?"
"Yes."
"Did you kill Kate Rich?"
"No."
"Do you know where Kate Rich or her body is now?"
"No."

The examiner then asked Lucas if he knew whether Mrs. Rich was in Texas, California, New Mexico, Arizona, Oklahoma, or Louisiana. Lucas answered "no" for each state.

Finally, the examiner asked Lucas about Becky Powell. He said she had been alive the last time he saw her and answered "no" when asked if he had killed her.

Afterward, Conway and the examiner talked outside of Lucas's presence. Conway asked for the examiner's opinion. The written report would phrase it more circumspectly, but the examiner said he believed Lucas was not telling the truth. That was encouraging information to Conway, but results of a polygraph test could not be used as evidence, only as an investigative tool.

As soon as he could get out of the courthouse in Decatur, Ryan went back to Montague for another session with Lucas, who by that time was back from Dallas. This time the Ranger planned to start shooting holes in Lucas's story.

Lucas was as friendly as he had been that morning. But Ryan was beginning to sense Lucas's weak spots. One was his relationship with Becky. Lucas did not seem angry that his young wife had run off with a trucker, only hurt. In fact, he showed no emotion at all, except when he talked specifically about Becky. He often teared up in response to questions about her. And then he changed his story altogether. There had been no truck driver, he admitted. Becky had been having a relationship with another man, someone they both knew. She had hitched a ride with a trucker to San Antonio to meet this man and Lucas had followed them. At a budget motel, the man had given Lucas the key to the room and told him that he and Becky were going to California.

The new story, Ryan thought, was sounding even more bizarre than the first. As troubled as Lucas seemed by Becky's absence, and as obsessed with finding her as he appeared to be, it did not make sense that Lucas would have so casually let Becky and her supposed lover go to the West Coast together.

Ryan looked at his watch. Lucas seemed to have no limits when it came to talking, smoking Pall Malls, or drinking coffee. The smelly little man might die of lung cancer before they could connect him to Mrs. Rich's disappearance, Ryan thought.

After the man left with Becky, Lucas continued, he stayed one night in the room, then went to Houston, where he sold some blood for money. Then he got a ride with an old couple and ended up in Amarillo, up in the Texas panhandle. Lucas said he could prove his story—he still had the motel room key.

The Ranger, reeking of Lucas's cigarette smoke, gave up for the night and went home for a few hours of sleep. On the drive back to Decatur, Ryan weighed what he had—a convicted murderer who had worked briefly for an old woman who had disappeared. A guy with a glass eye whose good eye teared up at the mention of the teenage girl he had called his wife, a fifteen-year-old he said had run off with a trucker. Like most good law officers, Ryan operated to some extent on instinct. He still had nothing concrete to go on, but his feeling was even stronger than before that Mrs. Rich was dead somewhere and that Becky Powell was not shacked up with a truck driver.

The next morning Ryan went with Lucas back to the House of Prayer. Lucas directed the Ranger to a place in his small trashed-out room where he said he had hidden a key. Ryan reached around for a moment and came out with a motel key with an orange plastic handle. The key was to room 67, but there was no motel name on the plastic.

Back at the sheriff's office, Ryan mailed the key to the office of Texas Rangers Company D in San Antonio with a request that a Ranger check to find out what motel it belonged to. The day after the key arrived in San Antonio, Ryan got a phone call from a Ranger colleague. The key was not from the motel where Lucas said he had spent the night. No one at the motel even remembered anyone who looked like Lucas having stayed there. Another lie, but Ryan wondered where Lucas had gotten the key and what motel it did belong to.

Confronted with Ryan's information from San Antonio, Lucas changed his story again. Actually, he said, he had stayed in a motel in Altus, Oklahoma. He had been there to help Rueben Moore on a roofing job. He had stolen a TV set that Moore had taken with him and sold it in Amarillo.

Ryan got a Ranger in Amarillo to check some of the places Lucas mentioned. The Ranger there showed Lucas's picture around and determined he had probably been there.

At least he had a theft case against Lucas, if Moore chose to press charges. But he did not seem any closer to finding Kate Rich or Becky Powell.

The Ranger decided to try a new tack with the drifter.

"Henry, I'm not too smart, I guess," Ryan began. "I'm having trouble believing your story. If you've got any ideas that can help us clear this up, I'd sure appreciate it. We need to find out where Mrs. Rich is and who burned her house down."

Lucas said he was more than willing to cooperate. The Ranger asked Lucas if he would place a telephone call to the man the drifter claimed had taken Becky from him and let Ryan listen in.

"The sheriff's office will pay for the call," Ryan assured Lucas. "If he says you're telling the truth, we'll be able to let you go as soon as we get that Maryland warrant cleared up."

After taping the conversation, with Lucas's written permission, Ryan knew what he had suspected in the first place: the man Lucas called clearly did not know anything about the disappearance of Mrs. Rich or Lucas's young companion. The whole story was as phony as Lucas's first version. The only item of truth was the fact that the man did know Lucas and Becky.

The Ranger spent virtually every moment he could spare talking with Lucas. Lucas's stories had more holes in them than a worn-out screen door, but Ryan could not get Lucas to admit any involvement in the disappearance or the fire at Rich's home.

Ryan began having trouble sleeping at night. He would lie in bed wide awake, thinking of some way to get Lucas to tell him what really happened to Kate Rich and Becky Powell. In one of their conversations Lucas said that Mrs. Rich had told him she was born in Oklahoma and was part Choctaw Indian. If she had been killed by someone, Lucas offered, her spirit was probably restlessly roaming the north Texas plains of Montague County. The Ranger considered playing on Lucas's apparent superstitions. Wonder what Lucas would do if he looked outside his jail window and saw Mrs. Rich, or at least a blown up photograph of her, glowing in the dark, illuminated by a hidden light? The idea was born of frustration—something he could never do—but he needed something.

Ryan consulted several retired Texas Rangers, looking for insight into the fine art of persuading a man to talk when what he could say might send him to death row.

But nothing worked. Lucas stuck with his story,

implausible as it was. Finally, early in November, a reluctant Sheriff Conway released Lucas from jail. Authorities in Maryland had declined the opportunity to extradite Lucas on the probation violation warrant. Both Conway and Ryan figured Lucas would quickly absent himself from Montague County. He knew they considered him the prime suspect in Mrs. Rich's disappearance. If they ever did get enough evidence to arrest him, they would probably have to hunt for him the next time, Ryan thought. Lucas, however, surprised them again. He stayed in the county, returning to his old apartment at the House of Prayer.

Later that month, one of Mrs. Rich's daughters consulted a psychic from Dallas. Ryan did not believe that would do any good, but he agreed to talk with him out of sympathy for the family. The two spent a day together. By the time they parted, Ryan was impressed at the caliber of questions the psychic had asked. He would have made a good cop, the Ranger thought.

About 7:00 A.M. on December 2, a young man was hunting along Belknap Creek. As he walked near the bridge that crossed the creek, he noticed something out of the ordinary—a purse. Moving closer, he saw that it was a large blue straw handbag, lying on its side. The purse was empty, but scattered around it was an assortment of papers and photographs. One plastic card caught his eye and he picked it up for a closer look. Stamped on the card was a familiar name: Kate Rich. He had gone to school with her grandchildren and had heard the news that the elderly lady was missing. A short time later, the hunter walked into the sheriff's office.

Neither Ranger Ryan nor Sheriff Conway were particularly surprised by the discovery. They did not think Mrs. Rich had ventured far from home on her own. The discovery of her purse, evidently tossed by someone from the bridge above, supported their fears that Mrs. Rich had met with foul play. The only suspect was still the one-eyed little man who inexplicably kept hanging around Montague County.

Ryan dropped by the House of Prayer as often as he could, just to check in on Lucas. When he told Lucas that Mrs. Rich's purse had been found, Lucas said, "My God, I hope she's not around here somewhere. You'll think I did it." You're right about that, Ryan thought.

Twice yearly, the House of Prayer held an encampment, a combination picnic and revival. Lucas and Becky had taken part in the previous year's meeting, and Becky had had a great time. Lucas, who attended services at the church, told the Moores and others that he still held out hope that Becky would be back.

"If Becky's not back by encampment, I'll know something's wrong," Lucas said.

Lucas then told the Moores he was leaving on another search for his missing wife. He thought she might be in California. Could he borrow $150?

Ryan and Conway also had reason to believe Becky might be in California. On May 16, they drove to Blythe, California, to talk with officers there about a skeleton that had been found off I-10 in February. A pathologist who examined the remains had said there was a 90 percent chance the skeleton was female, even odds that it was Caucasian, and a 70 percent chance the person had been between twenty and twenty-five years of age. But after talking with officials in Florida who had access to Becky's medical records, the Texas officers were satisfied the skeleton was not Becky Powell.

While in California, Ryan and Conway drove to Hemet to talk to Jack and Obera Smart, an interview that firmed up the dates Lucas and Becky had stayed with them. The two investigators then went to San

Bernardino, where they picked up the evidence found in Lucas's car the previous September.

On June 7, Sheriff Conway got a telephone call from an obviously relieved Rueben Moore.

"Henry called and said he's got Kate and Becky both and he's bringing them back," Moore said.

Learning of this, Ryan asked D.A.'s Investigator Smith to put out a teletype describing the 1973 Pontiac Lucas was in and asked any officer who spotted the vehicle to stop and identify the occupants. He wanted more proof than Lucas's word that Kate Rich and Becky were okay.

Then Moore got another collect telephone call from a truck stop in San Jon, New Mexico. Lucas told the preacher his car had broken down and that he did not have the money to get it fixed. Could Moore come pick the three of them up?

Moore agreed to make the trip and left as soon as he could.

Ryan could not understand how a minimally educated drifter could find two missing persons who had successfully escaped the attention of every law enforcement agency in the nation, nor could he understand why a woman in her eighties and a fifteen-year-old would have struck out on their own. But if Kate Rich and Becky Powell were alive and well in New Mexico, Ryan would be happy to close the case. He had no shortage of other investigations that needed his attention.

When Moore got to the Red X Truck Stop in San Jon, a small town near Tucumcari on I-40, he found Lucas alone. As Moore walked toward him, he could see Lucas was crying.

"Where's Becky and Mrs. Rich?" Moore asked.

"They've been kidnapped!" Lucas sobbed.

"What?" Moore was stunned. He had done for Lucas all that the Bible said a God-fearing man

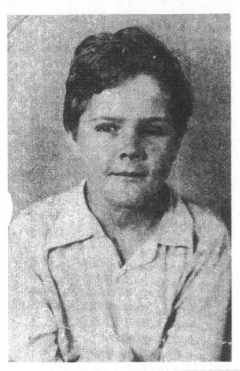

Henry as a young boy.

Lucas and Ohio Highway
Patrol Trooper H. W.
Lowe shortly after the
23-year-old Virginian was
taken into custody in the
1960 slaying of his mother.

Lucas undergoing
questioning for
his mother's
murder in 1960 by
Tecumseh Police
Chief George
Kilbourn.

Rita Salazar.
(Photo courtesy
Williamson County,
Texas, Sheriff's
Department)

Kevin Key. (Photo courtesy Williamson County, Texas, Sheriff's Department)

Texas Department of Public Safety forensic artist Karen Taylor prepared this sketch of the unidentified victim called Orange Socks from photographs of her body. (Photo courtesy Texas Department of Public Safety)

Investigators inspect spot off I-35 where Kevin Key's body was found. (Photo courtesy Williamson County, Texas, Sheriff's Department)

Ottis Toole, Henry Lucas, and Jacksonville, Florida, Sheriff's Detective Buddy Terry. (Photo courtesy Buddy Terry)

Lucas (far right) led officers to field where he said Becky Powell's remains would be found. (Photo courtesy Phil Ryan)

Ashes and human bone fragments were found in this rusted stove outside the converted chicken coop where Lucas and Becky Powell had lived for a time. (Photo courtesy Phil Ryan)

Texas Ranger Weldon Lucas (no relation) of Denton, Texas, and Henry Lucas, 1983. (Photo courtesy Weldon Lucas)

Kate Rich. (Photo courtesy Phil Ryan)

Ottis Toole. (Photo courtesy Phil Ryan)

Texas Ranger
Phil Ryan.
(Photo courtesy
Phil Ryan)

From left, El Paso Police Detective Benny Perez, Texas Ranger Buster Collins, Lucas, El Paso Detective Ed Uribe, Texas Ranger Clayton Smith, Texas Ranger Johnny Acock, and El Paso Detective Sgt. Santiago Apodaca. (Photo courtesy Benny Perez)

Lucas and Toole as they were being questioned.

Williamson County Sheriff Jim Boutwell. (Photo by Mike Cox)

Texas Rangers Captain
Bob Prince.

Becky Powell.

Lucas holding photo of
Becky that he kept in
his cell. (Photo by Mike
Cox)

should. He had offered food and shelter and the means for him to support himself and his young wife; he had taken Lucas's word when others doubted it. But this latest development was more than even a man of great faith could blindly accept.

As soon as he could, Moore excused himself to use a telephone. He called Sheriff Conway and reported Lucas's latest revelation. Moore said Lucas wanted to return to Stoneburg with him.

"Then give him a ride back," Conway told him.

The psychic brought in by Mrs. Rich's family had said he saw a large body of water and an old cabin in envisioning the missing woman's whereabouts. To Sheriff Conway that description fit Old Bowie Lake, a body of water only a couple of miles from the House of Prayer. Not having anything else to go on, the sheriff organized a search of the area.

Ryan, getting up early to take part in the search, bent over for something and suddenly went to his knees in excruciating pain. He finally was able to get up, but periodically his back would go into spasms again and the pain would be so fierce that he would come down. Even if he happened to be sitting at the time, the pain was so intense it would drop him to his knees. Finally, the Ranger went to a doctor. X-rays showed no obvious trauma.

"Your back," his doctor lectured, "is where both ends of the candle meet."

No question, Ryan thought, he had been burning the old candle at both ends and in the middle, too. Virtually every free moment he had was dedicated to the Lucas investigation, on top of his other day-to-day responsibilities as a Ranger. The pages in his red book were full. He had precious little time with his wife and family, and his wife was regularly reminding him of it.

Now, with Lucas once again back in Montague County and still a suspect, there was no letup in sight.

Ryan knew that for at least a while longer he would have to keep both ends of that candle burning.

Moore got back to Texas with Lucas the evening of June 10. As soon as he could, he telephoned Sheriff Conway.

"Can you meet me and Phil at Bevo's in the morning?" Conway asked. Moore said he would be there.

Bevo's was a restaurant in Decatur operated by Ryan's wife, Beverly. In addition to being a family business, it served as a convenient meeting place for Ryan. The coffee was always on the house.

That morning Ryan asked Moore to tell him everything he could about Lucas. The minister filled the Ranger and Sheriff Conway in on the latest developments and then began reflecting on Lucas.

Lucas never seemed to sleep when he was around the House of Prayer, Moore said. Often he heard noises around the place at night. He did not want to believe it, but he was beginning to suspect that Lucas was crawling between the ceiling and the common roof in the converted chicken barn to look down into his bedroom, which he shared with Faye Munnerlyn, a fellow church member he planned to marry. Moore had also discovered that a knife was missing from the church kitchen. When he had picked Lucas up in New Mexico, he noticed the missing knife in the drifter's meager luggage.

"Well, I know he doesn't have a gun," Faye Munnerlyn said. "He gave that to me."

"You're saying Lucas had a gun?" Ryan asked her.

"Yes, he gave me a pistol and some bullets and asked me to keep them for him," she said.

Finally, something has happened in my favor, Ryan thought. In Texas it is against the law for a convicted felon to possess a firearm. Now he could get Lucas back in jail. Maybe this time, he could get Lucas to tell him something useful. If he did not talk about Kate Rich, he still stood a fair chance of going back to prison on the firearms charge. At least he would be out of circulation for a while.

Jennie Conway, the sheriff's wife, left to take Faye to the House of Prayer to retrieve the pistol.

Ryan, meanwhile, called a justice of the peace in Nocona to get a warrant for Lucas's arrest. Later that day, paper in hand, the two officers drove to the House of Prayer to serve it. They split up, Ryan heading to Lucas's apartment, Conway to the church kitchen, where members took their meals and often sat drinking coffee. Lucas was in the kitchen.

"How you doing, Henry?" Conway asked.

Lucas eyed the paper stuck in the sheriff's shirt pocket.

"Don't look like I'm doing too good."

"You're under arrest, Henry," the sheriff said. "I'm going to read you your rights."

Lucas's mood soured.

"I always heard if the Rangers couldn't get a person one way, you'd get him another way," Lucas told Ryan when he came in. "I was going to help you find Kate, but not now!"

For the first time since Ryan had begun questioning the drifter, Lucas seemed angry, he realized with some satisfaction. The cooperative manner was gone.

"Whatever you think best," Ryan said.

After booking Lucas into the small Montague County Jail, the two officers discussed their strategy.

"I've got some other things I need to do," Ryan told the sheriff. "Let's just let him spend some time in jail before we talk to him again."

Conway said that was fine—it was plowing time anyway.

On Wednesday, June 15, Ryan was in his unmarked state car, heading home to Decatur from Jacksboro.

"Montague One to Six Seven Seven," Conway radioed Ryan.

"Go ahead, Montague One," the Ranger answered.

"I've got to talk to you," the sheriff said.

The two officers arranged to meet on the side of the road.

When the sheriff's car pulled off the highway where Ryan was parked, the Ranger saw that Conway had on his plowing clothes. He had obviously just got off his tractor.

Conway told the Ranger that Lucas had asked to talk to Joe Don Weaver, a jailer.

"A trusty came and got Joe Don and said Henry wanted to talk to him," the sheriff explained. "Joe Don went and looked in through the bean hole and Henry said, 'I've done me some bad things, Joe Don.'"

Weaver, who had come to work for Conway after getting laid off from a machinist job, studied the unshaven face framed by the small metal food service door.

"If it's what I think it is, Henry, you'd better get on your hands and knees in the corner and pray to God, because he's the only one that can forgive you. Man can't."

The jailer listened to Lucas for a few minutes and then left to go call the sheriff.

CHAPTER EIGHT

Shivering in his solitary Montague County jail cell, chilled by an air conditioner that did too good a job, Lucas paced the floor as the faces and bodies swirled around him in his mind—little girls, beautiful women, old ladies, flashing knives, blood smeared on pale skin. Some begged for life and struggled. Others, unable to believe something so horrible could be happening to them, died soundlessly.

Life had offered Lucas very little, and he had blown the few chances he had ever had. If he had any gifts, it was his memory. He had almost total recall.

"I have tryed to get help for so long and no one will believe me," he had written in the note he gave the jailer. "I have killed for the past ten years and no one will believe me . . . I cannot go own [sic] doing this . . . I allso [sic] killed The only Girl I ever loved. . . ."

One of the things he remembered was the first time he and Becky had had sex. He'd been on the bed with her, rough-housing around as innocently as a father might with a young daughter. She'd teased him about something and then started tickling him.

Suddenly, they were kissing. Then he was peeling off her clothes and his. Clothed, Becky was a playful little girl. Naked, at least to Lucas, she was a woman.

Just as clearly, Lucas remembered the last time he'd had sex with her: August 24, 1982. The day after his birthday. And the day Becky died.

Finally, the memory of what he did to Becky—and the others—became overpowering.

He passed a note to jailer Joe Don Weaver saying he needed to talk.

"I've been killing ever thing I can for the past ten years," he wrote. "I am to say a bout [*sic*] X different people." He had written in a number, but then scratched through it.

Lucas and Becky had argued about going back to Florida most of the day. Becky missed her brother Frank, her uncle Ottis, and her friends. She wanted to go back to Jacksonville. Lucas didn't. He couldn't put it into words, but he was afraid someone would try to take her away from him. Her uncle Howell, one of Ottis's brothers, had already tried that once.

Becky kept insisting. She cried. She switched to pouting. When that didn't work, she went back to crying. Finally, he gave in. It didn't take them long to get ready. She folded her clothes into two beat-up suitcases. He stuffed everything he owned into another. He rolled a couple of pillows into two blankets—they'd come in handy to sleep on.

When they were packed and ready, he asked Pop Moore to give them a ride to the truck stop at Alvord. Lucas knew he couldn't take his car. It didn't have license plates and he couldn't afford to buy them. He figured they could hitch a ride from the truck stop easily enough.

Shortly before eight o'clock that evening they left the House of Prayer. Rueben Moore offered his hand; Faye Munnerlyn had a hug for Becky. Moore told Lucas he'd always be welcome at the House of Prayer.

At the truck stop Lucas and Becky were lucky. They

got a ride to Decatur. Carrying their suitcases and blanket roll, they walked through town and then a gravel-truck driver gave them a ride to Denton, a college town thirty-seven miles north of Dallas.

They went to a nearby store, where Lucas bought himself a six-pack of beer and got Becky two cans of Coca-Cola. By this time it was getting dark. They sat for a while on the side of the busy interstate, watching traffic go by. They needed to get a ride headed south to I-10. That would take them east all the way to Jacksonville.

The beer tasted good but his mood had turned sour. Again Lucas tried to talk Becky out of leaving the House of Prayer. It wasn't too late to turn back, he insisted. He drank and they argued.

No one stopped to offer them a ride. Finally Lucas walked to a nearby motel and tried to get a room. The woman behind the desk looked at the unshaven, shabbily dressed man and the young girl, smelled the beer on the man's breath, and told the couple the motel was full for the night. Lucas knew the clerk was lying, but he didn't press it.

They walked back down the I-35 access road and sat with their luggage until about 2 A.M. Still no one stopped.

Becky was getting sleepy.

Off to the side of the highway was a large pasture knee high in grass and weeds, dotted with an occasional clump of scrub trees. Behind a mott of hackberry trees, they spread their blankets. Even this late at night the air was still hot and muggy. Lucas pulled his shirt and pants off and watched Becky strip down to her panties and bra.

The argument flared up again. Becky refused to consider going back to Stoneburg. She still wanted to go to Jacksonville.

Lucas was tired of arguing about it.

155

"We're either gonna go back to the church tomorrow or we're gonna go to Florida tomorrow—it don't matter which one," he later recalled saying.

"Well, I'm going to Florida," she said.

"All right, then, why don't you shut up?" he said, taking another pull of his now warm beer. He later recalled, "No matter what I tried to do for Becky she wouldn't grow up or take responsibility."

Becky started in on him again, using the rough language she'd picked up on the street. She was beginning to sound just like his mother, always harping at him about something, always cussing him.

Suddenly, Becky's anger boiled over. She struck out at Lucas, slapping him on the side of his face.

Lucas grabbed the ivory-handled meat-carving knife he carried for protection "in case someone came up on us." With the swiftness of a rattlesnake striking, he plunged the knife between her breasts. The sharp blade sliced into Becky's heart and she fell backward onto the blanket.

"Becky didn't say a word—she was gone before I knew it," he would remember.

He ripped off her bra and jerked down her panties, spreading her legs and plunging himself into her lifeless body. The constant roar of traffic on the nearby busy interstate was the only sound.

He didn't understand why he got such pleasure out of having intercourse with a dead body, he said, but it was far better for him that night than it had ever been when Becky was alive.

When he finished, he stood up and looked down at Becky's slashed body. He had known her for three and a half years and had lived with her on the road since January. He had never felt closer to anyone. Now she was gone, lying bloody and naked on a blanket in a field of weeds hundreds of miles from her home.

He couldn't afford to think about that now. There was work to do. First, he sliced off Becky's head, using the carbon-bladed knife to cut through the flesh, arteries, trachea, esophagus, and spinal column. He was surprised at how little blood there was. Next he cut off Becky's arms, taking time to sever her hands. He removed her legs at the hips. Then he cut the trunk of her body in two.

He looked down at his beloved Becky, now in nine separate pieces on the blood-soaked blanket. He yanked the pillows out of their cases and began stuffing the cases with Becky's body parts. His first idea was to drag the pillowcases off a ways and bury them, but he changed his mind. The ground was too hard to dig even a shallow grave. The only tool he had to dig with was his knife. He wouldn't risk dulling the finely honed blade.

Removing the gory pieces from the stained pillowcases, Lucas scattered Becky's body over the field.

He gathered up their luggage and walked through the grass to the railroad tracks that ran along the western edge of the field. Climbing the steep embankment Lucas tossed the suitcases into the dense brush below the tracks. For good measure, he pitched Becky's purse and all the canned goods they had been carrying.

To the east, he could see faint streaks of light. He came upon a creek and squatted down to wash the blood off his hands. After cleaning up, he walked into Denton and hung around town for most of the day.

Later, he hitched a ride back to Montague County. In Bowie he called Rueben Moore's brother to come and get him. He wanted to go back to the House of Prayer.

Texas Ranger Ryan listened to Lucas's confession with an uncomfortable mixture of satisfaction and disgust. The satisfaction came in knowing that his instincts had not failed him, that the many hours he and Sheriff Conway had invested in the case had not been wasted. But hearing how Lucas had calmly killed a fifteen-year-old girl, had sex with her corpse, and then butchered her with the same casualness that someone else might field-dress a deer came close to turning his stomach.

Lucas had been talking all night. He and Ryan had gone through cup after cup of coffee, cigarette after cigarette.

The evening had begun with Lucas's confession to the murder of Kate Rich, although he had butchered Becky three weeks before he killed the elderly Ringgold woman.

On September 16, 1982, Lucas said in his confession, he left the House of Prayer about six o'clock in the evening and drove to Mrs. Rich's house in Ringgold. Lucas stepped from the broken concrete walk onto the sagging wooden porch cluttered with rickety chairs and rusty pails. As he knocked on her screen door, he could see the old woman sitting inside alone, watching television.

"I asked Kate if she wanted to go to church and then go and look for Becky," Lucas said in his written statement to Ranger Ryan.

Lucas, however, had something else in mind. "I knew I wasn't going to look for Becky," he said.

If they had gone directly to services at the House of Prayer, Lucas would have driven south. Instead he headed north, to a small store just across the Red River in Oklahoma.

He had not been drinking when he first got to Mrs. Rich's house, but at the store he got a case of beer for himself and one soft drink for Mrs. Rich.

For Kate Rich, a once-active woman now forced by age to spend most of her time cooped up in her house alone, sewing, playing solitaire, or watching TV, a drive in the country was a real treat. Lucas headed south to an old graveyard near the House of Prayer, then back toward Ringgold. He had already had several cans of beer.

"About eight P.M. . . . I got the urge to kill Kate," Lucas said. "I went to the second dirt or gravel road to the left past the campground. This road goes left up to an oil tank after passing over the railroad tracks. There is a locked gate down this road. I pulled just over the railroad tracks and stopped."

Mrs. Rich had not paid any attention to the brown-handled butcher knife lying on the car seat between them.

"I got it in my right hand and stuck it all the way in Kate's left side," he told the Ranger. "Kate fell over against the door. I pulled the knife out and I don't remember if I left it in the car or threw it away. I opened the door Kate was against and she fell halfway out of the car. I stepped over her and pulled her down the embankment."

Mrs. Rich had bled some in the car and much more on the ground. Most of the bleeding, however, was internal. The knife had gone into her heart and she had died quickly and quietly.

Lucas stood over her for a moment, looking down at the lifeless old woman. His erection pressed against his pants as he bent down to undress her. He piled her clothes on the ground next to her body.

"I got naked and screwed her until I finished," Lucas told the Ranger. "I got dressed and drug her to the drain pipe that run under the road and put her as far as I could with my hands."

He stuffed her clothing into the pipe first, then used a two-by-four and a length of pipe to shove her body deeper into the pipe. When he was satisfied the old lady was hidden, he went back up the embankment and drove to his room at the House of Prayer. He washed the blood off his hands and opened himself another beer. He stayed up all night, drinking and remembering.

Now, nine months later, Lucas and Ranger Ryan were up all night, too. On tape and in two written statements Lucas described the murders of Becky and Mrs. Rich and what he did after committing the crimes.

At 5:00 A.M. on September 17, 1982, the morning after Mrs. Rich's murder, Lucas had decided he had better leave. When he got in his car, he noticed Mrs. Rich's shoes and purse on the right front floorboard. As he drove toward the House of Prayer gate, he saw that Gilbert Beagle was already up. Lucas pulled his car up and told Beagle he was headed out to see if he could find Becky.

"I'll be at work Monday," he said.

As soon as he felt he was far enough from the House of Prayer, he tossed Mrs. Rich's purse off a bridge into a creek. He drove a little farther and pitched her shoes.

He thought about driving to Jacksonville to see Ottis, but he would want to know where Becky was, so he headed west toward California. The old car got him there but broke down outside Needles. He didn't have any money and just left it on the side of the road.

He had drifted for a month, he told Ryan. In mid-October, a month after Mrs. Rich's murder, he came back to Stoneburg. That winter, after taking a polygraph examination, he had gone back to where he'd left Mrs. Rich and pushed her body from the drainage pipe so he could carry it back to the House of Prayer and burn it. The examiner had spread a map of the area and then tested Lucas's reaction as he pointed to various places on a map and asked if Mrs. Rich's body might be found there. Lucas worried they had finally figured out where she was.

At 1:55 A.M., Lucas's long confessional with Ryan

ended when he signed the second of the two written statements he had given. Ahead of Ryan now was the job of corroborating everything Lucas had told him.

Sheriff Conway, who had napped in his office while Ryan took Lucas's statements, walked Lucas back to his cell.

The Ranger and a deputy drove to the culvert described by Lucas. Searching with flashlights, they found a pair of panties that appeared to have washed from the drainage pipe. Still sticking in the north end of the culvert was a length of pipe similar to the one Lucas had described. The officers also found a two-by-four where Lucas said he had left it, as well as the hole Lucas said he had dug for the body before he changed his mind about burying it.

Realizing that finding anything else in the darkness would be a hit-or-miss proposition, the officers left until daybreak. Returning shortly after 6:00 A.M., they found two pieces of a broken pair of ladies' glasses on the side of the road near where Lucas said he had parked his car before stabbing Mrs. Rich.

At 8:00 A.M., Ryan and District Attorney's Investigator Paul Smith went to the House of Prayer with a consent-to-search waiver signed by Lucas. Behind Lucas's trashed-out apartment in the converted chicken barn, the two officers found a wood-burning stove like the one described by Lucas. What they found inside the stove sickened them, but it helped further support Lucas's confession: pieces of what appeared to be burnt flesh, somewhat preserved by wood smoke. Also inside the stove were several crisp pieces of bone. The ashes from the stove filled four plastic bags. At a spot where Lucas said he had dumped more stove ash, they found several larger pieces of bone fragments. All the material would be taken to the Southwest Forensic Laboratory in Dallas for analysis.

In Lucas's apartment, which was littered with empty Pall Mall cigarette packages and dirty clothes, the officers found a pair of green coveralls. Lucas said he had used them to carry Mrs. Rich's body back to the House of Prayer so he could cut her up and burn the pieces.

Shortly before noon, Ryan and the other officers returned to the sheriff's office to pick up Lucas.

"Henry, we'd like you to show us where you threw Mrs. Rich's purse," the Ranger said. "Can you take us there?"

Lucas directed the officers to the bridge where Mrs. Rich's purse had been found the previous December.

"Okay, Henry, will you take us to where Mrs. Rich was killed?" Ryan asked.

Again he guided Ryan straight to the culvert where the panties and partial eyeglasses, along with the pipe and lumber, had been found earlier that morning.

Ryan had lost track of how long he had gone without sleep, but there was more to do. After lunch he and a deputy headed for Denton with Lucas to give him a chance to take officers to whatever might be left of Becky Powell. Smith and Sheriff Conway went to Dallas with the evidence.

Thinking Lucas had killed Becky outside the city limits of Denton, Ryan contacted a friend with the Denton County Sheriff's Office, Lt. Ron Douglas. Douglas met Ryan and his prisoner in a convenience store parking lot near the intersection of I-35 and Highway 380. When Ryan pointed to the area where Lucas had said Becky's remains would be found, the sheriff's lieutenant realized the spot was actually in the city and radioed for city officers to come to the scene.

A short time later, Denton Police detective Larry Brearley joined the other officers. At first, Brearley didn't realize the unhandcuffed Lucas was a murder suspect. Seeing the unkempt man with Ryan and Lt. Douglas, Brearley took him to be a highway department maintenance worker who had discovered a body and then called police.

The Ranger handed Brearley Lucas's signed statement.

"You might want to read this before we get started," Ryan said.

Brearley scanned the written confession and then looked at Lucas with new interest. He stood quietly in the background smoking as the officers discussed how they would handle the crime scene search.

"All right, Henry, do you want to show us where Becky is?" Ryan asked.

The Ranger knew Lucas had been dreading the trip to Denton. Discussing the casual murder of Mrs. Rich did not seem to bother him, but talking about Becky often choked him up. Hoping to keep him cooperative, Ryan tried to be deferential to Lucas.

The little man pointed to a grove of trees that looked to be fifty or sixty yards off the interstate. Followed by a dozen officers, Lucas walked through the grass to the trees.

"Part of her's here," Lucas said, pointing to the ground a few feet beyond the trees.

As Lucas looked on, one of the officers probed with a shovel.

"No, move over a couple of feet," Lucas said, pointing to a different spot. Soon the deputy had uncovered two shoulder blades and some partially decomposed flesh, several pieces of cloth, and part of a bra.

Two weeks after killing Becky, he later recalled, he had returned to the crime scene and buried one bag of Becky's remains. "I wanted to bury the rest of her, but I just couldn't do it," he said.

Lucas walked due west to a point the officers later measured as fifty-nine feet from the spot where the first group of remains had been found. Here several human bones, including two pieces of a pelvis, were visible on the ground. Lucas led the officers in a clockwise, C-shaped route tilted slightly on a northwest–southwest axis. They found bones and body parts at seven different locations, scattered at varying distances on either side of a line about 130 feet long. A skull, lying amid a pile of tangled brown hair, was found on the ground at the sixth site.

Finally, Lucas led the officers over a fence that ran parallel to the railroad tracks on the western edge of the pasture. Scattered along a rocky ledge just west of the tracks was an assortment of feminine clothing and articles—makeup, fingernail polish, combs and brushes, costume jewelry, a purse, billfold. The items appeared to have been strewn from an orange suitcase and faded gray overnight bag found in the same area. At some point in the ten months since the murder someone had used the suitcase for target practice, riddling it with shotgun pellets.

By 6:00 P.M. Brearley felt that most of Becky's body had been recovered. A justice of the peace called to the scene for the legal formality of pronouncing Becky dead ordered a forensic examination of the remains.

By sundown the officers had thirteen plastic trash bags filled with evidence found in the pasture off the interstate. Each discovery site had been marked by a wooden stake with a red plastic strip stapled to it and then photographed. Lt. Douglas made a map of the field, noting the distances between each location. In the identification section at police headquarters, the skeleton was arranged on a white sheet and photographed.

Lucas was fingerprinted and photographed and then released to Sheriff Conway, who took him back to Montague County.

That evening, Brearley and the other officers who had searched the field off the interstate began to itch, angry red splotches breaking out on their legs: chigger bites.

Ryan, who had now been up for nearly two days, got to his house in Decatur at 7:10 P.M. and went straight to bed. Adrenaline, caffeine, and nicotine could carry a person only so far. Lucas, back in his cold cell, asked for more coffee.

When Ryan finally managed to get out of bed that morning, every cell in his body screamed for more sleep. But there was just too much to do. Until Lucas started talking, Ryan had assumed that all he had was a double murder case, as if that wasn't enough right there. Lucas, however, had kept talking, claiming murders all over Texas and the nation.

Ryan knew Lucas was a liar, but he had already pretty well corroborated Lucas's confessions to two brutal murders—one of an old woman, the other of a young girl. Neither looked like a rookie job to Ryan. He figured Lucas was blowing a certain amount of smoke, but he acted like a man who had killed before—and more than once.

If Lucas was telling the truth about killing and sexually molesting dozens of women, the Ranger knew that he was going to need some help. He had already notified his sergeant, Carl Weathers, and his captain, Charlie Moore, at Ranger Company C headquarters in Lubbock. Ryan had also called the Crime Analysis Section at the Department of Public Safety headquarters in Austin to get them started looking for unsolved cases that might match Lucas's claims.

Lucas had learned years before in Michigan that suicide threats could get him attention. Using half a page in a legal pad he had been given for notes and sketches, he wrote:

> Since you gave me this paper can you give me any thing to stop this offel torment and nerves before I do trye to stop it my self I cant keep going

by my self so please do something you all got what it takes so please do something for me

I need to get something soon before I brake like before and only hurt my self

Signed
Henry Lucas

Since his arrest, Lucas had been kept in a cell by himself. Sheriff Conway did not feel there was anything in the cell Lucas could use to hurt himself, unless he tried to stab himself with his pencil. However, on Sunday, June 19, Lucas broke a light bulb and used a piece of glass to cut his wrist. The wound was superficial, but Lucas was taken to a hospital in Wichita Falls for treatment.

Since Lucas had first started talking on Wednesday, Ryan had succeeded in his strategy to keep the case low profile. He was not antipress, but he definitely wasn't looking for any publicity. He wanted time to see if there was anything to Lucas's claims of multiple murders in Texas before officers from the other states Lucas had talked about got in on the act. For nearly a week it worked, though word was spreading rapidly among Texas law enforcement officers.

On Friday, June 17, it had taken the Montague County Grand Jury less than an hour to return a murder indictment against Lucas. The grand jury also indicted him on the charge of being a felon in possession of a firearm.

Shortly before 5:00 P.M. on Tuesday, June 21, Chief Deputy Sheriff Jesse Ramos and Deputy José Cordero escorted Lucas across the street from the jail to the Montague County Courthouse for his arraignment before District Judge Frank Douthitt. A news crew from a Wichita Falls television station, in Montague to cover what they thought was a murder story of only area interest, taped Lucas as he walked unhandcuffed between the two deputies toward the courthouse. His dark hair was tousled and he had several days' growth of gray-flecked beard. Two newspaper photographers snapped pictures.

Inside the second-floor district courtroom two newspaper reporters, one from Wichita Falls and one who had come from Austin after getting a tip from a friendly detective who had heard about Lucas, flipped open their notebooks to cover what they expected to be a brief courtroom appearance of the murder suspect. He would be warned again of his rights and asked if he had a lawyer or wanted the court to appoint him one.

At the outset of the arraignment, Judge Douthitt asked Lucas if he had read the indictment accusing him of Mrs. Rich's murder.

"I didn't read it, but I know I'm guilty of it," he said. "I didn't try to hide it."

The judge asked if he had an attorney. Lucas said he could not afford one.

"I don't even care if I have one," he said.

After District Attorney Jack McGaughey read the indictment accusing him of Mrs. Rich's stabbing death and the indictment returned against him on the charge of being a felon in possession of a firearm, Judge Douthitt asked Lucas if he understood the seriousness of the murder charge against him.

"Yes, sir—I have about a hundred of them," Lucas replied.

The two reporters in the courtroom scribbled furiously in their notepads. The unkempt little man standing in open court had just said he had killed a hundred people.

Douthitt, acutely aware Lucas was appearing before him without an attorney, did not ask Lucas to elaborate on what he had just said. Instead he pursued another line of questioning: Had he ever had psychiatric treatment? If so, what had been the diagnosis?

167

"Not that they told me," Lucas replied, evidently referring to the second question. "They turned me loose and told me to go back home. They said, 'You are all right.' I tell them my problems and they didn't want to do anything about it. I kept asking for help. All I could . . . figure out of my problem was I know it ain't normal for a person to go out and kill girls just to have sex with them. No matter how much trouble I try to prevent, I always end up in it."

The judge asked Lucas if he felt he was mentally competent to stand trial.

"I would say yes, I think so. I am guilty of it and whatever you or whichever one try it, I don't care what it gives me . . . whether it gives me a death penalty or not."

"Mr. Lucas, this case does not carry the death penalty," the judge said gently.

Douthitt told Lucas he was appointing attorney Don Maxfield of Wichita Falls to represent him and that he was entering a plea of not guilty in his behalf.

"Will I still be able to go on helping finding bodies?" Lucas asked the judge.

The judge was silent for a moment, as if carefully choosing his words. "After you and your attorney have discussed this matter, I will rule on it."

Douthitt's final action was to order Lucas held without bond on the murder charge. He set bond at $25,000 on the firearms charge.

After Lucas was led from the courtroom, the two reporters zeroed in on District Attorney McGaughey. The prosecutor would not speculate on how many people Lucas might have killed, but said seven murder cases had been discussed with officers by Lucas.

"There's a lot of work still to be done before any of his statements can be verified," he said. "It's not beyond imagination that he's just spinning yarns."

The two reporters who sat through the arraignment had their stories on page one of their papers the next morning. The wire services picked up the story. By midmorning that Wednesday, June 22, television station helicopters from Fort Worth and Dallas were circling the Montague County courthouse. Since Montague had no airport, the choppers landed wherever their pilots could find a safe open place. One local woman called the sheriff's office to report her freshly hung washing had been covered with dust kicked up by a low-flying TV chopper. Sheriff Conway, trying to be accommodating, dispatched deputies to give the reporters a ride to his office. Already more newspaper reporters than Conway had deputies were crowding the lobby of the law enforcement center and jail. The out-of-town reporters hurried to buy copies of a special edition of the weekly Bowie *News* with a long page-one story on Lucas beneath a banner reading: CONFESSES TO MASS KILLINGS. A sidebar story, primarily based on an interview with the owner of a small store where Lucas came to buy his cigarettes, proclaimed: STONEBURG RESIDENTS RECALL LUCAS "REAL NICE MAN."

Sheriff Conway, less used to the issue of pretrial publicity than colleagues in more populated areas, discussed the case freely with the local paper's editor, who wrote the banner story. "I wasn't surprised over the confession," he said. "He was my number-one suspect from the start."

Asked about Lucas's claim that he had killed a hundred women, the sheriff said, "I believe the statement. I wouldn't be surprised that it will turn out to be the worst mass murders ever."

A couple of years earlier, Sheriff Conway had come to Williamson County on a cattle-rustling case. He and Sheriff Boutwell had lunch and, talking shop, Boutwell had told Conway about the unsolved murders he had in his county along I-35.

On Saturday, June 18, Boutwell was out in his ham radio shack behind his house when his wife called him to the telephone. Building and maintaining his short-wave radio equipment was Boutwell's therapy. In his radio shack he lost himself in transitors and resistors. Unsolved murders, jail problems, and disputes with county commissioners faded from his mind like a weak signal.

Sheriff Conway went quickly to the point and Boutwell just as quickly forgot about his ham work.

"Jim, I've got an old boy up here you might like to talk to," he said. "His name's Henry Lee Lucas and he's cleaned up a couple of murders for us. He's said he's done a lot more around the country."

Boutwell left Georgetown on Tuesday, went to a law enforcement group fish fry that evening, and spent the night in Bowie. At 8:00 A.M. Wednesday, the morning after Lucas's open-court admission of multiple murders, Boutwell drove to the Montague County Sheriff's Office.

Conway told Boutwell he could have a small, private office in order to talk with Lucas and sent a deputy to get Lucas out of his cell. Boutwell had seen the type of prisoner that the deputy led into the room a thousand times in his long career. Lucas, wearing a light blue shirt and blue trousers, was unshaven and he smelled.

Still, Boutwell smiled and shook his hand.

"I'm Jim Boutwell, sheriff of Williamson County," he began. He made small talk with Lucas and offered him a Lucky. The sheriff shook one out for himself as Lucas lit up.

"You want some coffee?" Boutwell asked.

"I sure would," Lucas said.

Boutwell explained that Georgetown was near Austin.

"Oh, I've got some down there," Lucas said.

Boutwell soon learned, as Ranger Ryan already had, that Lucas tended not to use the word *murder*.

Lucas started talking about a blonde with dark

roots in a dark car in the Austin area. Boutwell made a mental note to mention that to the Rangers, if they had not already heard about it, but he was interested in Williamson County.

After about ten minutes, Boutwell laid a color photograph of a puffy-faced dead girl on the table. Her face had been wiped clean of blood and dirt before the picture was taken.

Boutwell deliberately held his thumb over her neck to cover the bruises, obviously caused by manual strangulation.

"Do you recognize this girl?" he asked.

Lucas's one good eye came to life. If he had been a hound dog, Boutwell thought, he would have come to a point.

"That's one of mine," Lucas said, almost pridefully. "She would have been strangled."

By midmorning, Boutwell had Lucas's story reduced to writing and signed.

Emerging from the sheriff's office later that morning, Boutwell told a reporter that Lucas had signed a statement confessing to the October 31, 1979, murder of the unidentified woman found nude in a culvert just off I-35 north of Georgetown. The sheriff also said Lucas had talked about a case in central Texas that sounded a lot like the murder of Sandra Dubbs, whose mutilated body had been found in a field south of Austin on October 8, 1979.

"He told me he has killed over a hundred women, starting when he was thirteen years old," Boutwell said. "He said it was a compulsion with him."

"He's a good suspect in nearly anything," Sheriff Conway added. "He goes everywhere—he's U.S. general delivery."

As detectives from Travis County headed to Montague to talk to Lucas about the Dubbs case and other unsolved slayings, Boutwell returned to Georgetown with Lucas's confession.

The following day, June 23, Judge Douthitt set Lucas's bail at $1 million, appointed three psychiatrists to examine him, and issued a gag order barring law enforcement officers and lawyers from further discussing the Lucas case.

On June 24, Travis County sheriff's deputies interviewed Lucas for two hours on videotape. He confessed to Sandra Dubbs's murder, but three days later Travis County Sheriff Doyne Bailey said no charges would be filed against Lucas in the Dubbs case.

"We're not in any hurry," the sheriff told a reporter in Austin. "We know where he is."

Since a gag order had been imposed in the Lucas case, Bailey could not say it more publicly, but he felt there were already enough murder charges against the drifter. And the only evidence he had that Lucas killed Dubbs was his statement, though he had recalled things about the crime that had not been released in the media.

Lucas, however, continued to talk, though he had imposed certain conditions himself. In a note to "Phill Rine" on June 28 Lucas set out two rules:

(1) At no time will I see any other officer or person pertaining [*sic*] to any other crime in any other area: Unless a member of Montuage [*sic*] Staff is present, or Texas Ranger. (2) The Description a/ location that I give must be sent to an area that pertains to that crime. Then if nessary [*sic*] to other Locations.

Lucas had been generating almost as many words and images as the reporters who had flocked to Montague to cover the spectacular story. Each day Ryan collected summaries of cases written by Lucas and drawings of female victims that generally shared two traits: large eyes and prominent breasts. Some of the women in the pencil drawings were clothed; others were nude.

In addition to the drawings, Lucas offered written descriptions of the victims and what happened to them. Typical was the story of "Cindy," a runaway "from north" whom he described as "very sexy and well built large bust. . . ." She was sixteen or seventeen, wore heavy makeup, and was hitchhiking when Lucas stopped to offer her a ride.

Lucas said he was already one six-pack into a case of beer and that she started drinking beer, too.

> We kept talking and I ask her to slide over beside me and she did. I become to feel of her tittys and she ask me if I like that and I said yes. She was only playing me I could tell so I said I wanted to fuck her and she said meby. I said I was going to stop and get some and she said not yet we'll have plenty of time and I said no we don't. . . .

When she tried to move closer to the passenger door, Lucas wrote,

> I pulled her back with my right hand and put my arm around her neck and she was pulling and hitting me . . . I almost recked.

In desperation the girl tried to grab the steering wheel. At that,

> I rammed the butcher knife into her. She said something but I could not make it out. She fell between the seat and dash next to the door. She stayed like that until I pulled her out of the car and while I was pulling her she began to moan or something.

Lucas said he dragged her into a field and choked her.

> [In] a little while I knew she was dead. I got sex from her and left her there. . . . I know that what I am saying is true and that I will find her some how no matter what happens. This picture is the best I can draw of her.

Ryan was careful to date each of Lucas's literary efforts and add them to his growing case file.

On August 2, with Lucas in Georgetown for arraignment on the "Orange Socks" case, Travis County deputies took him to Austin for further questioning in the Dubbs case. He led detectives south on I-35 and showed where Dubbs's car had been, pointed out the field where he left her body, and drew a diagram correctly showing the position her body was left in.

As he was being driven to Austin, Lucas startled detectives Jerry Wiggins and Gary Cutler by admitting to a crime he hadn't even been suspected of.

Southbound on the interstate with the detectives, Lucas pointed to a building and asked if it had been a liquor store at one time. The deputies said it had. Lucas went on to correctly describe the robbery and murder of a man and wife that had occurred at the location on October 23, 1979.

The two deputies, taking Lucas's confession on a tape recorder, were stunned at their prisoner's voluntary confession to the murder of Harry and Molly Schlesinger.

By the time Wiggins and Cutler returned Lucas to Sheriff Boutwell in Georgetown, they were convinced he had killed at least three people in their county.

In Montague County, Prosecutor McGaughey spent the rest of the summer preparing to go to trial. He felt confident he could prove that Lucas killed Mrs. Rich, despite the problem of not having a recognizable body.

But at a pretrial hearing on Friday, September 30, Lucas's attorney, Don Maxfield told Judge Douthitt that Lucas was ready to plead guilty. The judge recessed the hearing and said he would reconvene court at 4 P.M. after both sides had discussed the plea offer. Later that afternoon, Douthitt accepted Lucas's guilty plea and sentenced him to seventy-five years.

Since Lucas would have to serve a minimum of twenty years before parole would be possible, the seventy-five-year sentence would amount to life, Douthitt told reporters after the hearing.

Before Boutwell could get Lucas down to Williamson County to face trial, he had to be tried in Denton County. At Lucas's arraignment on August 12, he pleaded not guilty to Becky's murder, despite the written confession taken by Ryan and the videotaped confession Lucas had given to Detective Brearley on June 17.

Court-appointed defense attorney Tom Whitlock's only real hope was to get Lucas's confessions tossed out of court. In a hearing on Friday, October 7, Whitlock argued that the confessions should not be allowed as evidence against his client since Lucas mentioned other offenses on the tape made by Brearley, including the slaying of Mrs. Rich.

District Attorney Jerry Cobb played the videotape to a packed courtroom. The video was the first public airing of what Ryan and other officers had been living with for nearly four months. Spectators and court officials alike were stunned at Lucas's calm account of Becky's murder and dismemberment.

"I didn't do it because I didn't love her or anything like that," Lucas said in the on-camera interview. "It was because of the arguments and the difficulties I've been having through my life."

After describing Becky's murder and how he cut her body into "little teeny pieces," Lucas commented on his interest in having sex with dead bodies. "It was one of those things that got to be a part of my life—having sexual intercourse with them after they were dead."

At the end of the tape Lucas told Brearley: "I hope you can find all of her. I hope you can. I didn't leave her in a pretty sight."

The judge ordered that the tape be edited, with any references to other offenses deleted. When that was done, he said, the confession to Becky's murder would be admissable.

Whitlock's other line of defense would be insanity. At the attorney's request, the judge appointed a psychiatrist and a psychologist to examine Lucas. A week later, the judge issued another order that Lucas be taken off all medication prior to the examinations.

When the mental evaluations were completed, Whitlock's insanity option was out. As had been the case in the evaluations ordered by Judge Douthitt in Montague County, the professionals who interviewed Lucas found no indication of insanity.

Cobb told Whitlock he could have his client plead out, but it would have to be for a life sentence. The defense attorney opted for a trial. In Texas, the murder statute provides a punishment range of five to ninety-nine years. He might get lucky.

A seven-man, five-woman jury was seated on November 8 in Judge W. C. Boyd's 16th District Court. Testimony began at two o'clock that afternoon.

Twenty-three years before, on trial for the murder of his mother, Lucas had taken the witness stand. His attorney's strategy had been to show the terrible childhood Lucas had had, but Lucas's testimony had helped the people's case as well. Now Lucas wanted to testify again. It was as if Lucas wanted to assure his conviction by telling all, but Whitlock hoped his questions of Lucas might raise other questions in the minds of the jurors.

"I'm not denying taking her life," Lucas testified. "I'm not going to deny that. I hit her with a knife. I don't know how."

As he had done for Ryan and Brearley, Lucas described how he and Becky had argued and how she had struck him on the right side of his face.

In his confessions, he had said he stabbed Becky almost immediately after she hit him. In court, however, he was not as sure. "I can't say if it was ten minutes or ten hours. I don't remember what happened after I got hit. I could see her sitting there with the knife in her and I realized what had happened."

He was crying.

In the final argument to the jury Cobb asked that they assess Lucas a life sentence to "remove this animal from the streets." Whitlock sought the minimum possible sentence of five years.

"Henry came to the halls of justice to be punished," he said. "The band has played and he has faced the music. He deserves some credit for telling about Becky."

The jury deliberated Lucas's punishment more than four hours before deciding on sending him to prison for life. Lucas showed no emotion when the sentence was pronounced.

"You did a good job," Lucas told Cobb.

In a press conference after Judge Boyd dismissed the jurors, Whitlock read a statement written by Lucas.

I have not tried to win, if I ever decide to win I can do so. But because I was responsible for taking Becky's life, and my love for her, I do not wish to win and I have set forth to see that no man can win a case for me unless I want it done.

I'm sorry that people have to be used to gain

what I want to happen. But that is why justice can be used in every walk of life either for or against wrong.

You saw what I wanted you to; you heard what I wanted you to; and you read what I wanted you to. I used you all to gain my own peace of mind.

After the trial, deputies hurried Lucas back to the Denton County Jail, where Sheriff Boutwell was waiting for him with a bench warrant ordering him taken to Williamson County to stand trial in the "Orange Socks" murder. Lucas was glad to see the tall sheriff, who treated him with respect, always keeping his word with him.

Boutwell drove back to Georgetown nonstop. On the way, Lucas chain-smoked and talked about Becky, Mrs. Rich, and his friend, Ottis Toole, Becky's uncle.

The trial, set for January, would be Lucas's third since his arrest in June 1983. But the Williamson County case would be different from the others. District Attorney Ed Walsh was going for a capital murder conviction. He hoped he could persuade a jury to oblige Lucas with the punishment he'd said in Denton he had already decided on for himself—death.

CHAPTER NINE

The isolation cell on the first floor of the Williamson County Jail was little more than a steel box. Lucas's only view was through the "bean hole," the small opening in the metal door used to pass in food.

On November 12, 1983, five months and a day after his arrest in Montague County, Lucas sat on his bunk, writing on a notepad.

Dear Ottis, I have tryed to write you many times but with ever thing happening to me, I couldn't.

The reason I have not told you about Becky was I never wanted to hurt you, and knowing what happened to her. She was my life and I loved her more than any thing else. we both have did wrong but I believe God will soon let us to return to each other in Heaven and I pray ever day that it will happen real soon

But still I must clear the Books here on earth first.

Lucas needed Toole's help.

You know the different times we took lifes together. I'm trying to clear up my own wrong, and I relise you may not want me to involve you but I haft to ask for your help to clear up the cases that have happened. . . . I have not told them you were involved nor have I gave any thing they could use against you.

Lucas went on for four pages. He thought of Toole daily and wished "that I could turn back time and not have to go through this But I cant."

He hoped Toole would cooperate with the police: "If you deside that you wish to help clear up this I will try and get it arranged so we can get the hole thing out in the open."

Concluding with the hope that "ever thing is alright with you and that all is well with the family," he asked that Toole give his family his regards . . . "and tell them I'm sorry that ever thing has went wrong as it has . . ."

He signed the letter: "As always, Henry."

When Lucas said in his letter to Toole that "I have not told them you were involved," he was lying. But even before Lucas started talking in Texas, his homosexual lover was having legal problems of his own back in Florida.

About the time Lucas had been arrested in Montague County on the charge of being a felon in possession of a firearm, two juveniles arrested for setting fires in the Springfield area of Jacksonville had fingered Toole as their fellow arsonist. He'd been arrested on June 6, 1983, and charged with two counts of arson. After pleading guilty to both charges, Toole was sentenced on August 5 to fifteen years in prison for one of the fires and five years for the other. The terms were to run consecutively.

Within a month of his arrest at the House of Prayer, Lucas had started talking to Ryan about Toole and murders around Jacksonville. The Ranger contacted the Jacksonville Sheriff's Office to relay the information. Jacksonville detective J. W. (Buddy) Terry, assigned to look into Lucas's claims, mailed Ryan summaries of eleven unsolved cases.

Ryan was already well aware of Lucas's propensity to take credit for homicides that either weren't his or had never even occurred. With that in mind, the Ranger was careful in discussing the possible Jacksonville cases. On July 15, he showed Lucas photographs of the victims, but did not provide him any details on the crimes.

After going over all the cases with him, Ryan felt Lucas did know something about several of them. He sent his notes to Terry, who called Ryan to get a better feel for what he was dealing with in Lucas. Cutting out the middleman, Ryan surprised Terry by putting Lucas on the phone with the detective. When Lucas told Terry he had committed some murders in Jacksonville, the detective got his lieutenant's okay for a trip to Texas to talk to Lucas in person.

Terry tape-recorded his August 11 interview with Lucas in Montague three months before Lucas would write Toole asking his help and assuring him he had not done anything to incriminate him.

"Henry, you said that Ottis has committed some homicides on his own," Terry asked.

"Yeah, he's committed homicide of his own," Lucas replied.

"Were you on any homicides that he committed in Jacksonville?"

"Well, the one that was burnt. He died from burns."

"Which one are we talking about?" Terry asked, not expecting to hear about a fire. "Who died from burns?"

"Well, some old man in his fifties, somewhere around there."

"Black, white?"

"White guy."

"When did this happen?"

"That was back in December of eighty-two," Lucas replied. "He set fire to an apartment house . . . and, uh, we were hiding over there in the back alley there when he set the fire. We went around back . . . and the Fire Department was there fighting it. They brought the old man out there on the front porch and tried to save his life, but they couldn't."

Lucas filled Terry in on the details of the fire and eight other Jacksonville homicides that he had confessed to in the taped interviews.

Back in Florida, Terry found that the fatal arson Lucas had described fit the January 4, 1982, death of George Sonenberg, a case that had been carried as accidental. On August 30, Terry and Detective S. W. Higginbotham, who had investigated the fatal fire, drove to the Florida State Prison reception medical unit at Raiford to talk to Toole about the fire.

Toole readily admitted setting the fire. The only difference between his story and Lucas's was that he had ignited a mattress with a match and had not used gasoline to start the blaze. When Higginbotham asked Toole why he had started the fire, he broke into a big grin, exposing his bad teeth. He loved fires, he said. He had started about a hundred of them during the past several years.

Terry wrote out a statement based on what Toole had just told him and Toole signed it. Based on that, Toole was charged on September 8 with first-degree murder.

By September 22, Terry and other Jacksonville law enforcement officers were confident enough in their investigation of Lucas's Duval County activities to hold a press conference at which they announced they believed he had killed eight women in the county. The murders had occurred during a twenty-three-month period from 1979 to 1981. The female victims ranged in age from eighteen to seventy-six. Some had been strangled, some stabbed, some beaten; one had been shot. The only thing they had had in common, apparently, was coming into contact with Henry Lee Lucas.

Duval County Sheriff Dale Carson said his department had closed the books on the murders and intended to ask the state attorney's office to look at the evidence and determine if the cases should be presented to a grand jury.

"As far as I'm concerned, the mystery is over," said Dr. Peter Lipkovic, Duval County Medical Examiner. "After confirming those eight cases, I trust him. I don't think he is going to take credit for something he did not do."

All they had, however, was Lucas's word that he killed the people he said he had. Statements from Toole fairly matched Lucas's claims, but there was no physical evidence.

Sheriff Boutwell sat in his office staring at the stuffed rattlesnake on the shelf across from him. His desk was covered with yellow telephone message slips. He hadn't taken time to count, but he figured he had sixty to seventy phone calls to return, some from reporters, but most from law enforcement agencies across the country. Everyone wanted to talk about Lucas. The problem was, he still had a sheriff's office to run.

Up in Montague County, Sheriff Conway had had a similar headache, thanks to Henry Lee Lucas. As the publicity surrounding Lucas's arrest increased, so had the sheriff's workload. Boutwell remembered Ranger Ryan telling him that at one point the crush of calls to the sheriff's office was so intense he'd "volunteered" his son to come in and answer the phone for a while.

Conway had one thing in his favor: his county was considerably less populated than Williamson County, which meant he had less crime to deal with. He could afford to spend most of his time on Lucas. Like

Conway, Boutwell knew he could count on help from the Texas Rangers. He worked closely with Ranger Clayton Smith, who had been assigned to Williamson County after Joe Davis, the Ranger who had helped in the "Orange Socks" case, was transferred to Kerrville. Judging by the number of calls he'd already received, Boutwell realized the workload was going to be too much for two men, even if they had 100 percent of their time to devote to the Lucas case.

In 1980, worried about all the unsolved murders he had in his county along I-35, Boutwell had asked the Department of Public Safety for help. Calling on the state law enforcement agency now seemed like an even better idea. On November 22, as he had done three years earlier, he wrote a letter to Chief Floyd Hacker, head of the Criminal Law Enforcement Division of the DPS. This time he asked that the DPS create a task force to assist local, county, and out-of-state agencies in their investigation of possible homicides committed by Lucas and Toole.

Specifically, Boutwell suggested that the task force be used to respond to police officers seeking interviews with Lucas; that DPS crime analysis personnel be used to track Lucas and Toole's movements over the years; that DPS Criminal Intelligence investigators look into Lucas's claim that he and Toole had belonged to a cult; that the department furnish air and ground transportation so Lucas could be taken places he claimed to have committed crimes to assist in locating victims; that the department consider flying Toole to Texas or taking Lucas to Florida so that they could "assist each other's memories in some of the crimes they have committed"; and that the DPS look into holding a nationwide conference to be attended by officers from states where Lucas had claimed to have cases.

Boutwell said his department had VHS videotaping

equipment if agencies wishing to interview Lucas would furnish their own tapes and that he would provide an office and telephone for the task force. He asked that the state pick up the cost of the long-distance calls.

Hacker took up the request with his boss, DPS Director Col. Jim Adams, who had risen to the number-two job in the FBI under J. Edgar Hoover before retiring and coming home to Texas. Republican Gov. William P. Clements had appointed Adams as the head of the DPS when longtime director Col. Wilson E. Speir retired in 1980. Adams gave Hacker the go-ahead to get the task force up and running.

On the day after Thanksgiving, November 25, Adams announced the creation of a task force to coordinate the exchange of information among law enforcement agencies investigating cases in which Lucas or Toole might have been involved. Texas Ranger Sgt. Bob Prince, the second in command of Ranger Company F at Waco, would supervise the task force, Adams said.

A short time later, Chief Hacker put out a teletype to all Texas law enforcement agencies inviting them to send a representative to a one-day seminar at the DPS headquarters in Austin on December 7 "to discuss the activities of murder suspects Henry Lee Lucas and Ottis Toole."

On the morning of December 7, Colonel Adams and Sheriff Boutwell had a press conference before the seminar began.

"Lucas claims about a hundred twenty murders, and at this point about thirty-five murders have been cleared from the standpoint of confirming his involvement in them," Adams told reporters. "The main thing we have learned thus far is that an individual like this, traveling around the country for an extended time, can escape detection where he really has no

motive for killing the individual . . . has no association with that individual, and more or less takes
advantage of targets of opportunity."

What brought Lucas down, Adams said, was killing
someone he knew. Since his arrest, Lucas had been
"extremely cooperative," the colonel said.

"That unusual cooperation . . . has created the
need for the task force approach to make sure everyone who has an interest has an opportunity to interview him," Adams said.

Adams knew the task force job would not be an easy
one. Lucas had said many of his crimes were committed while he was under the influence of drugs or
alcohol, he had bragged that he never left evidence,
and Ranger Phil Ryan had already demonstrated that
Lucas would lie about cases. Then too, as a drifter,
Lucas would not have left an easy paper trail to
follow—no credit card slips, bank accounts, or mort-
gages. Henry Lee Lucas was not an average person—
or average killer.

When Oklahoma-born, Texas-raised Bob Prince
was a star tackle for the Texas Christian University
Horned Frogs from 1956 to 1960, a career in the Texas
Rangers never occurred to him. In his junior year his
team won the Southwest Conference and played Air
Force to a scoreless tie in the Cotton Bowl; in 1960,
Prince and his fellow Horned Frogs played in the
Bluebonnet Bowl. After graduation, he was hired by
the Birdville Independent School District in Tarrant
County to teach American history and coach football.

But Prince's older brother Johnny was a police
officer, and on weekends Prince rode with him as he
patroled the Tarrant County community of Benbrook.
At six feet four inches and 275 pounds, Bob Prince
made a handy sidekick on some of the calls. Prince
liked teaching and he loved football, but he began to

realize he had an even stronger desire to wear a badge. In November 1964 he joined the DPS as a recruit, graduating from the training academy in the spring of 1965. After two years in the Highway Patrol, he returned to teaching for a couple of years but decided to reinstate with the DPS.

On September 1, 1974, he earned promotion to the Texas Rangers. He made Ranger sergeant in April 1979.

As a Ranger, Sgt. Prince had had training in everything from cardiopulmonary resuscitation to investigative hypnosis. But he had no textbook to turn to in working with Sheriff Boutwell to set up the task force. The idea of a homicide task force was not new, but the only task forces Prince was familiar with had been organized to catch a killer at large. In this case the state had its suspect in custody. The job at hand was to make Lucas available to law enforcement agencies across the country with unsolved cases and to try to make sure Lucas did not confess to crimes merely for the sake of confessing. Prince would see that each officer who came to talk to Lucas was told that Lucas would try to take cases that were not his. They would be told to be very careful about providing him with any information on any particular murders.

However, it was not the Rangers' job to oversee the other officers' questioning of Lucas; the reason for the task force was simply to provide a means for officers in other areas to be able to talk with Lucas about crimes in their jurisdiction. Many of Lucas's confessions were videotaped, and in this way the Rangers hoped that any officers who might be tempted to ask leading questions would be discouraged by the fact that they were on camera. If officers who had interviewed Lucas were satisfied that he had committed the crime, either to the point of filing charges or closing the case based on his confession, again, it was not the Rangers' place to question this: The case would be declared "cleared" by the questioning officers.

Obviously, the system was open to possible abuse. It was definitely in the best interests of the law enforcement agencies to solve these crimes, many of which had been on the books for years. And indeed, it was at no extra cost to their jurisdictions, except for the officers' travel expenses to visit Lucas. Once a confession was obtained, the police could go home and mark the case closed, which was often of great consolation to the victims' families. And their county would not have to pay for prosecuting Lucas; the thinking went that since he was already convicted on charges resulting in life imprisonment, there was no point in going through a long and expensive trial locally when the killer was already off the streets.

Prince found that much of the groundwork had already been laid by Ranger Ryan, who had operated what amounted to a one-man task force in the nearly five months since Lucas's first night of confession. Ryan, using a seventy-leaf stenographic notebook with the simple label of "Henry Lee Lucas w/m 8-23-36," had listed "Info given by Henry without any or little prompting as he remembered. . . ." The Ranger started with short summaries of the Kate Rich and Becky Powell cases, followed by 126 other homicides claimed by Lucas. The first twelve cases were in Texas, followed by cases claimed in twenty-two other states plus the District of Columbia, and then more in Texas.

Of course, it was probably impossible that Lucas could have killed so many people over such a vast area. Yet the Rangers felt a responsibility to allow law officers who did feel strongly that Lucas might have committed crimes in their area to speak with him. And if officers did "clear" Lucas on a murder, the Rangers would add this to the growing list, since it was not their responsibility to make sure that the many law agencies were correct in their findings. In fact, this would have been impossible.

Ranger Sgt. Bob Prince also kept a chronology that was made available to other officers who came to talk to Lucas. Whenever a fact about Lucas's whereabouts was discovered, it would be entered into the chart. This was made available to all the investigating agencies to try to avoid conflicts of location and also to attempt to identify which of Lucas's crimes were actual and which were his fictions.

In addition to the notebook, Ryan fielded calls from other agencies, questioned Lucas enough on some cases to determine whether an investigator should come to talk with him, and developed biographical information.

The results of Ryan's work, along with background put together by the DPS Crime Analysis Service, went into a fact sheet on Lucas made available to officers wishing to question the prisoner. Sgt. Prince reviewed that material and talked with Ryan, Boutwell, and Ranger Smith to learn more about Lucas. By the time Boutwell brought Lucas to Williamson County, he had been charged in ten homicides and had claimed responsibility for as many as 150 murders across the nation.

The Ranger sergeant had also followed the case in the media. After months of intense press attention, Lucas had a name recognition that would equal a rock star's. Some people, in fact, were getting sick of it. The mother of one of Lucas's alleged victims said, "We're trying to put this horrible thing behind us, but how can we when every time we pick up a newspaper there's his smiling face."

Prince realized all the publicity would have considerable impact on the task force he now headed: It would continue to attract more reporters and it would interest more law enforcement officers in talking with Lucas. There was another consideration. As the media built Lucas into America's most notorious criminal, the Ranger had a growing fear that a distraught parent or relative of someone Lucas claimed as a victim might decide to hurry justice and kill Lucas. With that in mind, there would be no advance publicity on any trips Lucas might be taken on in the course of an investigation.

Prince also realized that despite Lucas's cooperative attitude, his prison records showed he was an escape risk and suicide-prone. If Lucas had killed as many people as he claimed, his good-natured demeanor could not be taken for granted. He might snap and decide to go out in a blaze of glory, grabbing for an officer's weapon or maybe a hostage. The Ranger intended to see that nothing like that happened.

Since Waco was about seventy miles from Georgetown, Prince decided to rent an apartment in the nearby community of Pflugerville to avoid spending more than two hours a day on the road. He'd go home to his wife, Elizabeth, and kids on the weekends. Clayton Smith, the other Ranger assigned to the task force, lived in the Williamson County city of Round Rock, halfway between Austin and Georgetown.

Prince's first step was to set up an appointment calendar for officers wanting interviews with Lucas. Lucas's time was quickly blocked out for weeks in advance. He would be available until mid-March, when his trial for the Orange Socks murder was scheduled.

Boutwell and the Rangers were growing increasingly interested in Toole. If Lucas and his Florida friend had traveled as much as Lucas said, and judging from the letter Lucas had written asking him for his help so he could "give back the Bodies," Toole might be able to shed light on other unsolved cases.

Against the advice of his attorneys, Lucas agreed to let Boutwell and the Rangers record a phone conversation between him and Toole. Boutwell called Detective Terry, who arranged to have Toole available at a set time in an office at the Florida State Prison. With Parker McCollough, one of Lucas's court-appointed attorneys, listening in, Boutwell placed the call. As the tape rolled, Lucas talked to Toole for the first time in nearly two years. Lucas told his friend they were being recorded.

"I don't know whether you're like me," Lucas said, "but I've got just about every law enforcement agency in this country wantin' to talk to me, and I've gotta give them information that will prove that what I tell them is the truth."

Lucas smiled as he said that, savoring the attention.

"Well, when they get rowdy with me I won't even say nothin' to 'em," Toole said. "I just don't tell 'em nothing."

"Well, don't. . . . If they get rowdy with ya, don't say a word," Lucas advised.

"I'll tell ya something . . ." Toole's voice trailed off, the thought never completed.

"If they can't treat you as a man, then they don't need to talk to ya, and, uh, I know I'll continue to talk as long as people treat me as a man," Lucas said.

"Yeah."

"I've taken and refused I don't know how many people up in Montague because they started treatin' me like dirt."

"Well, you'll always be a man in my book, you know," Toole said.

"And that's the way I'm gonna continue to be. Ever crime that I committed no matter where it's at, if I've got enough time to finish what I started, then I'm gonna turn every one of the bodies up somehow."

"Yeah."

"I just don't want you to feel that I'm doin' it as a revenge or anything else. I'm just doin' it because I know that what I'm doin's right."

"And I don't want you holdin' nothing back now, Henry. If you know I was involved, I don't want you just to say it, I want you to spit it out."

Several times during the conversation, they talked about cannibalism, turning the stomach of nearly everyone in the room—except Lucas's.

"Well . . . there was that time when we cut them like that," Ottis interjected. "Uh, I would pour some of that blood out of 'em."

"I know that," Lucas said.

"See what the man tastes like," Ottis laughed.

"Well, you know why it was done, too, don't ya?"

"Yeah."

"Because we are, in other words, you and I have become the same thing people look at as an animal."

"Yeah," Toole said flatly, as if he didn't quite grasp what Lucas meant.

The conversation had lasted more than thirty minutes.

The cannibalism claim made a good story, but Boutwell and other officers didn't put much stock in it. On the other hand, there was definite evidence of mutilation in some of the cases Lucas claimed.

It was Christmas Eve, but the sound in the Williamson County Jail was not a medley of Christmas carols. The inmates who had radios seemed more interested in hard rock music than "Jingle Bells." Their radios generated a pounding base that seemed to make the stone and steel inside the old jail throb to an alien rhythm. White-clad prisoners added to the din, shouting from cell to cell, arguing, threatening, propositioning, bragging. For the sensitive ears of forty-six-year-old Clementine Schroeder, a part-time piano teacher schooled in the classics and married to a music professor, the noise was almost too much to bear. Yet God had told her to be where she was and she would endure.

For three years she had operated a nondenominational jailhouse ministry, delivering word of the Gospel to anyone who wanted to hear it. Just about every day, the Catholic lay worker, born on a cattle ranch in south Texas but educated at the Cincinnati Conservatory of Music and Boston University, walked the steel catwalks inside the Williamson County Jail. This Christmas Eve she was giving away Bibles to anyone who would have one.

"Hello," she called out to the prisoners she passed. "The Lord loves you."

Now she stopped at the cell that held the man she'd heard was the most prolific killer in American history, Henry Lee Lucas. She'd seen him once, being escorted from his cell. That time she'd shrunk back in horror, afraid even to look at him.

Opening the small food door to Lucas's cell, she peered inside. Looking back at her through the square hole was the one good eye of a man said to be a notorious killer. Inside that eye Clemmie thought she saw a spark of something else, something kinder.

"I have one Bible left," she said. "I'll give it to you if you won't destroy it."

Lucas didn't seem in too talkative a mood, but he said he'd take the Bible.

Clemmie left the jail and went home to spend the rest of Christmas Eve with her husband and family.

The telephone talk with Toole had made Lucas happy and had given the Texas officers a better understanding of what they were dealing with in Toole. Despite leading questions from the cooperative Lucas, Toole had not said anything of substance. The task force members wanted to get the two suspects together in person.

On December 27, 1983, an icy morning in central Texas, a DPS twin-engined Cessna 421 left Austin, heading east. On board was DPS pilot-investigator Jim Field, a co-pilot, Sheriff Boutwell, Ranger Smith, DPS crime analyst Don Overstreet, Lucas, and Parker McCollough.

A contingent of Jacksonville detectives met the DPS plane at the airport. For security reasons, and to avoid news media attention, Lucas was booked into jail for the night in a nearby county under a phony name. When Boutwell went to get him the next morning, Lucas was as angry as any of the officers had ever seen him.

"I've never been ashamed of my name," he told Boutwell. "Anytime I've sold blood or applied for welfare, I always sign my right name."

Boutwell explained the subterfuge had been for his own protection, but Lucas was still mad. Jail personnel had fastened a plastic identification band with the assumed name around Lucas's wrist. When the sheriff pulled his pocketknife from his trousers and cut off the tag, Lucas calmed some, but not much.

When they got to the sheriff's office in Jacksonville, Boutwell took Lucas into a room for a one-on-one talk.

"We've brought you twelve hundred miles to talk to Ottis," the sheriff said. "There's no need acting this way. Just settle down."

Boutwell had learned he could talk to Lucas like a father dealing with an errant son. He was firm, but not threatening. He gave him reasons for things, and he had proven he would keep his word.

Beneath Lucas's anger over the assumed-name incident, Boutwell suspected, was his nervousness about seeing Ottis again. Lucas didn't know how Ottis was going to react to him, knowing that he'd killed Becky.

When the tall, broad-chested Ottis was led into the

interview room to see Lucas, their greeting was low-key.

"How you doin'?" Lucas smiled. "How you being treated?"

The two sat side-by-side in a small interview room, facing a roomful of officers and a video camera. Ottis, wearing a dark sweater with the sleeves pushed up to just below his elbow, often looked up at the ceiling, his mouth open, before answering a question. Lucas, wearing an old suit someone had donated, had grown a short, dark mustache since he and Toole had last been together. Boutwell thought the mustache and the almost V-shaped way his hair bushed out made Lucas look something like Charlie Chaplin minus the bow tie and bowler hat. But there was nothing comic about Lucas, who seemed to be having trouble looking directly at anyone, including Ottis.

Finally, the topic Lucas had dreaded most came up. Ottis, however, did not seem to be at all troubled by Becky's murder. His compassion was for Lucas, not the little girl Lucas had confessed to butchering in Texas.

"It just happened, that's all, Henry," Toole said, almost tenderly. "There ain't nothing you can do about it."

"No, I can't change it, it happened," Lucas said. "Why it happened . . ." His voice, barely audible, trailed off. He didn't seem to have a good explanation for killing his friend's niece, but he knew what it had led him to do. "That's the only reason I'm telling this: this one person that really changed me."

Toole reflected on that for a moment.

"I don't think if that [hadn't happened] you would a told on yourself," he said.

"I wouldn't," Lucas said.

A moment later, Toole tried to comfort his friend and lover.

195

"No, I don't hold it against you, Henry—it was just time for her to go. If God wanted her to live, she would have lived. That's the way I see it in my mind myself."

Even people that "lived right" had to die, Toole offered. "Like Mama—she lived right. She believes in God and all that. She didn't drink. They took her, you know. God took her. It was time for her to go. Once she passed away she was in a new spirit."

Lucas pulled a pack of cigarettes from his shirt pocket and lit one with a match. He wasn't looking at Ottis.

"You know I don't hold it against you, Henry," Toole repeated. "It was just time for her to go. So don't feel bad about it."

Lucas wiped a tear that came from under his glass eye, but others followed.

Toole reached out with one of his big arms and gently wiped away Lucas's tears.

"Come on, don't feel bad about it. Don't crack up about it."

Lucas dropped his head and sobbed. For a moment Toole held a hand across Lucas's forehead.

Suddenly Lucas stood, still sobbing. "Let me walk a little bit," he said, and one of the officers switched off the camera.

That session was the only time Lucas and Toole got to spend together. For the rest of the trip, Lucas was kept busy talking to Jacksonville detectives about the murders there. He definitely seemed to know things about the cases that no one else knew—descriptions of victims, how they were killed, and where their bodies were found.

Sipping from his coffee cup, Ranger Smith sat at his desk in the small task force office, beginning his workday on Wednesday, January 4, 1984, by rereading a letter from a detective with the Kennewick, Washington, Police Department. On the wall behind him was a large color map of the United States dotted with pins representing places where Lucas was believed to have killed someone. The Ranger pulled a set of photographs from a manila envelope, shuffled through them, and shook his head. The first photograph was from the driver's license of Lisa M. Martini, born on December 7, 1959. Long dark hair framed a pleasant face. The next photograph showed a nude woman lying in a pool of blood on her left side, her right leg cocked upward to expose her rectum and vulva. Someone had nearly hacked off her head and slashed a deep upside-down Y on her back. Martini had been found in her apartment on November 1, 1978. The autopsy showed she had been stabbed beneath her right breast and twice in the upper back. The examination indicated she had had vaginal intercourse recently, though it was not determined if it had occurred before or after death. Additionally, there was evidence of trauma to her anus, either from intercourse or insertion of a foreign object, possibly a knife handle.

Smith finished his coffee and went to get Lucas from his cell. They made small talk for a few minutes, then Smith explained he wanted to talk about a case in Washington State. At 9:40 A.M. in the task force interview room, the Ranger turned on the tape recorder. Lucas smiled as Smith once again advised him of his constitutional rights, a litany Lucas could have recited as easily as the Ranger.

For the record, he asked Lucas if he was aware that the interview was being taped. "Yeah," Lucas replied.

"Henry, I call your attention to a photograph," Smith began. "This involves . . . a woman out of Kennewick, Washington, and you have a map there before you and you have spotted the town on that map and we had been talking about Washington prior to this tape. . . . Do you recall being in Kennewick, Washington?"

"Yeah, I've been through there," Lucas replied. He had been in that part of Washington at various times between 1976 and 1981, he said.

"Okay. Henry, I showed you a photograph. It's a photograph of a girl. . . . She's alive in this picture right here. Do you recognize anything about this girl? Does she seem familiar to you?"

"She seems familiar with a girl that I killed in a house in seventy-eight," Lucas said.

The Ranger asked Lucas to describe the house. Lucas said it was a one-bedroom house.

"Just a one-bedroom?"

"Yeah. That's all, one bedroom."

"Now you described it as a house."

"Yeah, well, it's known as an apartment house, is what it's known as."

Lucas said it was a two-story apartment complex with about eighteen units near a "big school."

"Okay. What was the circumstances surrounding you being with this girl," Smith asked.

"I was traveling and I came in and pulled in the parking lot and she was out there in the parking lot when I came in and we got to talking and she invited me up to her apartment," Lucas said. "We went up there and sat down and drank some beer and we sat there and talked for a while and then I talked her into going to bed with me and had sex with her. Then after I had sex with her . . . we started arguing about some boyfriend that she had. . . . I ended up stabbing her to death. . . . I can remember stabbing her in the chest and back. . . . I think it was four times she was stabbed. I think twice in the chest and twice in the back."

Lucas said he used a seven-inch butcher knife.

"That's something I carried all along," he said. "I usually carry one on my belt. It's one of them cut-down butcher knives. The blade was thinner than it was originally because I cut the back end of the blade down."

"What happened after you killed her?" the Ranger asked.

"Well, I cleaned the apartment up," Lucas said. "As far as anything I touched or handled while I was in there, I took and throwed it away."

"Did you clean up . . . I mean clean up yourself inside the apartment?"

"Yeah, I did, in the bathroom. I washed up."

Smith turned off the tape recorder at 10:25 A.M. With no prompting from him, Lucas had fairly well described the victim, correctly recalling that she had lived in an apartment complex. He was right in the manner of her death and the weather at the time (upper 40s), though he had been wrong on the time of year. As soon as he could, Smith would call the detective in Kennwick. Someone from Washington needed to come talk with Lucas about Lisa Martini.

One hundred and seven officers from eighteen states and the District of Columbia gathered at the Holidome in Monroe, Louisiana, for the second Lucas homicide conference, held January 17–20, 1984. The first conference had been held there the previous October.

"To date we have cleared seventy-two cases total on both Lucas and Toole," Ranger Smith told the officers at the beginning of the conference. "Lucas has cleared twenty-three by himself, and Toole has cleared thirteen by himself. There have been thirty-six cases that have been cleared together. They are suspects in seventy-one additional cases."

Smith said Lucas was booked up until February 26.

His latest trial date in the "Orange Socks" case was in early March.

"We are trying not to schedule any officers on the weekends," Smith continued. "He has probably talked with more than one hundred officers." He asked that officers with scheduled interviews call a few days beforehand to reconfirm and told them to be prepared to work around Lucas's trips to a dentist and sessions with his lawyers as they prepared his defense in the upcoming "Orange Socks" trial.

"When Henry was first arrested, he would play games with the officers," the Ranger continued. "Henry has become much better to interview since he has been in custody. At the time of his arrest he was on Thorazine, which was driving him up the wall. Since he has been in Georgetown he has been taken off all that medication and his mind seems much clearer. He is able to recall details and facts in these investigations that amazes me."

Lucas, in fact, was like a new man. For the first time in his life, he was important. Newspaper reporters and magazine writers sought interviews with him. Visiting police officers even asked him to pose with them for photographs. Television cameras recorded his public appearances; a smaller video camera took in his private confessions. Confession, he was learning, was good for more than the soul.

"He is bouncy these days," Don Higginbotham, one of two attorneys appointed to represent him in the "Orange Socks" case, said of his client. "He is getting all this attention, all the coffee and cigarettes he wants, he's getting dental care, and visitors on a daily basis."

Lucas was beginning to joke about the room used by the task force in the Williamson County jail as being "my office."

While on one hand the task force members hated to see a convicted killer living so well, at least in comparison to most jail inmates, they felt it was the key to keeping Lucas in a cooperative frame of mind.

Ranger Smith then offered a few suggestions in dealing with Lucas: Don't ridicule him or otherwise abuse him. It could end his cooperation with officers, which so far had been excellent.

"He recalls photos very well," Smith said. "If you give him too many details, he will take the case for you, so you must be careful when you interview him and not give him all the details."

For four days the officers compared notes on cases.

"We had a visit with Mr. Lucas which resulted in the solving of three cases," said Leo Mock, Jr., of Conroe, Texas, a deputy with the Montgomery County Sheriff's Office. "In all three we have Lucas indicted for capital murder. In all three cases, with his attorney present, Lucas led us to all three crime scene locations."

The partially burned body of Laura Jean Domez, sixteen, had been found in a pine forest in northwestern Montgomery County on April 13, 1983. She had been beaten, strangled, and set on fire—the blaze spread and left three hundred surrounding acres charred.

Mock told the officers Lucas had led deputies to the spot where the body was found.

"He described to a tee the way he left the body," Mock said. "His attorney was present and was amazed at his perfect recall."

Lucas also directed deputies to the spot where an unidentified woman had been discovered on March 17, 1983. Like that of the victim that would be found a month later, her body had been partially burned after being doused with diesel fuel.

In this case, Mock told his law enforcement colleagues, Lucas said he picked the victim up as a hitchhiker on I-45. He raped her, beat her, strangled her, and then tried to burn her body, the deputy said.

No attempt had been made to burn Lucas's third claimed victim in Montgomery County, thirty-two-year-old Gloria Ann Stephen. Her body was found October 2, 1982. She had been stabbed and beaten, and her throat had been cut. She was nude from the waist down.

As he had in the other cases, Mock said, Lucas led investigators right to the crime scene.

Even before the formation of the task force, DPS crime analysts had been compiling information on Lucas and Toole's method of operations. They were traveling serial killers, their victims selected at random. Hitchhikers often were targeted. Lucas almost always killed women; Toole preferred men. Lucas favored knives with strangulation his second preference; Toole was more partial to firearms, particularly cheap, easy-to-get .22 handguns.

Neither were clean killers. Lucas claimed to have bitten women and slashed their bodies, sometimes eviscerating them, sometimes mutilating their genitals. Occasionally, he claimed, he would decapitate the victim, or try to. Once, he said, he traveled through several states with a woman's head in the backseat of his car. Toole also would mutilate victims.

Sexual gratification was the motive in the majority of the murders, though they occasionally killed someone in the course of a robbery. Lucas preferred sex with the victim after she was dead; Toole often killed homosexuals.

Lucas had tried to convince Boutwell and other officers that he and Toole had belonged to a Satanic cult Lucas called "The Hands of Death," but the claim was never substantiated, and the task force never gave it much credibility.

Though DPS analysts doubted Lucas had been a member of some killing organization, they learned he was a killer with a good sense of geography. He was a walking road atlas. An investigator could ask Lucas how to get from one city in one state to a distant city in another state and Lucas would tick off the route quicker than a travel agent using a computer terminal. Mostly he favored the interstate highway system, but he occasionally took back roads.

He traveled the country in older-model cars and by hitchhiking, often with truckers. He was good at charming people into doing him favors. Truck drivers often would use their C.B. radios to arrange a ride for him from the next truck stop. On one long trip he took to California with Toole, Becky, and her younger brother Frank, they covered some of the distance by hopping a freight train.

If Lucas was traveling by car and it developed mechanical difficulty, if he could not fix it, he would abandon it. When he needed gasoline or oil and didn't have any money, he'd syphon fuel from other abandoned vehicles or from cars in parking lots.

His car was usually his home when he was on the road. When he absolutely had to sleep, he pulled over at a roadside park or turned down a side road and slept in the car or outside, depending on the weather and location. For food, he got by on what he could bum or steal. In his many interviews with investigators, he claimed he used Becky and Frank to approach people for help, knowing that most people would have a hard time saying no to a thirsty or hungry child. Often, Becky's knocking on some unsuspecting woman's door was the beginning of an evening of murder and sex for Lucas and Toole, Lucas told officers.

Lucas was almost as familiar with rescue missions and churches with outreach programs for the needy as he was the nation's highway system. For spending money he sold blood or stole things he could sell. He seemed to be able to sustain himself on very little—except murder.

While law enforcement officers across the country scrambled to get an appointment to interview Lucas in Texas or Toole in Florida, Sister Clemmie was spending as much time with him as she could. He told her he had become a Christian in his jail cell in Montague County when he saw a bright light and heard a voice. From then on, he said, he had been doing everything he could to clear up the murders he had committed.

"The deputy told him he was hallucinating," Sister Clemmie would recall. "But he says the light became more and more beautiful and he felt loved and knew it was Jesus. He said he felt a struggle inside him."

On January 25, she baptized him, though both agreed that at a later date they would get a minister to do it for him again.

"He told me he'd been praying for someone to baptize him," she said. "He was ready."

Lucas took a Styrofoam cup, filled it with water, and handed it through the bars to Sister Clemmie. They both prayed. As Lucas kneeled in his cell, she poured the water over his head. For communion, she offered a piece of bread pulled from a heel and a cup of Kool-Aid for wine.

With each visit, Clemmie felt closer to Lucas. They prayed, discussed the Bible and his "cases," as he called them. Sometimes they held hands through the bars.

On February 23, two Kennewick, Washington, detectives took a statement from Lucas about the Lisa Martini murder. Lucas remembered driving from Reno, Nevada, northwest to Kennewick sometime in the fall of 1978, he told them. He had been driving all night when the headlights on his 1965 Ford station wagon began flickering. He made it to Kennewick, where he stopped to fix the lights.

He turned off of Highway 14 in Kennewick and after a series of turns pulled up in the parking lot of an apartment complex.

"While I was looking at the lights I met a female, early twenties, approximately five feet eight to five feet nine, a hundred thirty pounds, dark hair. The female invited me up to her apartment and after a short period of time we had sex. . . . After a while the female and I began arguing about her boyfriend coming home because she did not want me to be there when he arrived. . . . The female made me mad so I took out my seven-inch butcher knife and stabbed her."

After listening to Lucas's account of the killing, one of the Washington detectives asked him if he had injured himself at any point during the attack. He was careful to use the word "injured" and not to ask about a specific type of injury.

"I recalled that I did cut the lower heel portion of my right-hand palm," Lucas said in his statement. "I remember wiping the blood off my hands with a bathroom towel."

Before leaving for Texas, the investigators had a voluntarily given sample of Lucas's blood compared with the unidentified blood found at the crime scene. On January 9, the Washington State Patrol crime lab had reported that the two blood group profiles matched, eliminating 96.2 percent of the population. In addition, the report noted, analysis of the semen found in Martini's vagina during the autopsy showed it had come from a nonsecretor. Lucas was a nonsecretor—someone whose blood type can only be determined from a blood sample, not from other bodily fluids. "Considering this factor, 99.43 [percent] of the population could be eliminated as sources of the biological material found at the scene," wrote criminalist Joseph J. Gorski. "Mr. Henry L. Lucas is in the 0.57 percent of the population which are possible sources of the biological material."

On February 29, 1984, Lucas was charged with first-degree murder in the Martini case.

Each week Sgt. Prince prepared a report for Chief Hacker in Austin summarizing cases believed to have been committed by Lucas and Toole.

Since it was not the task force's role to independently verify the cases, Prince listed a case as cleared if the law officer who talked with Lucas about a particular case said he was satisfied Lucas or Toole had been the perpetrator. Each report bore this caveat: "The certainty of clearance of each offense is unknown to writer, and no recommendations are made as to their authenticity." The number grew with each report. By March 14, seventy-eight cases were listed as cleared. No one knew how much bigger the list would get.

CHAPTER TEN

The bluebonnets and other wildflowers that normally line the sides of central Texas highways by early March, filling the air with their natural perfume, hadn't taken a chance on coming out yet. The winter of 1983–84 had been a hard one, with heavy snow as far south as San Antonio—a rarity. It seemed like winter just wasn't ready to give up, no matter what the calendar said.

As Sheriff Boutwell drove into San Angelo that afternoon in March after the two hundred-mile trip from Georgetown, an unseasonably cold north wind rustled leafless tree limbs. He checked Lucas into the Tom Green County Jail, a fairly new facility just across the street from the imposing county courthouse, a long, three-story stone building with eighteen Corinthian columns lining its front. On Monday, jury selection would begin for Lucas's trial in the death of the still unidentified nude woman found in Williamson County on October 31, 1979. After seeing that Lucas was settled into a cell for the night, Boutwell drove back to the downtown Holiday Inn that would be the headquarters for a sizable delegation of Williamson County residents for the next several weeks —those who came to get Henry Lee Lucas convicted of capital murder, those who came to prevent it if they could, and one man who came to see that, either way it worked out, justice prevailed.

Also arriving in San Angelo that weekend was the Williamson County prosecution team: thirty-seven-year-old District Attorney Ed Walsh, First Assistant D.A. Ken Anderson, and investigator Jim Treffetz. In town to represent Lucas were Georgetown defense attorneys Don Higginbotham and Parker McCollough. Another guest at the Holiday Inn was the man who would hear the case, State District Judge John Carter, an affable, heavyset, tobacco-chewing forty-two-year-old known for his no-nonsense approach on the bench. He was fresh from another high-profile case, the murder trial of nurse Genene Jones, a woman found guilty of injecting a fourteen-month-old baby in her care with the paralyzing drug succinylcholine. The trial had been moved on a change of venue from Kerrville to Georgetown. Like the man Carter would try next, Jones was suspected in additional deaths. For a time Jones had something else in common with Lucas: the same address. During her trial, which received national media attention, she had been kept in the Williamson County Jail. A San Antonio newspaper even suggested a romantic link between the two accused killers, a story Jones indignantly denied and one that gave Boutwell and members of the task force a good laugh. Lucas and Jones never had any contact.

Monday morning, March 12, as the winnowing of the jury panel got under way, Higginbotham made a last-ditch effort to have Lucas's confessions ruled inadmissible. That battle had already been fought in an earlier pretrial hearing, and as attorneys for both sides expected, Judge Carter denied the defense motion.

The process of picking a jury dragged on for the rest of the month. During the day, the prosecution and defense questioned potential jurors, each side sizing up who they wanted to try to get on their jury and who they wanted struck from their lists. At night they relaxed in the motel cocktail lounge and went out to dinner with each other like the old friends they were.

Lucas sat impassively through the jury-selection process each day, wearing the same ill-fitting blue Western-cut suit. Sheriff Boutwell, three inches taller than Lucas, had retrieved the old suit from the back of his closet and given it to Lucas to wear during the trial. Though the blue suit was all Lucas had, he did occasionally change his shirt and underwear—when reminded by the sheriff.

After two and a half weeks of questioning, a jury of seven women and five men, plus two alternates, was selected on March 28. (One of the men was later excused, replaced by an alternate, changing the make-up of the jury to eight women and four men.) They ranged in age from twenty-nine to fifty-six, by avocation from housewife to junior high school coach. Testimony was to begin on Monday, April 2.

Before Walsh could prove Lucas had killed the girl in the orange socks, he had to prove she had been murdered.

The state's first witness was Williamson County resident R. V. Barker, a meat-processing worker, who testified briefly on how he came to find the dead woman off the side of I-35 that Halloween four and a half years earlier.

Walsh next used testimony from Williamson County investigator Ray Hardison to set the scene that cool afternoon the body was found. Hardison's crime scene drawing and photographs of the body in the culvert were introduced into evidence.

Next to testify was Travis County Medical Examiner Dr. Robert Bayardo, the pathologist who performed the autopsy on the victim.

Jim Wilson, Sheriff Boutwell's chief deputy, described how he had found two matchbooks—one from a Motel 6 and the other from a Holiday Inn in Henrietta, Oklahoma—near where the body appeared to have been dragged through grass on the side of the roadway before being tossed into the culvert. The only other physical evidence he found on the scene, he said, was a used homemade sanitary napkin.

On the second day of the trial, Walsh introduced the words of his star witness—Henry Lee Lucas. Lucas had signed a written confession and also admitted to the murder on two audiotapes and two videotapes. The confessions were the heart of the state's case.

To get to the confessions, Walsh led Sheriff Boutwell through a brief summary of the crime scene and his efforts to identify both the dead girl and her killer. After recounting how he had driven to Montague County on June 21, 1983, to talk with Lucas, which he did on the next day, Boutwell identified the statement Lucas had signed.

"The actual writing out of that statement, Sheriff—did Henry Lee Lucas do that or did you do it?" the tall, slow-talking prosecutor asked.

"No, sir," the sheriff replied. "I wrote it out myself, read it back to him, allowed him to read it prior to his signing it."

"And that instrument is signed 'Henry Lee Lucas'?" the prosecutor asked.

"Yes, it is."

Walsh offered the confession into evidence. The defense objected, but was overruled.

"May I read this to the jury, Your Honor?" Walsh asked.

"Yes, you may," Carter replied.

"My name is Henry Lee Lucas, and I am forty-six years of age," Walsh began.

"In 1979—I'm not sure of the time of the year—I picked up a girl who was hitchhiking in Oklahoma

City about the second exit off the turnpike. It could have been in one of three cars I had. I think her name was Joanie or Judy; I don't remember exactly. We stopped at a truck stop and ate. I don't recall if she had a hamburger or a plate lunch. I was drinking beer. I had sexual intercourse with her at a roadside park or picnic area. I think she was wearing something; I don't know if it was a Kotex or what. I didn't get satisfied. I don't know if something was wrong with her or something wrong with me.

"I killed her not long after that by strangling her with my hands. She was later undressed, and I had sex with her after she was dead. She was in the backseat laying down. I still couldn't come. Something was wrong with either her or me; I don't recall what. She didn't feel right. I drug her out of my car somewhere on I-35, southbound toward San Antonio, and dropped her into a culvert. I remember an iron guardrail with curved iron because I skinned my knee on it.

"Signed June twenty-second, 1983, by Henry Lee Lucas."

After getting the statement from Lucas, the sheriff testified, he had returned to Georgetown. On July 31, he said, he went back to Montague County with a bench warrant to take Lucas to Williamson County for arraignment on the capital murder charge he had filed on the basis of Lucas's statement. At the sheriff's office in Montague, he said, he interviewed Lucas again, this time using a tape recorder. Boutwell wanted to see if he could get additional details from Lucas on the murder.

All of the audio- and videotaped interviews were edited to remove Lucas's claims of other murders. In each, Lucas offered his confession to the murder of the nameless girl found sprawled in the culvert. The admissibility of the tapes had been hashed out in the pretrials. Judge Carter ruled they could be used against Lucas, though Higginbotham and McCollough continued to object to their introduction.

The second interview with Lucas to be heard by the jury was a videotape made the afternoon of August 2, 1983, after Boutwell had driven Lucas from Montague to Georgetown for a pretrial hearing. With Higginbotham present, Lucas showed Boutwell the culvert in Williamson County where he said he had left the girl's nude body. Boutwell got another videotaped statement from Lucas in an interview in his office, done after they returned from the crime scene.

Throughout the videotapes, Higginbotham, appointed that day to represent Lucas, repeatedly warned Lucas not to make any admission of guilt, cautioning that anything he said could lead to "a very possible death penalty case against you."

"I've got to go my way," Lucas replied on the tape. "It's the only way I can get peace of mind. . . . I have to take what's coming to me. I've already tried to kill myself. If they [do it] for me, it don't make no difference."

Each time Higginbotham interrupted to warn Lucas against incriminating remarks, Lucas ignored him and went on talking. "I've got to make a statement," he repeated several times. "If people don't realize the truth, there's no use in me being alive anyway. I've fought for thirty-six years to get something done. . . ."

In one segment of the videotape played for the jury, Boutwell and Lucas are seen standing near the culvert where the body had been found. Lucas demonstrates how he dragged the girl over the guardrail and dropped the body. He claimed the first time he had had sex with the victim it had been voluntary. He killed her, he said, when she refused to have sex with him a second time.

"She went to jump out the car," he said. "I grabbed

212

her and pulled her back in. She was fighting so hard I pulled off, because I almost had a wreck. I grabbed her by the neck and choked her so she died. I had sex with her again."

He drove on from the scene of the murder, the dead body in the backseat, until he finally decided to get rid of her.

The fourth statement, an audio recording, had been made on November 10, 1983, when Boutwell drove Lucas from Denton to Georgetown after his sentencing in Becky Powell's murder.

In the "Orange Socks" murder, he said, he had acted alone. Asked by Boutwell if Ottis Toole had been with him at the time, Lucas replied, "Not on this one, no. I won't take credit for something I didn't do. The one near Georgetown, I know I did it and I'm going to face my responsibility whether my lawyer or anybody likes it. To me, the death penalty for something I done is right. It's not wrong. . . . The one in the culvert is the one I done."

After the jury had heard all of the tapes, Judge Carter recessed the trial so Lucas's defense team could have copies made of the segments that had been edited from the tapes by the prosecution.

Outside the courtroom, a reporter caught up with Higginbotham and asked him what effect he thought Lucas's taped confessions had had that day on the jury.

"I can only tell you if I were to hear it, I would assume that I had somebody on my hands who had real mental problems," the attorney said. "I would think he was suicidal [but] that he wanted someone else to do it for him. Anybody who says they are not afraid to die is crazy."

When the trial got under way again at 9:00 A.M. Wednesday, April 4, the jury got a chance to hear Lucas's confessions once again. This time the tapes were edited by his lawyers. In the defense version of

213

the tapes, Lucas was suddenly a witness in his own behalf. The defense-edited versions showed what seemed to be confusion and lapses of memory on Lucas's part.

In the audiotape made July 31, 1983, Lucas said he could not remember where he had picked up the hitchhiker.

"I believe she's the one I picked up hitchhiking . . . on [Interstate] Thirty-five. I'm pretty sure it was in Texas," Lucas said on the tape.

"That's not what you told me before," Boutwell said. "You told me before it was Oklahoma City."

"Yeah," Lucas answered.

Lucas also was unsure whether the girl had been a brunette or blonde, whether he had dumped her body to the north or south of Austin; whether he had left the corpse in a field or culvert, and whether she had been wearing orange socks.

"I drug it [the body] out in a field, out there on the edge of the road," Lucas said in his second recorded confession.

"Okay . . . well . . . refresh your memory again," Boutwell had said.

"Oh, that's the culvert on Thirty-five," Lucas said. "I was gonna throw her in the culvert. . . . I remember it. On Thirty-five, this side of Austin. No, on the other side of Austin. West of Austin."

"No, you said it right the first time," Boutwell said. "This side of Austin."

Walsh knew the exchange, and others that day, sounded bad, but the jury still did not have the whole picture. During the long voir dire process, they had individually denied having any detailed knowledge of the Lucas case. Officially, based on the evidence they had seen and heard so far, they did not know Lucas had confessed to many other murders in addition to the various confessions he had given in the "Orange Socks" case. Lucas, the prosecutor believed, was confused because of the number of women he had killed, not because he didn't kill the girl found in the culvert.

Max Parker, a San Angelo attorney who was assisting Lucas's two court-appointed attorneys, put Boutwell on the stand to ask him about Lucas's evident confusion in his confession. The sheriff confirmed that he had had to refresh Lucas's memory at times during his interviews.

That afternoon, after a frenzied lunchtime editing session, Walsh questioned the sheriff about the defense version of the July 31, 1983, tape.

"Sheriff Boutwell, the edited version of the July thirty-first, 'eighty-three, conversation which was played in evidence by the defense, how would you characterize the editing of that exhibit?" Walsh asked.

"It seemed to me, Mr. Walsh, it is slanted and out of context."

"Are there other conversations and statements on that seven thirty-one interview which we have not previously introduced that are necessary to explain and fully understand the context of that conversation?"

"Yes, sir."

With the jury out of the courtroom, Walsh played the newly edited version of the Lucas tape for Judge Carter. He said the jurors would be confused about Lucas's admissions and the apparent inconsistencies until they heard a more inclusive editing of the tape.

"These contradictions or discrepancies or whatever you want to call them that the defense has chosen to introduce cannot fully be understood unless the jury realizes this man is talking about a hundred forty—a hundred fifty-six—people. . . ." Walsh argued.

The state had scrupulously tried to avoid any mention of extraneous offenses in its evidence, he said, but "the defense has totally opened this conversation up by putting in the information they put in."

After spending the afternoon reviewing a transcript of the July 31, 1983, interview—seventeen legal pages long—and listening to the edited versions of the tape, Judge Carter ruled the jury could hear additional portions of the tape in which Lucas offered an explanation for his confusion in his confessions: "I can't think offhand about her because I've got all these others in my mind. And she has been pushed aside, so to speak."

But Carter ruled the jury could not hear Lucas say, "She—to me, they're just one of a hundred forty-some. That's not much to say about a girl, but that was all I ever picked one up for, was to have sex with her."

The net result was that Walsh got more of Lucas's statement heard by the jury, though not as much as he would have liked. Still, he felt he had answered the defense effort to show Lucas was confused in the details he provided on the "Orange Socks" case. Shortly after the jury heard the reedited tape, Walsh rested the state's case.

Walsh knew what was coming next and thought he and Anderson were pretty well prepared for it.

Back in October, at the first Lucas homicide conference in Monroe, Louisiana, police officers comparing notes on possible cases involving Lucas and Toole had learned of work records from Jacksonville, Florida, that apparently documented when Lucas and Toole were on the job and when they were not. Texas Ranger Smith and Deputy Hardison had flown to Florida to look into the records and reported back to Boutwell that it appeared that Lucas and Toole had participated in a kickback scheme in which they collected money though they hadn't actually been on the job every day.

Since the state was required to make available to defense attorneys any exculpatory evidence it developed, Higginbotham and McCollough were well aware of the existence of the Florida work records.

Now they were going to try to show that Lucas was working for a roofing company in Jacksonville the day the body was found in Williamson County, Texas— more than a thousand miles distant.

First to testify for the defense was Eilene Knight, a bookkeeper for Southeast Color Coat. She brought payroll records showing Lucas had been employed by the roofing company from February 1979 to March 1980.

The next defense witness was former employee Fred Ellis, who had worked as a substitute foreman for the company on October 30, 1979. He testified that Lucas had been checked present on the job each day of the week from October 29 to November 2 that year, though he had not done so himself every day. At the time, he said, his company had been doing a roofing job on a building at the Jacksonville Naval Air Station. The work records reflecting that were introduced into evidence by the defense.

When Anderson stood to begin cross-examining Ellis, he quickly moved to impeach the defense witness. In response to Anderson's questioning, Ellis acknowledged he had a criminal record, including arrests for assault, driving while intoxicated, and driving without a license.

After Ellis had listed the arrests, Anderson asked him if he had had any other arrests, reminding him he was under oath.

When Ellis said he had had no other arrests, the prosecutor produced records showing Ellis had been convicted twice of writing hot checks.

The witness's criminal history exposed, Anderson asked him if he ever took a bribe to falsify work records.

"Never," Ellis replied.

The next defense witness was Mack Caulder, the regular foreman for Southeast Color Coat during Lucas's employment. He testified he had marked

Lucas as being on the job on Monday, October 29, 1979, and on Wednesday, October 31.

But on cross-examination Anderson revealed that Caulder, too, had a criminal record. He had served three years in an Alabama state prison on a forgery conviction and two years in federal prison on another forgery conviction.

The final defense alibi witness was Monir Yazgi, a Syrian grocer from Jacksonville. Yazgi, who owned a store in the Springfield area where Lucas and Toole had lived, said he had frequently cashed checks for Lucas. He identified one check he said he had cashed for Lucas on November 1, 1979—the day after the girl in orange socks had been found in Texas.

In rebuttal the prosecution introduced portions of Boutwell's November 10, 1983, tape-recorded interview with Lucas.

"I know that circumstances show that I didn't do it, and, ah, but I'm still the guilty person, regardless of what circumstances show," Lucas said on the tape. "A lot of times you can pay a foreman to show you were working when you're not."

The state's rebuttal witness was Kenneth Emery, another Southeast Color Coat employee. He testified that very often Caulder did not call the roll to see who was on the job; he also testified that he was aware that payoffs were being made and that during the months of October and November 1979 Lucas and Toole missed a lot of work, often disappearing for two or three days at a time.

On Friday, April 6, the jury began to learn more about Lucas as his lawyers began their effort to prove their client was insane.

Austin psychologist Tom Kubiszyn, hired by the defense to examine Lucas, testified Lucas had an IQ of 84, a strong desire to feel important, a hatred of women, and a sense that he was "at the mercy of various forces."

Kubiszyn testified that he felt Lucas was schizophrenic, unpredictable, and with "dull normal" thought processes. He said Lucas was a fifth-grade dropout, read at a sixth-grade level, spelled at a fifth-grade level, and understood mathematics at a fourth-grade level.

The psychologist said tests indicated Lucas had "very strong feelings of inadequacy and inferiority" and "strong, pervasive feelings of sadness, guilt, and of inner turmoil."

"He is not an individual who is at peace with himself by any means," Kubiszyn said.

The basis of Lucas's problem went back to his abuse during childhood, Kubiszyn said. "He suffered repeated abuse at the hands of his mother."

As Kubiszyn began describing that abuse, an insight that he said came from six and a half hours of interviews with Lucas and from an examination of his Michigan prison records, Lucas began weeping quietly, tears rolling from his good eye and the socket with the glass eye.

When Lucas continued to cry, Judge Carter recessed the trial early for lunch and deputies led Lucas back to his cell across the street.

In his cross-examination that afternoon Anderson brought out that Kubiszyn had had only limited experience in interviewing criminal defendants, that he had been hired by the defense to diagnose Lucas, and that schizophrenia, first mentioned in Lucas's prison records, once had been something of a catchall diagnosis, much overused, especially in the 1960s.

On Monday, April 9, McCollough and Higginbotham continued their efforts to convince the jury that their client was insane.

Dr. Jay Fogelman, who later testified under cross-examination that he was being paid $125 an hour by the defense, also described Lucas as a chronic schizophrenic.

"It's not a license he asked for," the Austin psychiatrist testified. "It was a gene that he was born with."

If Lucas had killed the hitchhiker, he said, he had been legally insane at the time. Still, he was capable of going from being out of control to thinking logically.

In addition to being schizophrenic, Fogelman said, Lucas had personality disorders, including being psychopathic and antisocial. "He's able to cover his tracks," he said. "That's where the antisocial behavior comes in."

The psychiatrist said Lucas still was extremely upset over the killing of Becky Powell, breaking into tears anytime he talked about her. "I think he had empathy for Becky," he testified. That Lucas could kill someone he cared for so much, Fogelman said, was "the crazy part."

Lucas's guilt over the teenager's violent death, Fogelman said, had led him to confess to the "Orange Socks" murder.

After Friday's testimony on Lucas's horrible childhood, Fogelman said, he had had to increase his patient's dosage of Thorazine to 300 milligrams daily.

"He was so upset that he was virtually begging for more medication," Fogelman said.

Lucas, he said, needed to continue receiving antipsychotic medication, "locked up forever" in a maximum-security mental institution.

Higginbotham had been planning for five weeks to put Lucas on the stand in his own behalf, but changed his mind at the last minute.

The decision surprised and, to some extent, disappointed Walsh. He had spent the weekend planning his cross-examination of Lucas. Having Lucas on the stand would have been an excellent way to get more details on Lucas's many other confessions brought out into the open.

"He's just too crazy," Higginbotham told a reporter after court that evening. "He's crazy right now."

"He is ambivalent, because of his sickness," Higginbotham told another reporter. "Every day's a different story."

McCollough was more circumspect in his answer. Evidence already presented was sufficient to prove Lucas's innocence, he said. Testimony from Lucas "would not substantially bolster our case."

Lucas's mental condition, of course, was the mainstay of the defense, along with the work records from Florida. On Tuesday, Walsh and Anderson set about convincing the jury that Lucas was not legally insane, just a cold-blooded killer.

When Dr. E. Clay Griffith of Dallas took the stand as a prosecution witness Tuesday morning, about the only thing he found to agree with Lucas's insanity defense witnesses on was that the defendant was "a little below the average intelligence level." Lucas, the doctor said, "was not suffering from any mental disease or defect."

The psychiatrist, reading from notes, testified he had examined Lucas in June and October 1983 and that he had found nothing to indicate Lucas suffered from hallucinations or delusions—hallmarks of schizophrenia. Lucas, he said, was "faking it" when he evidenced symptoms of mental illness, including his several suicide attempts.

"Mr. Lucas is a real manipulator," the doctor said, looking at Walsh above the half-glasses on his nose.

The prosecutor wanted the jury to know that Lucas was more than a manipulator.

"Henry Lee Lucas knows how to kill?" Walsh asked the psychiatrist.

"From the record, it appears he does," Griffith replied.

"Yet he never found a way to kill himself?" Walsh continued.

"Apparently not," Griffith said.

Though not insane, the psychiatrist said, Lucas

definitely had personality disorders, including his fondness for sex with animals and dead bodies. Even so, he continued, Lucas knew right from wrong and could abide by the law if he chose, which was the basis of legal sanity.

"It is your opinion that Henry Lee Lucas is not insane?" Walsh asked.

"That is my opinion, yes," Griffith replied.

"Do you have an opinion as to whether he's dangerous?"

"He very definitely is dangerous," the doctor replied.

Walsh, seeking to bring home the point to the jury as strongly as possible, asked Griffith to rate Lucas's dangerousness on a scale of one to ten.

"I think you would have to raise the scale some to find a place for Mr. Lucas," Griffith said.

The prosecution drew Griffith out on his credentials to show he had plenty of experience in evaluating killers. Over the years, he testified, he had examined three hundred to four hundred persons accused of murder and at least thirty persons charged with capital murder.

Also testifying as a rebuttal witness for the state was Dr. Richard Coons of Austin, who said Lucas had "personality problems, drug problems, moral problems." Coons agreed with Griffith that Lucas was not legally insane. Lucas was a man with a "defective conscience," he said.

As further rebuttal to the defense testimony that Lucas had been working in Florida when the girl in orange socks was murdered, Walsh wanted help from Lucas. The way he intended to get it was to play a videotape of Lucas made in the Williamson County Jail on February 16. On the edited tape Lucas had said he had paid off his job supervisor to falsify his work records.

Judge Carter cleared the jury from the courtroom so he could see it and then rule on its admissibility. The press and general public were allowed to see it, too.

"I've got three hundred sixty murders in the United States," Lucas said on the tape. "I'd go from one state to another one, go to one place and end up in another one, and go from there to someplace else," Lucas continued as the judge, prosecutors, defense attorneys, reporters, and spectators looked on, fascinated by Lucas's matter-of-fact discussion of mass murder.

The murder binge started, he said, "when I killed Mom."

Referring to Toole, he said, "We killed 'em most every way there is except poison."

"There's no way possible that anybody in the country could do what me and Ottis have done," he said, estimating he had more than sixty murders just in Texas.

Victims were killed by "shooting them, hanging them, running them down with cars," he said, adding, "we've beat them to death. There's crucifixions, filleting people like fish, people that have been burnt, shot in their cars."

The gruesome laundry list of death was numbing, but the tape was hard to understand because of poor sound quality. The tape was played several times as Judge Carter and the lawyers strained to make out certain passages. At one point, Carter got down from the bench and sat in the jury box in an effort to hear better.

In the tape Lucas said he was making his confessions because "it's the right thing to do. It's what I promised God I was going to do."

Walsh would love to have played all of the tape for the jury, but he knew that was impossible. Judge Carter finally ruled that the portion of the tape that emphasized Lucas's travels was admissible, but the jury would not hear Lucas's categorical recitation of murder methods.

Both sides rested their cases and Judge Carter read his formal charge to the jury, explaining to them what constituted a capital case under the law and the questions they would have to answer to determine whether Lucas was guilty of killing someone in the course of committing or attempting to commit kidnapping, robbery, or aggravated rape—capital murder—and whether he was guilty of the lesser offense of murder, or was not guilty.

The courtroom began to fill for the next step, the final arguments of the prosecution and the defense. This was Walsh's second capital case, but it was the biggest trial of his legal career. He knew, as did his colleague and the three defense attorneys they were about to face, that a case might turn on rhetoric alone. By law, a jury could only consider what it had heard in evidence, but he knew the lawyer who most logically and eloquently argued his case usually won the lawsuit. The law does afford the state one advantage: it opens and ends the argument. The defense argues in the middle, with the state getting the last word. Both sides would recount the evidence presented—from their perspective, of course—and add as much subjectivity as they could get away with. Now, after eight days of testimony, the fate of Henry Lee Lucas rested to a large extent on the outcome of a debate among five lawyers.

Anderson began at 3:07 P.M., first explaining the points in Judge Carter's charge item by item. Then he bore down on Lucas's defense.

"Now, the defense in this case is really two defenses," Anderson said. "It's what I can only refer to as an insane alibi, because what it involves is two totally inconsistent defenses. . . . One is this alibi they raised—that he was somehow in Florida at the time he was killing this woman—and their other defense is this insanity defense."

What the defense would have to have proved, he said, was that Lucas was legally insane. "Not that he was different, not that he was abnormal, not that he was strange, but that he was insane under our legal definition, which means at the very time he was choking the life out of that woman, at that very time he was suffering from a mental disease or defect, and that he didn't know that that was wrong or that he couldn't help himself from doing that." The best evidence to dispute that, he said, were the facts of the case.

"He didn't know it was wrong?" Anderson asked. "Of course he knew it was wrong. He didn't do this in front of a bunch of eyewitnesses. He premeditated it; he thought about it. He said, 'I know I've made up my mind, I was going to kill her.' He concealed the body—that's not the act of somebody who doesn't know what they're doing is wrong. He hid it in the culvert. And finally, he didn't sit around waiting to get caught—he fled the scene. And those facts do not show somebody who is out of touch with reality at the time."

The prosecutor moved into his attack of the alibi defense with a geography recitation. The distance between Austin, Texas, and Jacksonville, Florida, was 1,050 miles. At a conservative fifty miles an hour, it would take a little more than twenty-one hours to make the drive.

Dr. Bayardo, he said, had testified the victim could have been dead from six to thirty-six hours before her body was found. Even if Lucas had dumped the body in the culvert only one minute before it was found, Anderson argued, he would have had plenty of time to drive to Florida in time to cash the November 1 check introduced by the defense.

Max Parker, the San Angelo attorney, opened the

argument for the defense. After offering his perspective on the court's charge and the issue of reasonable doubt, he concentrated on the evidence in the case. No fingerprints were found on the guardrail, the body, or the matchbooks; no skin or foreign material had been found under the victim's fingernails; no foreign pubic hairs were found on her body; no semen was found in her vagina and crime scene photographs did not show evidence that the body had been dragged through grass.

"What it all boils down to is, there is absolutely no evidence, none other than perhaps this one bit of matches, that links Henry Lucas to this unidentified white female other than his confessions—that's it," Parker argued.

That brought him to the matter of the confessions, which he spent the rest of his argument attacking. Parker said Boutwell, an elected official with an unsolved case on his hands "is not going to be too picky on getting a confession." Additionally, Parker said, Lucas was happy to confess because, "It's obvious on these tapes Henry Lee Lucas wanted to die. Henry never disagrees with the sheriff on anything."

Even if Lucas had killed the woman, Parker argued, the state had presented no evidence of rape or attempted rape, one of the elements needed to make the crime capital murder.

Parker read a quotation from one of Lucas's videos. "After I pulled over, I grabbed her by the neck. I choked her until she died. I had sex with her again."

"I don't remember any testimony that she was not already dead," Parker said. "At the most, that's a murder, and that's desecration of her corpse."

Next to rise for the defense was McCollough, who concentrated on the work records alibi. In response to the prosecution's exposure that two of the alibi witnesses had criminal histories, McCollough said, "I would like to have brought you the president of the Rotary Club of Jacksonville, but we couldn't."

Higginbotham closed for the defense, reiterating that Lucas had confessed out of grief over Becky Powell's death. "I submit to you the reason he confessed to this case is remorse," Higginbotham said. "To say you want the death penalty is a real good indication you're insane." Despite that, Lucas's work record alibi was solid, despite the character of the two foremen for the roofing company, he argued.

"It's a very unique case, ladies and gentlemen, because it's the first time I've ever had to stand before a jury and try to save my client by trying to convince them that he's lying," Higginbotham said.

He urged the jury not to find Lucas guilty just because he had a bad reputation.

"And Henry does have a bad reputation—there's no question about it. But he's got his rights to be heard in this case on this evidence, just like any of the rest of us."

When Walsh stood to begin the closing argument—the state's last shot at convincing the jury Lucas was a killer—he was nervous and a little angry at some of the things said by the defense, particularly the intimations that Boutwell had taken Lucas's confession merely to clear up an unsolved case. He knew the butterflies would go away once he got started and that Lucas's lawyers were just doing their job.

The courtroom, recently remodeled, was packed with spectators—trial junkies, local lawyers, courthouse employees—and the press. Despite the knot in his stomach, for him the final argument was the most satisfying part of a trial. It was a powerful tool, especially if you had a good case. And he believed that he did.

Before the arguments began, he'd drawn a line down the middle of several pages. He'd used the right side of each page to list the defense arguments and the left side to note his points of rebuttal. Earlier he'd jotted down a rough outline of the basic points he intended to cover, though he relied a lot on intuition and his ability to read the jury.

"Don't you think for a minute that I would be up here trying to railroad someone into the penitentiary —or into the electric chair or needle or whatever you want to call it now," Walsh said.

"Mr. Parker said this is a life-and-death situation for Henry," the district attorney continued. "Poor old Henry. It's a life-and-death situation for that unidentified girl, and it is a life-and-death situation for the future victims of Henry Lee Lucas."

Walsh zeroed in on the defense's argument that their two-pronged defense was not inconsistent. "It seems a little inconsistent to me that, number one, he wasn't there, or, number two, if he was there he was crazy, or, number three, if he was there and he wasn't crazy, it was just a simple murder—it's not a capital murder."

Finally, after trying to parry the various defense arguments point by point, Walsh was down to the last five minutes of his time.

"You've heard about Henry Lee Lucas, and what I'm asking you people to do is put Henry Lee Lucas in a position [where] he can get what he should have gotten years ago, after he killed his mother. How many people would have been saved if he would have gotten the death penalty then? It is about time that somebody put a stop to Mr. Henry Lee Lucas."

Walsh then invoked the "they" argument, an old standby for prosecutors. "You watch the TV and read the papers and you read about these things every day of the week. And you may have turned to your husband or your wife on . . . occasion and said something like, 'I wonder why they didn't do something about that? I wonder why they didn't do something?" Well, today you have an opportunity to do something about it. You are the 'they' . . . today."

As the jury filed out of the courtroom to begin its deliberations at 7:20 P.M., Lucas sat twiddling his thumbs. He had alternated between the thumb twiddling and rolling his tie up and down throughout the trial. Three hours later, the jury sent word to Judge Carter that it would like to call it a night and begin again in the morning. Reporters covering the trial got up a pool on how long the jury would be out.

The jury resumed its work Thursday morning, asking that Lucas's confessional tapes be played for them again. During the day, as the verdict was awaited, the man with the most at stake seemed the least nervous. Lucas, smiling frequently, talked casually with his attorneys and Boutwell. While the defendant seemed calm, Walsh and Anderson were beginning to feel the effects of the long wait. Both knew the longer a jury is out, the more likely it is that the final news will be bad for the prosecution.

Walsh knew he could have worked out a guilty plea with Lucas and his attorneys, which didn't make the long wait any easier. In fact, when it appeared that Lucas might have known something about another young woman missing from Williamson County, Walsh offered him the opportunity to plead out for more prison time if he would assist in locating the girl, who had disappeared from a community college campus. In the interim, her car, with her body still inside, had been found in a creek just off the roadway she would have taken home from class. The death was determined to have been accidental, possibly due to a seizure that caused her to lose control of the car and plunge off the bridge over the creek. After that, Walsh had pressed on with the capital case, believing it was important for someone to try for a death penalty for

Lucas. Now, if Lucas was found innocent, about $50,000 in tax money would have been wasted—and a lot of people's time.

As the hours went by, the D.A. and his assistant tried to guess what the jury was thinking, playing and replaying their mental tapes of the trial and final arguments. Could they have done or said anything differently?

Walsh was just about ready to chalk up his political career as something else killed by Lucas when the bailiff reported that the jury had reached a verdict. They had been out for nine hours and fifteen minutes.

When Lucas walked into the courtroom with his lawyers, he was smiling. Moments later, the smile sagged when the jury foreman announced the verdict: guilty of capital murder. Judge Carter immediately warned those in the courtroom against any outbursts and ordered the jury sequestered for the night, since they would have to consider Lucas's punishment the next day.

As Lucas was led from the courtroom, his mouth slightly open, Walsh felt like he had years before when he'd found out he'd passed the state bar exam. This was the biggest case of his career. Now there was only one other step.

"It's been a long day and night for us," the clearly relieved D.A. told a reporter after court had recessed. "We intend to do the most important thing tomorrow —convince the jury that Lucas needs and deserves the death penalty."

That part, Walsh felt, would be easy. Now that the jury had decided Lucas was guilty of capital murder, he was almost sure they would vote for his execution.

Fitting for a murder case that began on Halloween, the matter of Lucas's punishment was taken up on Friday the thirteenth.

All Walsh had to do now was get the jury to answer

yes to two questions: Had Lucas killed the unidentified hitchhiker deliberately and was he a continuing threat to society? To sway the panel that the answer was yes to both questions, Walsh introduced the sworn confession Lucas had given to Travis County investigators in the Sandra Dubbs case. Then he offered Lucas's confession to the March 18, 1980, murder of a forty-three-year-old Abilene, Texas, woman. In that statement he said he was running short of cash when he passed through Abilene on I-20, drifting toward California. Armed with a shotgun, he went into the temporary office of a savings and loan company and collected a thousand dollars from the teller. He shot her in the back of the head and fled.

The jury then heard ninety minutes of final argument, Lucas's lawyers pleading for mercy, Walsh for a death sentence.

"It says in the Bible, 'Judge not lest you be judged,'" Parker argued. "What right do we have to say that a man should die? What makes us better than Henry Lee Lucas if we sentence a man to death?

"I can't tell you Henry is not a killer," he continued, "but Henry Lucas is not an animal. He's a human being."

Higginbotham argued for a life sentence: "Get him out of society. Give him the help he's asking for."

McCollough, in his argument, asked the jury how Lucas could continue as a threat to society since he already had a seventy-five-year sentence, a life sentence, and other cases still pending against him.

Walsh argued that Lucas might someday escape from prison. "Can you take the chance that this man might someday get back on the streets?"

Waving photographs of two of the women Lucas had confessed to killing, Walsh said, "If you want to feel sorry for Henry Lee Lucas, look at these. . . . This is what Henry Lee Lucas is all about."

Forty minutes after they left the courtroom, the jury

was back. Their answer to the two crucial questions was yes. Lucas should die by lethal injection.

Lucas, standing before the bench, smiled grimly as Judge Carter read the verdict.

Surrounded by reporters as he was led in handcuffs back to the jail cell where he'd been for thirty-five days, Lucas was asked how he felt. "I still feel the same as I did," he said, smiling again. "I haven't changed. I didn't do it, but I'm happy anyway."

Boutwell had been keeping in close touch with his office throughout the trial. When he called Friday night to check in, he got some bad news. One of his deputies had taken an anonymous call: Lucas was going to be killed on the way back to Georgetown. There had not been enough time to trace the call.

The sheriff was inclined to dismiss it as a nut call, but he didn't want to take any chances. Though investigators had never been able to prove it, Lucas had said that he was a member of a cult. He had intimated they might want him killed because of his confessions.

Boutwell called Ranger Sergeant Prince, who arranged for a DPS escort when the sheriff headed back to Georgetown with Lucas.

Before they left San Angelo, the sheriff told Lucas about the threat.

"Henry, if something starts happening, I want you to drop to the floor of the car," Boutwell instructed him. "If you don't, you're fixing to see one hell of a gunfight."

But the drive back to Georgetown was uneventful. Even while keeping on the alert for anything that might signal trouble, Boutwell and Walsh still were able to admire the bluebonnets along the highway. Spring had finally returned to Texas.

CHAPTER ELEVEN

For someone facing the death penalty, Henry Lucas was for the most part a happy man.

He had been in the Williamson County Jail for seventeen months now, his longest stay at any one address since his last hard time up in Michigan. But being locked up in Georgetown was like staying in a fancy motel compared to the old walled prison in Jackson. Sister Clemmie Schroeder had given him a television set and paid for a cable hookup. In addition to the regular jail food, task force officers, Clemmie, and visiting homicide investigators kept him supplied with hamburgers, pizza, and strawberry milkshakes. Last fall, Clemmie had even brought him a home-cooked Thanksgiving dinner. He had all the coffee and cigarettes he wanted, which was a lot; he had his canvas and paints; and he had Clemmie, who came to pray and visit with him at least twice daily.

The beige metal walls of his cell were covered with his artwork, including a portrait he'd painted of Clemmie and inspirational posters from Clemmie. One poster featured a color photograph of a spotted fawn standing alertly in a field of white flowers. The caption said, "Peace on the outside comes from knowing God within." Clemmie, a sweet, intensely religious woman, had taken the manipulative Lucas into her heart. At times Lucas could seem very affable—many of the law officers had been amazed at the small, friendly-seeming man's penchant for violence. These qualities had probably helped Lucas in disarming many of his victims. For Clemmie, he was the perfect object for reformation—the convicted killer who now wanted to save his soul through Jesus. Also prominently displayed in his cell was a school photograph of Becky. Anyone seeing the picture, not knowing the circumstances of her relationship to Lucas, might have thought the girl with the long dark hair was his daughter.

Except for being behind bars, in many ways Lucas lived nearly a normal life. Like most people on the outside, he had a day job—working with Sheriff Boutwell and the Rangers with the task force to clear up murders across the country. The job involved occasional travel, though he hated being away from Clemmie. But most of the time he got weekends off. He had a regular stream of reporters wanting interviews—his picture was in the papers as often as some sports figures—and he got a lot of interesting mail on a variety of subjects, from Christians praising his conversion to other convicts pleading with him to confess to murders they were in prison for. Someone even wrote a song about him and sent it to the jail in Georgetown. He kept the correspondence stuffed under his mattress, though he gave the song to Sheriff Boutwell.

Henry Lucas dealt with death every day in the downstairs task force office, and, according to his confessions, had brought violent death to many innocent people. But he thought about his own mortality only occasionally. He knew the appeals process would take years, and he didn't think anyone in Texas would be in too much of a hurry to get him on death row in Huntsville as long as he kept cooperating with law officers by clearing cases for them. Even when his final moment came, it would be easy, like going off to sleep. No struggle, no pain, no blood. Just an injection. And after it was over, he was convinced he would be in heaven, united forever with Becky, cleansed of sin by his earthly confessions. He would miss Sister Clemmie, but someday she would be in heaven, too.

For now, considering what most of his life had been like, he was enjoying his own paradise on earth.

On Friday, April 12, 1985, Lucas was looking forward to the weekend. The previous Saturday he'd wrapped up a five-day, 2,200-mile trip across Georgia, spending sixteen-hour days leading state and local officers to ten crime scenes where he claimed either he or Ottis had left bodies.

Lucas usually was happy to talk to reporters, but he didn't pay too much attention to what they wrote. The Atlanta *Constitution* didn't interview him while he was in Georgia and treated the story almost routinely, devoting only fourteen paragraphs to his claims. He was not likely to be tried in Georgia because he already was under a death sentence in Texas, the story pointed out. "He made a sincere effort to clear these cases," a Georgia Bureau of Investigation agent told the reporter. "He certainly was not boastful or filled with braggadocio, nor did he show much emotion about the crimes."

Since being back in Georgetown, Lucas had been busy confessing to other cases elsewhere. Now he'd have a couple of days to take it easy, do some painting, and spend time with Sister Clemmie.

Sheriff Boutwell liked his weekends off, too. Lucas didn't expect to see him or any of the Rangers until Monday. They had gone home to their families. So when the lawman appeared outside his cell about 7:00 P.M., Lucas knew immediately that something was wrong. The sheriff was usually pretty easygoing and smiled a lot. This time his mouth was set in a firm, even line.

Boutwell and District Attorney Ed Walsh had been at a reception near the small county airport, not far from where the sheriff lived, when his dispatcher contacted him with the news that Sheriff Jack Harwell from Waco had shown up at the jail with a warrant for Lucas. It wasn't like Harwell, a man Boutwell had known for several years, to show up unannounced with a warrant for someone in his custody, especially after 5:00 P.M.

"Henry, I've been served with a bench warrant for you from a judge up in Waco," Boutwell said. "Ed's looked it over and we've decided to honor it. You better pack up whatever you need. You're going right now."

Boutwell listened as Lucas fumed about having to leave.

"I don't know how long you'll be up there, but Sheriff Harwell says he doesn't think it'll be too long."

Boutwell was disgusted by the bench warrant, though he had expected something like this sooner or later. The signs had been building for months. He'd heard that the young district attorney for McLennan County, Vic Feazell, was planning a grand jury investigation into Lucas's confessions to several murders in that county. He also had heard that Jim Mattox, the state's attorney general, was looking into the matter as well.

As early as January 1984, Lucas had written a letter to a reporter with the Fort Worth *Star-Telegram* intimating that he hadn't killed all the people he said he had. Members of the task force had questioned Lucas about it, and on videotape he had assured them he really had killed all the people he said he had.

That had barely died down when a case up in

Lubbock started generating news stories that cast doubt on Lucas's claims.

Deborah Sue Williamson had been found stabbed to death on the patio of her Lubbock residence on August 24, 1975. The murder of the eighteen-year-old newlywed had gone unsolved until May 17, 1984, when Lucas confessed to it. At first, Deborah's parents, Bob and Joyce Lemons, had been relieved to hear that police had solved the nearly nine-year-old case with Lucas's confession.

But when police and prosecutors let them read Lucas's statement, they became convinced Lucas could not have killed their daughter. For one thing, Lucas had only been free from prison for two days when the murder occurred. He would have to have driven straight to Lubbock, Texas, from Michigan to kill Deborah. But Lucas had gone directly to Maryland after his release—his family as well as neighbors knew he'd been there during that period.

The Lemons had begun their own investigation, spending their own money to look into Lucas's past. The deeper they dug, the more sure they were that Lucas had not killed their daughter—and possibly not some of the others he had claimed. Their contention first got local newspaper coverage in Lubbock, then spread statewide with a story in the September 1984 *Texas Monthly,* "True Confessions? Henry Lee Lucas admits to hundreds of murders. But that doesn't mean he committed them all."

Boutwell, too, had doubted that Lucas had killed as many people as he said. It strained logic to think he could have left as many bodies across the country without slipping up and getting caught. But the longer he was around Lucas, the more he began to believe the little man was an accomplished serial killer. Boutwell had seen him direct officers to crime scenes too many times. On the other hand, Lucas also was an accomplished liar. The trouble law enforcement faced, Boutwell knew, was separating truth from fiction.

Now, Boutwell realized, the question of Lucas's credibility had sprouted up in public again—this time in Waco, where Lucas had claimed three murders. One of those cases was the killing of Rita Salazar, the murder that had begun in Williamson County in 1978, when Salazar's date, Kevin Keys, ran out of gas on I-35.

The other murders were that of Glen Parks, forty-seven, who was shot seven times in his home during a robbery, and that of the twenty-five-year-old Dorothy Collins, who died of multiple stab wounds and a cut throat. In both cases Lucas had led officers to the locations of the crimes; he'd described the floor plan of Parks's home and had taken McLennan County investigators to the place where Collins's body had been dumped.

A story in that morning's Waco paper had reported that three investigators with the McLennan County Sheriff's Office had testified before the grand jury there the day before about the murders Lucas had claimed in their county. Also appearing before the grand jurors was Hugh Aynesworth of the Dallas *Times-Herald*.

Boutwell first met Aynesworth during the "Orange Socks" trial in San Angelo. After Lucas's conviction, the newsman had made news himself when he said he didn't think Lucas was guilty. Co-author of a book about Florida serial killer Ted Bundy, Aynesworth sat through the San Angelo trial to gather material on Lucas. He had interviewed Lucas in Denton before his transfer to Williamson County and since then. He'd written a story about Lucas that had run in *Penthouse* magazine. Boutwell had heard that Aynesworth was working on a long newspaper story about Lucas and the task force. He didn't expect it to be complimentary.

The story broke on Sunday, April 14, just two days after Lucas's sudden transfer to Waco on the heels of Aynesworth's grand jury appearance. HENRY LEE LUCAS: MASS MURDERER OR MASSIVE HOAX? was the headline. Aynesworth shared the byline on the long, copyrighted page-one story and inside sidebar pieces with another reporter.

The thrust of the stories was that Lucas had confessed to far more murders than he had actually committed and that the task force had "ignored or failed to pursue leads that would have proven the deceit of his confessions." The implication was that Lucas had either been fed information by officers anxious to clear cases or had been able to trick investigators into giving him enough information to "confess."

The stories used records furnished to other law enforcement agencies by the task force to show that some cases initially listed as cleared had later been removed from the list, indicating that the agencies had changed their minds in some cases about Lucas's guilt. It also pointed out that Lucas and Toole would have to have driven hundreds of miles in a short period of time to have committed all the crimes they had claimed.

Lucas, the story said, had told his court-appointed defense attorneys and Aynesworth that all but three of his many murder confessions (his mother, Becky Powell, and Kate Rich) were a hoax intended to "show that law enforcement doesn't do its job."

"I'm gonna show 'em," the story quoted Lucas. "They think I'm stupid, but before all this is over, everyone will know who's really stupid."

Some of the law enforcement agencies probably were overeager in their questioning of Lucas, despite the Rangers' repeated warnings not to ask leading questions or to provide information to Lucas. The task force also told officers to show Lucas only photos of victims when they were alive (so as not to give away the manner of death). The officers would give Lucas a photo to study and then ask him to provide information about the homicide. At times, the officers would show Lucas several photos of victims and have him pick out which was the person he'd killed. At times, an officer would present a photo of a crime scene with an area of the picture covered, in order to see if Lucas could fill in the blank.

It is important not to overlook the fact that Lucas had, by this time, become very adept at the questioning process. While not intellectually intelligent, Lucas was very quick to pick up on subtleties like tone of voice and facial expression, and he could be very manipulative. It's quite possible that when he sensed that he was coming close to what the investigator was looking for, he could sway his answers in that direction. And he was very good at remembering small details in the murders he did commit—so much so that one court-appointed psychologist diagnosed him as "hypernesiac" (as opposed to amnesiac). This ability to recall details may have helped him in piecing together what the law agencies were leading to in their questioning.

The newspaper story brought up the discrepancies in some of Lucas's confessions, particularly given the distances between some of the alleged crime scenes. Certainly it is hard to imagine that Lucas killed people in twenty-two states. However, it was a fact that Lucas would get wired up on coffee and pills and take off for days at a time, either with Toole, or with Toole, Becky, and her brother Frank. And in January 1982, Lucas drove and sometimes hitchhiked with Becky from Jacksonville, Florida, to San Diego—a distance of some 2,090 miles. Leaving Florida in mid-January, he showed up in Houston, where he sold blood on January 20. Then, after his car broke down on I-10 in Texas, he and Becky hitched to California, arriving in San Diego on January 25—a distance of about 650 miles from El Paso, on the border of Texas. A trip from Austin, Texas to Provo, Utah (where law officers suspected him of crime) would have been a distance of around a thousand miles. Certainly Lucas lied about many of his crimes, but in several instances it was documented that he had traveled a great distance in a small amount of time.

Boutwell and the Rangers would have been the first to admit that Lucas had tried repeatedly to take cases that weren't his. He had been questioned in several thousand homicide cases; Lucas was considered a suspect in only a couple of hundred cases, and in only about one hundred cases had he been able to lead officers to crime scenes. The sheriff still firmly believed, as had been demonstrated in the "Orange Socks" trial, that the work records showing Lucas elsewhere when some of the murders occurred had been falsified as part of a kickback scheme. Another problem with dates, Boutwell felt, was that all the murders were listed by the date the victim's body had been found; in many of the cases, no one knew for sure when the death had actually occurred.

The lack of physical evidence to back up many of Lucas's cases was not surprising to the sheriff. Lucas was good at what he did, and he seldom killed anyone he knew. Boutwell had seen Lucas bring up cases that officers didn't even suspect him of on too many occasions to believe he was lying about everything.

Before he finished reading the five Lucas stories in the Sunday *Times-Herald,* Ranger Sergeant Prince felt like someone had landed a hard punch to his stomach. Few things in his life had ever hurt him more. The stories seemed not only to question his professional abilities, but his personal integrity as well. And he had not been afforded a chance to respond to the allegations in the articles.

Sergeant Prince and other Rangers who dealt with

Lucas had repeatedly warned other officers to be careful when they interviewed him, pointing out that he tended to try to take cases that weren't his. Ranger Ryan early on had tested Lucas's credibility by pitching him a phony case. Lucas had tried to take it. Officers with other agencies had done the same thing, with the same result; they were well aware of Lucas's tendencies to confess to crimes he didn't commit.

The Monday, April 15, editions of the *Times-Herald* offered four more Lucas stories, including an article headed: "Lucas gets death on his word only." The main story was based on a comparison of the various edited transcripts of Lucas's assorted confessions in the "Orange Socks" case—the same material that had been brought up in the trial and rejected by the jury as it went on to convict Lucas of capital murder.

In Austin, Department of Public Safety Director Colonel Jim Adams also pored over the Lucas stories. After talking with his staff, Adams decided to meet the allegations head-on with a press conference the next day.

By Tuesday morning, through Sister Clemmie, Lucas had already reversed himself in print again. Sister Clemmie told the Austin *American-Statesman* that she had gone to Waco on Sunday and had spent seventy minutes with Lucas in his cell. She said they had discussed the *Times-Herald* story and that Lucas had told her he had made his claim to Aynesworth of only having killed three people at least fourteen months earlier, before his religious convictions had deepened and before he had decided to cooperate fully with law enforcement officers.

"He said he wasn't worried about [the hoax story] hurting his reputation, but he didn't want to make a mockery of the Lord," Clemmie said. "I know he's a killer. There's no doubt in my mind. He really feels he needs to confess to every one of his cases because that's the only way to undo the evil he has done."

Asked about the hoax allegation by the Austin newspaper, Sheriff Boutwell said, "No professional officer believes everything [Lucas] has claimed. But if he can describe a crime and lead you to the scene and is accurate on most details and does not have an airtight alibi, he either did it or he's the biggest psychic the world has known."

Boutwell was angry that his integrity had been questioned.

"I think a lot of it is political, and I don't mind saying so," he said.

The sheriff didn't think Feazell was out to get him personally. They had never even met. But Boutwell believed that Feazell saw the Lucas case as a way to get state and national publicity, achieving a name recognition that would come in handy if he decided to run for attorney general of Texas in the Democratic primary. The situation was further complicated because Ed Walsh, the Williamson County D.A. who had gotten the capital conviction against Lucas, had switched to the Republican party a month earlier. He, too, was thinking about running for attorney general. If Feazell could make the Lucas case look like a farce, he was attacking a potential political opponent before he even had his campaign going.

Later that Tuesday morning, Colonel Adams had a press conference at the state agency's headquarters in Austin.

"I am satisfied that he killed a substantial number of people," Adams said of Lucas. If Lucas had indeed claimed to have killed only three people, the colonel continued, "Such an assertion . . . is ludicrous."

The DPS director quickly went to the defense of his agency's Lucas Homicide Task Force. The task force, he said, had been set up to collect information and

MIKE COX

coordinate law enforcement interviews with Lucas, not to investigate whether all of Lucas's confessions were true.

"It's never been any secret . . . that Henry has claimed more killings than have ever been confirmed," the DPS director said.

The colonel said 189 murders had been listed as "cleared" (i.e., the various law agencies felt convinced of Lucas's guilt in the cases they had investigated) by agencies that had questioned Lucas about unsolved cases, but he would not speculate on how many murders he felt Lucas had actually committed.

"I don't think he will ever tell everything—or perhaps even remember everything," he continued. "I don't think we will ever know."

But Adams said he was sure of one thing: no one had entered into any "wholesale" effort or "conspiracy . . . to just write off a bunch of killings" with Lucas. Some cases Lucas had confessed to had been reopened because of holes. In other cases, Adams said, inconsistencies could be attributed to Lucas's heavy drug and alcohol use when he was on the road.

"I am satisfied that the task force operated within its charter," Adams said.

Adams was not the only lawman to disagree with the Lucas hoax allegation. Police in California, Utah, and Texas, contacted for reaction by reporters in their areas, said they were still satisfied that Lucas was responsible for cases they had talked with him about.

Capt. Dennis Rhoten, chief of detectives for the Arlington, Texas, Police Department, told reporters his department had interviewed Lucas concerning six murders, two of which had been cleared when Lucas related details only the killer would have known. "If he wanted to make us look like fools, why didn't he confess to the others?"

Steve A. Egger, a criminologist on the faculty of

244

Sam Houston State University in Huntsville, Texas, told a reporter for the Houston *Chronicle* that he had interviewed Lucas on a dozen occasions—totalling fifty hours—as part of his doctoral research on mass murder. "I have no doubt he committed all except a very few of the homicides that have been attributed to him in twenty-six states," Egger said. "There is no way they [law enforcement officers] could have asked Lucas leading questions in that many cases. I have more faith in law enforcement than that."

A letter writer to the Houston *Post* saw the issue in simple terms: "What's the difference if Henry Lee Lucas killed three or three hundred? He's just stalling. Execute him."

While Colonel Adams was busy fielding questions from the press, Attorney General Mattox was on his way to Waco, one hundred miles north of Austin, to meet with Vic Feazell and the famous prisoner now held in the McLennan County jail.

After talking with Lucas, Mattox told reporters, "I am convinced Lucas is not guilty of some of the cases he has confessed to. But I cannot tell you how many he has committed, how many of the confessions are good, or how many are bad. I'm not sure anybody really knows. I'm not sure even he knows."

Under the Texas Constitution, the attorney general is empowered to be the state's civil lawyer. No mention is made in the charter of the attorney general having a role in criminal cases, as is the case in the federal government, though the attorney general does represent the state in the review of death penalty cases. Mattox said that after meeting with Feazell he intended to ask Governor Mark White (Mattox's predecessor in office) for funds to investigate Lucas's confessions. He was willing to take on such an investigation, he said, because he felt that Colonel Adams believed the Lucas task force's "primary responsibility . . . was to simply serve as a clearing-house, making Lucas available to different law enforcement agencies."

Mattox, whom some Texas political observers expected to run for governor in 1986, said he knew of no evidence indicating that Lucas had been coached by law enforcement officers "or led specifically in any criminal form." However, he also added, "We have determined that even though Lucas is not well educated, he is astute and streetwise and has the capability of picking up very quickly from the mere suggestions of certain questions. [Lucas] has most certainly led us to believe that the law enforcement work that has been accomplished, in some circumstances, has not been of the highest order we might expect."

But, Mattox continued, "Our purpose is not to investigate the task force. Our purpose is to try and determine whether or not Henry Lee Lucas committed some of these crimes and whether or not he committed those in McLennan County."

While the director of the DPS and the attorney general were circumspectly slugging it out in the press, some intense behind-the-scenes activity was under way.

Jan Patterson, an assistant U.S. attorney, was something of a modern-day circuit rider. Her office was in Austin, but her area of prosecutorial responsibility included Waco. She made the two hundred-mile round-trip often; the employees at the Dairy Queen in Salado, a small town on I-35 about halfway between Austin and Waco, recognized her as a regular customer.

An Austin native, she had graduated from the University of Texas law school and had worked in Manhattan as an assistant U.S. attorney for the Southern District of New York, prosecuting mobsters and dope dealers. In the summer of 1984, the petite, blue-eyed prosecutor had transfered to Texas, leaving her Manhattan office at 5:00 P.M. on a Friday and showing up at the federal offices in Austin at 8:00 A.M. the following Monday.

An admitted workaholic, Patterson was still in her office after 6:00 P.M. when a colleague called her from the main office for the Western District of Texas in San Antonio. He said that Floyd Hacker, chief of criminal law enforcement for the DPS, had called him to say that the sheriff of Williamson County was concerned that the civil rights of one of his prisoners had been violated. The prisoner was mass-murder suspect Henry Lee Lucas. Patterson said she'd go to Georgetown to meet with the sheriff right away.

After returning to Georgetown from her visit with Lucas, Sister Clemmie had contacted Sheriff Boutwell. She did not like the way Lucas was being treated in McLennan County. Lucas had said he had been unable to sleep since his transfer and had been denied medication he had been receiving in Georgetown. In general, he was distraught. He also had not been provided with a lawyer in Waco, she said.

Patterson listened to a tape-recorded statement Boutwell had taken from Clemmie and then talked privately with her. Until her trip to Georgetown that night about all that Patterson knew of Lucas was what she had read in the papers and seen on television. But she was well aware of Vic Feazell, the district attorney who had gotten Lucas transferred from jail in Williamson County to appear before his grand jury in McLennan. The previous fall, in fact, she had quietly begun looking into stories she was hearing that dismissals to criminal charges could be obtained in McLennan County for a price. Now, after listening to Boutwell's tape and talking with Sister Clemmie, it seemed to her that the Lucas situation in Waco deserved attention.

On the way back to Austin later that night, Patterson thought about Sheriff Boutwell and the task force officers she'd met a few hours earlier. One of the first things she tried to do when looking into a case was determine the motivations of the people involved. The officers at the sheriff's office that night had all seemed sincere and dedicated.

Sister Clemmie was not as easy to read. How could the lay minister be so close to a confessed killer? Clemmie had seemed tremendously upset not only by Lucas's purported treatment in Waco, but by his sudden absence from Georgetown. The prosecutor concluded that Clemmie's faith must have been very strong. Just looking at Lucas's picture in the newspaper gave her the creeps. Headed south on I-35, Patterson reached over and locked her car door.

Early Wednesday morning, April 17, three FBI agents came to the McLennan County Jail and asked to see Lucas. Jail personnel, after checking with D.A. Feazell, told the federal officers they would not be allowed to talk with their prisoner.

When State District Judge George Allen, who had empaneled the grand jury looking into Lucas's confessions, got to work later that morning, he found a note on his desk to call Feazell. When the judge called the district attorney, Feazell told him Lucas needed a lawyer. Allen said he would appoint Guy Cox, a former assistant district attorney who had a civil and criminal practice in Waco.

At 9:00 A.M., Lucas was moved from the jail to the grand jury room in the courthouse. He spent three hours before the panel. After a lunch break, Clemmie Schroeder entered the grand jury room to testify.

Later that afternoon, when reporters learned of the attempt by the FBI to see Lucas that morning, the district attorney would not comment on the reason for their visit, but he did confirm that they were denied access to the prisoner.

"They can see him later," Feazell told a reporter. "This is a state investigation."

The three federal agents, Greg Rampton and Jim Echols from Austin and Tony Ball from Waco, had been asked to keep their visit low-key. All Jan Patterson had wanted was for them to talk with Lucas and attempt to assess his condition. When the agents were told they could not see Lucas, they did not press the matter.

Attorney General Mattox, who also would not say anything about the FBI's sudden interest in Lucas, sat in on the Waco grand jury proceedings throughout the day.

"I don't want to comment specifically on what he said to us," Mattox told reporters later in the day, "but he's led us to believe he did not commit a very large number of these crimes."

Lucas had spent more than eleven hours before the grand jury. Since grand jury proceedings are secret under Texas law, no one but the twelve men and women on the jury, plus Feazell, Mattox, and various staff members, knew what Lucas had talked about. Judge Allen ordered an extension of the panel's term for another ninety days, and Feazell said the jury would reconvene to further consider the Lucas matter on May 3.

Again, however, some events occurred that did not make the newspapers. Based on what Sister Clemmie had said about Lucas's behavior since his move to the jail in Waco and Feazell's refusal to allow FBI agents to talk to Lucas, Patterson's boss, U.S. Attorney Helen Eversburg, decided to bring Lucas before a federal grand jury in San Antonio. On Friday, April 19, U.S. District Judge Edward Prado signed a warrant ordering Lucas to appear before the federal panel in San Antonio the following Wednesday. That Friday, two deputy U.S. marshals, expecting to pick up Lucas and take him to San Antonio, served the warrant on Sheriff Jack Harwell in Waco. But after talking with Feazell, the McLennan County sheriff told the federal officers he would not surrender his prisoner, though he would consider the writ as a detainer.

When he learned of the federal move, Attorney General Mattox ordered his staff to begin work on a motion requesting that Lucas be allowed to remain in custody in McLennan County until Feazell's grand jury completed its investigation.

The next morning, Feazell said he would be prepared to go to jail himself rather than turn Lucas over to federal officers.

"They [federal officials] were not interested in this case back when Lucas was confessing to all these crimes he didn't commit," Feazell told a reporter. "They weren't interested in this case back when cases were being cleared and the real murderers were out walking the street. Now, all of a sudden, when something is being done about this situation, here come the feds."

Attorney General Mattox wrote Governor White asking for $120,000 to press his investigation of the Lucas case, a request quickly turned down by the governor, who had approved the creation of the task force. "We don't have any money," the governor said at a press conference. Asked by a reporter if he felt the task force had mishandled the case, White said, "I don't think so. The Rangers in this case were there at the request of the sheriff of Williamson County to coordinate access to this individual by other law enforcement agencies across the country and had very little role to play in the detailed investigation."

On Monday, with his motion to keep Lucas in Waco about to be filed with the San Antonio federal court, Mattox sent a photocopy of the brief and a short, testy letter to U.S. Attorney General Edwin Meese III. "Helen Eversberg . . . has charged that state officials have violated the civil rights of Henry Lee Lucas by denying him access to counsel during an ongoing state grand jury investigation. Her charges are bogus." The U.S. attorney's planned grand jury investigation, Mattox continued, would "disrupt the ongoing state grand jury investigation. . . ." The state attorney general told Meese: "I doubt that [Eversberg] has cleared her plans through the Justice Department. I urge you to review the steps she has taken. This country simply cannot have U.S. attorneys attempting to intimidate state officials and undermine state criminal investigations."

Tuesday morning, Mattox went public with his letter to Meese at a press conference in Austin, claiming collusion between Williamson County officers and federal authorities in the effort to get Lucas out of Waco. If his motion was not granted or set for a hearing, Mattox said, he would appeal it to the U.S. Court of Appeals for the 5th Circuit in New Orleans.

Both Mattox and Feazell seemed to be relishing the publicity connected to the state–federal tug-of-war over Lucas. Unnoticed in the midst of the media circus was that Lucas was agreeing with whomever asked him something, no matter if his answer to one person's question contradicted a previous answer. In a little more than a week Lucas had denied in print that he had ever killed anyone except his mother, Kate Rich, and Becky Powell; he had told Clemmie Schroeder he had not recanted his confessions and that he was being denied his civil rights in the Waco jail; and then he had signed an affidavit on Monday, April 22, that "I myself have no complaint. I am being well treated."

Tuesday afternoon, with his lawyer by his side, Lucas was made available to the press in the 54th District courtroom at the courthouse in Waco. This time he denied even having killed Kate Rich and Becky Powell. "I have killed Mother, and that is the only one," he told the roomful of reporters. With the video cameras and tape recorders rolling, he then went on to take a verbal knife thrust at the Texas Rangers and law enforcement in general: "I've been aided by the Texas Rangers' Bob Prince. I've been aided by Clayton Smith of the Texas Rangers. I've been aided by other police departments in the investigations."

Lucas then went on to describe how he had been able to confess to so many murders: "They'll show you pictures of crimes. They'll give you all the information in the crime. They'll even take you back and point the crime out to you, and all you have to do is stand there and say, 'Yeah, I did it.' And they've been cleared that way, and this is what has got to stop."

As if his blast at the Rangers was not enough to excite reporters, Lucas went on: "I think it should be known that if I go anywhere from here, there's no guarantee that I'm going to live. I'll either end up escaping, they'll say, or I'll end up stabbed in some cell where an inmate does it. I don't feel safe anywhere because of what I've done. I've put the truth on the street by coming forward and telling them I didn't do these crimes. People isn't going to just stand by and say, 'Well, we're going to forget it.'"

Texas Ranger Sergeant Prince responded to Lucas's allegations.

"He is a convicted murderer," Prince told the Waco newspaper. And, he added, "he is a habitual liar. It's so important to believe only what you can confirm. . . . We know the credibility of Henry Lee Lucas. He's got everything in the world to gain by getting people to believe he didn't kill anyone."

Lucas's claim that the only person he had ever killed was his mother, Prince continued, "is absolutely absurd."

"If anyone thinks there's been a mass conspiracy— and that's what it would have had to have been—of officers throughout the United States to clear those cases, it's ridiculous."

Why did Lucas keep switching his stories? Perhaps he simply wanted to please whoever was questioning him at the moment. It is also probable that, since he knew he'd continue to be treated well as long as he kept confessing, he simply decided to continue to confess as long as he was in the Williamson County jail. Then, when he was transferred to Waco, perhaps he felt betrayed by the Rangers for allowing him to be transferred and for that reason turned on them. Or, once he got to Waco, perhaps Feazell's contention that he hadn't committed any crimes took hold and he decided to try to get all the charges reversed so that he could go free. At any rate, his prevarication kept the press hopping.

Wednesday morning, millions of Americans getting ready for work got to see Lucas in a live interview on ABC's "Good Morning America." Lucas was no newcomer to the nation's airwaves. He had been featured on ABC's "20/20" and other TV news shows and documentaries, but this was his first live appearance on network television.

Speaking from Feazell's office before a camera provided by the ABC affiliate in Waco, Lucas repeated his accusation that the Texas Rangers had coached him in his confession spree. He went along with it, he said, because of his treatment after his arrest in Montague County for possession of a pistol.

"I was put in what they call a cold cell and I was deprived of every right I have," Lucas told the nation. "I asked for an attorney. I couldn't get one. I was harrassed for nine months. I lost all kinds of jobs because of it and I made up my mind that . . . people weren't going to walk on me."

Lucas said God was the reason he had finally "decided to tell the truth" and recant his confessions.

"I have found God at last," he said as he looked

with his one eye into the camera. "He has . . . at last He won't let me go any further and I have to stop."

Attorney General Mattox also got some coast-to-coast airtime during the broadcast.

"We want to see if some of these cases were improperly closed and if necessary reopen them," Mattox said on camera.

The attorney general and McLennan County prosecutor Vic Feazell were getting the kind of publicity most politicians could only dream about, but their effort to keep Lucas in Waco failed. When Judge Prado refused to grant the state motion, Mattox made a last-minute appeal to U.S. Supreme Court Justice Byron White. Justice White also denied the motion.

Shortly after his national television appearance, Lucas was driven to San Antonio by a deputy U.S. marshal and the McLennan County sheriff to be questioned before federal grand jurors by prosecutors about whether his civil rights had been abused in Waco. Handcuffed and chained around the waist, Lucas was quickly led past a mob of newspaper and television reporters into the rear entrance of the federal courthouse. U.S. Marshal William Jonas, Jr., met his deputy and Sheriff Harwell inside and escorted Lucas to the grand jury room on the third floor. Feazell and Lucas's attorney, Cox, waited in the marshal's office as Lucas testified before the grand jury.

Patterson and two other assistant U.S. attorneys chatted with Lucas before he was taken to the grand jurors.

"Everyone was being very deferential to him," Patterson would recall. "At one point, I challenged something he said and he stopped abruptly and gave me that cross-eyed stare. 'What did you say your name was?'"

Despite Clemmie's concerns about his health, Lucas seemed to have all his senses during his grand jury appearance. By the time the questioning was over, Patterson and the other prosecutors realized that it would be very difficult to proceed with a civil rights case. They were not comfortable with the way Lucas had been jerked from the Williamson County Jail without notice, nor with the time that had gone by before a lawyer had been appointed to represent him. But Lucas had signed an affidavit that he had not been concerned about his civil rights and had no complaints with his treatment in McLennan County. That afternoon, Lucas was returned to jail in Waco.

On Monday, April 29, Lucas changed his story again.

Bob Larsen, a rock-and-roll musician who gave up fast music and the fast life in his conversion to Christianity, had found another medium of expression: radio evangelism. His Denver radio program, "Talk Back with Bob Larsen," was carried by most Christian radio stations via satellite to millions of listeners. He was the Larry King of Christian radio, a broadcaster with a penchant for topics relating to mysticism, astrology, pyschic phenomena, cults, and satanism. His interest in Lucas had been piqued when he saw in one of the Denver papers a wire service photo of Lucas wearing a T-shirt with Jesus on it and read of Lucas's conversion from self-professed killer to born-again Christian. In September 1984, Larsen had finally been able to arrange an interview with Lucas through Sister Clemmie. In the interview Lucas freely discussed his many murders and his involvement in what he said was a cult called the Hands of Death. Afterwards, Clemmie sent Larsen a peaceful church scene painted by Lucas. The radio minister had it framed and hung in his studio. He began a correspondence with Lucas, by letter and cassette tape.

After Larsen heard Lucas had begun denying he was

a mass murderer, he contacted Clemmie and arranged for another interview. At Clemmie's request, Feazell gave it his blessing.

Larsen came to Lucas's cell that Monday morning with his wife and Sister Clemmie. Mostly they discussed spiritual matters. They knelt and prayed together. Shortly after Lucas's transfer to Waco, Feazell, the son of a Baptist minister, also had gotten down on his knees with Lucas and prayed.

While waiting on Lucas's attorney, who had said he wanted to be present during the interview, Larsen asked Lucas about his recent denials that he had killed anyone but his mother.

"I killed the people," Lucas told Larsen.

Larsen asked if he could get that on tape. Lucas said yes.

Before Cox joined them, Larsen pulled that tape out and put another cassette into his recorder. Barely five minutes into his second interview, Cox asked Larsen to stop. The attorney felt Lucas was incriminating himself. As Larsen later told his listeners, he erased that second tape at Cox's insistence, but kept the first tape.

When a reporter for the Waco paper interviewed Larsen after his visit with Lucas, the evangelist stuck to religious matters, saving Lucas's latest turnaround for his radio show. He did say, however, that a portion of his interview with Lucas had been "one-on-one" before Lucas's attorney arrived at the jail.

Ed Walsh, the prosecutor whose courtroom efforts the previous spring had led to Lucas's death sentence, called a press conference on Tuesday to respond to the allegations being made by his counterpart in Waco and by the state attorney general.

"They are attacking the integrity and credibility of all of the officials involved in those cases and causing further pain and doubt to the families of the victims," he said.

Walsh accused Mattox and Feazell of "irresponsible, unprofessional actions" and of using Lucas for political gain. Their actions, he continued, were "jeopardizing cases by implying wrongdoing on the part of Texas law enforcement agencies."

Asked by a reporter if he, too, were using Lucas for political reasons, Walsh replied, "If he's a political football, I didn't start kicking him around—Jim Mattox and Vic Feazell did."

Larsen broadcast his interview with Lucas the next day, May 1.

"Did you or did you not kill the people you said you did?" Larsen asked.

"I have killed the people I said," Lucas replied. "They may have somewhere along the line [found] other dates, but they were supposed to have went back and checked on each case to make sure there was no conflict. They also know that these work records [the ones from Florida that had come up in the "Orange Socks" trial] are phony work records. They knew that the people that I've took back to the crimes themselves did not help me to get back to those crimes. I went back to them on my own.

"Every time I say I didn't kill the people it only helps these people here [in McLennan County]. In order for me to stay here I have to do what I'm told. But I told the people in Georgetown the truth, and they know it's the truth. Regardless of what I do, they're going to try and block it. I've asked the sheriff [Boutwell] to come up here, I've asked the FBI to come up here and talk to me privately so we can get this straightened out. And they won't do it. The only way I can come forward with it is to have people behind me."

Larsen asked Lucas again about his recantations.

"No, it's not true. It's only what they want to hear, and that's all. It's not what the actual truth is. The truth is I killed three hundred sixty people and the only way I can prove it is with the help of the police in Georgetown and the Rangers who have turned their backs on me. And that's the only way I can do it."

Larsen had one other piece of news for his listeners: Moments before his show had gone on the air, Lucas had telephoned him in Denver and asked if he still intended to broadcast the tape he had made two days before. Larsen said yes.

"What I said to you Monday was a lie," Larsen said Lucas told him.

After the broadcast, Feazell's office issued a short written statement that "Henry Lucas claims that he did not make the statements to Mr. Larsen as aired on the radio. . . . It is our position that no matter whether Henry Lucas says he did the murders or didn't . . . he can't be in two places at once [an apparent reference to Lucas's work records from Jacksonville, which had been contested in court]."

Later that afternoon, in Georgetown, Boutwell released excerpts of a letter from Lucas smuggled to him from Clemmie Schroeder. In the letter, Lucas said that the Hands of Death cult, which no one in law enforcement had ever been able to prove existed, was "going to shut my mouth one way or the other.

"After I even gave you all the information about all these killings, you and the Rangers spent two years almost with the world's most worst killer, and now the Hands of Death is going to win and I can't believe that from law enforcement," Lucas said in the letter to the sheriff. "I guess I didn't tell you they were going to shut my mouth one way or the other."

Judge Allen had had enough of Lucas's media performances. On Thursday he signed an order barring any further media access to McLennan County's star prisoner. The order also prohibited any law enforcement officer from talking with Lucas unless his lawyer was present. On Friday, May 3, the McLennan

County grand jury resumed its deliberations, hearing testimony from Bob and Joyce Lemons, who had moved to Gainesville from Lubbock. Before they went into the fourth-floor grand jury room, the Lemons told reporters they remained convinced that Lucas had not killed their daughter or anyone else.

"I don't believe Henry has ever killed anybody," Lemons said. "I don't think Henry is capable of killing anyone."

Judge Allen's order had the desired chilling effect on publicity in the Lucas case, though things were continuing to happen. The federal investigation into Feazell's conduct in office, begun by Jan Patterson months before the Lucas controversy arose, began to gain momentum. The DPS was assisting her in the investigation. They were investigating various claims that Feazell was taking payment from defense attorneys in exchange for not prosecuting some cases.

In early June, another fight broke out over custody of Lucas. Denton County District Attorney Jerry Cobb got a bench warrant from District Judge Jack Gray in Denton ordering Lucas transferred to the state prison in Huntsville to begin serving his life sentence in Becky Powell's death. But the same day the warrant was issued, Judge Gray withdrew it at the request of the district judge who had sentenced Lucas to death for the "Orange Socks" murder, John Carter. Carter then signed a warrant ordering Lucas returned to Williamson County. Since the McLennan County grand jury investigation was about over, D.A. Feazell didn't try to fight the order that would send Lucas back to the Georgetown jail.

Colonel Adams and several other DPS officers, along with Sheriff Boutwell, appeared voluntarily before the McLennan County grand jury on June 13. Ranger Sergeant Prince spent nearly five hours in the grand jury room, followed by Adams, Bob Werner, assistant chief of criminal law enforcement for the

DPS, Ranger Clayton Smith, DPS Criminal Intelligence agent Ron Boyert, and Sheriff Boutwell.

Attorney General Mattox, back in Waco for the day's grand jury session, led the questioning of Colonel Adams.

Adams told the grand jurors he believed his agency's handling of the Lucas case had been proper. "To this point, I have no indication of any wrongdoing on the part of any Ranger," he said to reporters after his testimony. "I still feel comfortable . . . that Lucas did kill a substantial number of people. I don't think we'll ever know how many."

The day after the Rangers appeared before the grand jury, Lucas was transferred back to Williamson County. Two months earlier, when he'd been transferred to Waco on the bench warrant, the task force still had a list of law enforcement officers waiting to talk with the celebrity prisoner about unsolved cases in their jurisdictions. Sheriff Boutwell and the Rangers had hoped they could gear up operations again, but it was over. In a letter written on June 11, Lucas's new lawyer had put the task force on notice that they were not to talk with Lucas without permission—in effect putting an end to any ongoing investigations.

Since his return from Williamson County, Boutwell had found Lucas to be a changed man. Now he was more like the sort of prisoner Boutwell was used to seeing in his jail—sullen, calculating, ready to tell anyone who listened he was an innocent man, victim of a law enforcement conspiracy. The sheriff, reflecting over his evening sip of bourbon and water, saw a couple of possibilities. Maybe Lucas had finally worked through most of his grief over the killing of Becky, an act for which he had once said he wanted to commit legal suicide in repentence. Now, sobering to the reality that his confessed crimes might actually send him to the death chamber, he saw a chance at reversal of his capital conviction and, incredibly, even the possibility of eventual freedom, through his allegations of a law enforcement hoax. Another possibility was that Lucas had found he could satisfy his thirst to hurt other people in another, bloodless way, through manipulation. Whatever had happened, Boutwell thought, the old Henry was as dead as his victims.

On June 17, one of Lucas's attorneys filed a 1.5-million-dollar federal lawsuit alleging that his client's civil rights had been violated during the time he had been in custody in Williamson County. Named as defendants were Boutwell and Williamson County, Colonel Adams, and the three DPS members of the task force. Specifically, the suit charged that Lucas had been given Thorazine "in order to secure confessions from the defendant," that Lucas had been questioned without having an attorney present, and that he had not been told he did not have to make any statements.

Lucas had been given Thorazine—he had first been treated with the strong tranquilizer while he was in custody in Michigan—only a short time during his stay in Williamson County, and then it had been at his request after he claimed he was suicidal. And Lucas had consistently waived his rights to counsel during questioning by task force members and other officers.

The Waco grand jury was still deliberating, but on June 19 Feazell told a reporter that he did not expect the jury to find fault with the DPS or the Texas Rangers. The jury's concern was whether Lucas should be prosecuted in McLennan County for the three murders he had claimed there.

"From the beginning, we've never been investigating the DPS or the task force," the prosecutor said. "I do not anticipate any allegations of illegality or wrongdoing on the part of the task force."

Less than a week after his lawsuit against Williamson County and the DPS was filed, Lucas, handcuffed and chained at the waist, was transferred from the Williamson County Jail to the state prison in Huntsville. Sheriff Boutwell had escorted Lucas from Florida to California during his confession spree, but he would let his deputies handle Lucas's trip to death row.

But Boutwell stood by as Lucas and some other prisoners were led from the jail to two waiting patrol cars. As Lucas walked past, he fixed his good eye on the tall sheriff, a man he'd once said was one of the few police officers who'd ever treated him with respect.

"I'll be a free man in a month," Lucas sneered.

Boutwell could have said a lot of things, but all he did was look back at Lucas and smile. He was willing to bet Feazell had told Lucas he could end up doing time in some plush federal prison if he cooperated with the grand jury up there in Waco. He'd heard Feazell had told Lucas he could take up golf in federal prison. When Boutwell pictured Lucas on a golf course, his smile got bigger. There wasn't a golf course where he was headed today.

Lucas's transfer, ending what had been the major focus of two years of his life, left Boutwell with mixed emotions. In a way, he was glad his one-time star boarder was gone; throughout Lucas's stay in his jail, Boutwell had worried about his prisoner's security. On the other hand, the sheriff was disappointed the task force would not get to complete its work. The federal lawsuit didn't particularly worry him, but something else did, and it hurt a lot worse than Lucas's taunting good-bye—a lot of murder cases were going to go unsolved.

Lucas made the trip to Huntsville with six other prisoners carried in two patrol cars. A third car followed as a precaution against any escape attempts. They arrived at 12:30 P.M. on Friday, June 21, two years to the day after Lucas had blurted out in open court that he had killed a hundred or more women. Texas Department of Corrections personnel were not particularly impressed by Lucas's celebrity status.

"He's just another death row convict," a prison spokesman told a reporter. "He's number two hundred ten right now."

On July 2, 1985, eighty-three days after it began its examination of Lucas's three McLennan County murder confessions, Feazell's grand jury declined to indict Lucas in any of the cases. The panel had heard from twenty witnesses. Despite the publicity the investigation received in its early stages, the foreman of the grand jury, J. R. Closs, had little to say after informing Judge Allen of the jury's decision. "We're glad we're through and can go back to work, but I don't have any comment at all," Closs said.

Feazell, aware his office was under federal investigation, seemed more careful in his choice of words when talking to reporters than he had been in April. He said the attorney general's office was preparing a report on Lucas's travels since his release from prison in 1975. "I think it will give local authorities some indication of where Henry Lee Lucas was and when instead of having to guess about the validity of his confession," Feazell said.

In Austin, Mattox said he was still concerned about cases having been closed on the basis of Lucas's confessions. "We want to see that the actual murderers are brought to justice," he said.

In Huntsville, Lucas granted his first death row interview. He was not surprised by the Waco grand jury's refusal to indict him. "They know I didn't do the crimes," he said.

Boutwell read the story in his morning paper. Lucas had said he was sorry for all the problems he'd caused.

"I'd like the opportunity to tell the truth," Lucas said. "I've lived a decent life." At that line, the sheriff could only shake his head in wonder.

When the reporter asked Lucas when his next trial would be, Lucas said he expected it to be in El Paso, where he was charged with killing "some old woman who was chopped up with an ax."

CHAPTER TWELVE

First Assistant District Attorney Bill Moody looked up from the yellow legal pad on his desk and allowed his eyes—and his mind—to rest on the view. From his office on the fourth floor of the El Paso County courthouse, Moody could look out on the Franklin Mountains, the foothills of the Rockies. Here, at the far western tip of Texas, the Rio Grande cut through the Franklins on the north and through the Sierra Madres to the south on its way to the Gulf of Mexico. Across the river was Juárez, the largest Mexican city on the border.

Moody pondered the twists of fate that had brought all the players—including himself—on stage for the bizarre drama now unfolding. The thirty-six-year-old prosecutor knew that the pass between the mountains was the source of his county's name and the reason for its existence.

In 1581, the first Spanish explorer who splashed across the Rio Grande where the mountains parted decided to call the place El Paso del Norte (the Pass of the North). The pass quickly became a crossroads for travelers.

For the first two centuries of its history, El Paso was a stopping place on the long journey from Mexico

City to Santa Fe. Later, the axis shifted from north–south to east–west as the pass became the southern-most route connecting the Atlantic seaboard with the Pacific coast.

Part of that same long-ago trail was now Interstate 10, the multilane highway that stretched from Jacksonville, Florida, to San Diego, California. Interstate 10 helped support El Paso's economic life.

Interstate 10 also led Henry Lee Lucas to El Paso.

Moody forced his attention back to his task. Writing in a forceful hand, he drafted the state's brief, the written argument detailing the facts of the case—as he saw them—for the court's consideration. It was the most important brief in his twelve-year career as a prosecutor.

Since joining the staff of District Attorney Steve Simmons in October 1975, Moody had handled more than a hundred jury trials, including thirty homicides. In all five of the capital cases he had prosecuted, the defendant had been convicted and sentenced to death, though none of the executions had yet been carried out.

In case No. 43314-120, *The State of Texas* versus *Henry Lee Lucas,* Moody was seeking his sixth capital conviction. And now it all hinged on admissibility of Lucas's confessions, the subject of his brief.

"In all of American history," Moody began, "there has never been a case even similar to the Henry Lee Lucas case." He continued:

No one has ever confessed to over one hundred murders. No one has ever been believed by over one hundred law enforcement agencies throughout the United States. No one has ever been interrogated by so many law enforcement agencies over such a prolonged period of time. None of the recent serial murderers have confessed and

266

then recanted all of their confessions. Henry Lee Lucas stands alone in the annals of the criminal justice system and there are no cases that this court can look to that even appear similar in nature to the Lucas phenomenon. This Honorable Court is proceeding into a wilderness heretofore never explored.

Moody looked over what he had written and started a new paragraph with a sentence that perfectly summarized the situation: "This court stands face to face with the greatest mass murderer in American history, the greatest liar in American history, or both."

Lt. Jerry Smith had talked with Lucas most of the evening Thursday, September 19, 1984. A detective with the Odessa Police Department, Smith was investigating an unsolved murder in his city, a blue-collar town in the oil-rich Permian Basin in West Texas.

Satisfied that Lucas knew nothing about his case, Smith followed through on a favor for his friend, El Paso Police detective Benito (Benny) Perez. Detective Smith knew Lucas had been interviewed by El Paso officers who visited him at the Georgetown jail in December 1983. On February 14, 1984, Lucas was brought to El Paso in an attempt to have him lead officers to bodies he claimed were buried in the desert. The attempt was unsuccessful.

But Benny Perez had not been one of the officers who talked with Lucas in El Paso. Perez had a hunch. He wanted to question Lucas about the death of Librada Apodaca. Lieutenant Smith asked Lucas if he knew anything about an elderly Mexican woman who had been killed with an ax in her home in El Paso.

"No, I told them [El Paso police] that I was out there but they didn't. . . . They called me a liar so . . ." Lucas trailed off without finishing his thought.

"Sir?" Sometimes the simplest response was the most productive.

Lucas fidgeted in his chair, fishing for a cigarette.

"I told them that I was out there but they called me a liar, so I let it go."

"Is that right? Well, this is some different guys that I talked to," Smith said, thinking of his friend Perez, "and they . . ."

"That's what I call north of El Paso," Lucas interrupted.

Smith took that as an admission that Lucas had something to talk about. He asked Lucas directly, "You chopped the lady up with an ax?"

His reply was confusing, an evasive yes-no answer. But Smith got the impression that Lucas was saying he was involved in something.

"Well . . . I broke in her house."

"Is that right before you [got] locked up?" Smith prompted.

Lucas paused. "About, ah . . . I don't know, about two or three weeks before I got locked up . . . not too long."

"Anything you can tell me [about that] particular murder?" Smith asked.

"Ah, well, the woman was in her bedroom . . . and it seem like I took her out of her bedroom. I think it was in the living room that . . . I killed her at, I don't remember right now. And, ah, I took some jewelry and some money and I can't remember whether I took the television."

Lucas elaborated on the jewelry, which he described as "Mexican jewelry" that looked like silver and had green stones.

"Turquoise?" Smith asked.

"Turquoise, yeah, it had that stuff on it."

Lucas offered a description of the woman. She was about sixty, maybe older. She was five feet two or three inches tall, between one hundred and one hundred twenty pounds. "Skinny-looking, ah, if I can remember," he said. "I did a good job on her, sure did a good job on her." Lucas smiled, exposing his rotting, stained teeth. "I really worked her over."

"What'd you use? Where did you get it?"

Lucas said he'd used an ax he found inside the house. He gave a general description of the residence, an old house, where the murder occurred.

"Oh, I had sex with her, but just sex," he added.

Smith had no jurisdiction in El Paso and did not have any detailed information on the case. Lucas was scheduled to be taken to Sierra Blanca the next day.

"Tell you what I'll do," the detective told Lucas. "I'll call this buddy of mine who works for El Paso Police Department. I'm going to see if I can get him to you."

When Lucas agreed, Smith quickly ended the interview.

By this time, it was 12:30 A.M. Lucas was checked into jail for the night. Smith called El Paso to let Detective Perez know what information he had gained from Lucas during the talk.

"You don't have to play any games with him," Smith told Perez after filling him in on what Lucas had said. "You don't have to break him . . . he's already broke."

The next day, Friday, detective Sgt. Jimmy Apodaca called Assistant D.A. Moody and told him about the Odessa officer's conversation with Lucas.

"Just because he said he killed her, big deal," Moody said. "He's said that about hundreds. What can we corroborate?"

"Perez and I are going to talk to him later today," the detective replied.

"Make sure you tape-record the interview," Moody told him, "and let me know how it turns out."

The two detectives drove the ninety miles from El Paso to Sierra Blanca, in the next county downriver from El Paso. They sat down with Lucas in a room in the county jail and Perez turned on his recorder. He began by giving Lucas the Miranda warning: "You have the right to have a lawyer present . . ."

"I understand my rights," Lucas replied. "I know them by heart." Being "Mirandaized" had become a familiar ritual for him.

"You can proceed with the interview, Mr. Lucas," Perez began formally.

"Well, it starts before I was arrested [June 11, 1983]," Lucas said. "This was when I was coming back from Tucson, Arizona. I had been out there running around, and I came back into El Paso and left Interstate Ten. . . . And I traveled about thirty . . . thirty minutes off of Interstate Ten, driving around in different neighborhoods. And I ended up on this one street, so I decided that I'd park the car and get out and walk."

Lucas said he was looking for a house where no one was home.

"And I come up on this one house and I could see a light on in it, you know, and, uh . . . I couldn't see nobody moving around in the house nowhere so I figured they just left the light on for security. So, I went on round back of the house and went in the little walkway there behind the house and went up, I think, two steps or something like that and went in the kitchen door. It was open, so I went on in.

"I got through into the living room, and I heard a noise. I went to where I heard the noise from, which was the bedroom, and as soon as I walked in the door of the bedroom, why, the woman jumped by the bed and run. She run right by me.

"When she did, she pushed me back against the edge of the wall. There's an ax fell on me," Lucas continued. "And I grabbed the ax and took after her, you know. And I caught her just before she got to the front door of the house and, when she did, I hit her, pretty close to centerways of the back with the ax. And, uh, she screamed . . . and she fell towards the, uh, center part of the living room and when she did, I hit her, I think, four maybe five times after that, with the ax. And, there was blood spewed on me and on her and I went, you know, where's her body. I took and had sex with it after that. . . ."

Lucas told the officers that after he was finished, he walked back into the woman's bedroom, carrying the bloody ax.

"I got to thinking, you know, I said, well, I better wash up."

He put the ax down and went into the bathroom to wash the blood off his face, arms, and hands.

After cleaning up, he walked back into the bedroom and started looking around for anything of value. He took some money from her purse, which was on a nightstand, and found some old silver coins in her closet.

He went into the woman's dining room, where he noticed a radio on a table. He collected that and a few other items.

"From there I went back into the living room and . . . checked her to see if she was dead. And she was, so I . . . went on back out through the back of the house."

Outside, Lucas switched the radio on to see if it played. "It did. I went on down the street playing the radio till [I] got to my car."

Lucas talked nonstop.

"Do you remember the clothing . . . that the lady had?" Perez asked when Lucas showed signs of running down.

"Yeah, it was, uh, a pink, uh, slip, an old pair, I called them an old pair, it's an old-fashioned pair of white panties."

"What did you do with the clothing?"

"I think I just took them off and threw them down there on the floor," Lucas said.

Lucas said that after leaving El Paso he crossed the state line into New Mexico. He headed north to San Jon, on I-40, twenty-three miles east of Tucumcari, where he abandoned his red-and-white 1973 Pontiac.

"Yeah, I blew the engine up in the car. I took my clothes out, some of them anyway, and, uh, took them back to Stoneburg."

The interview had lasted ten minutes. Perez switched off the recorder.

Listening to Lucas describe the murder, Benny Perez and Jimmy Apodaca began to believe Lucas was the killer. With no prompting from them, he had fairly well described the way they believed Librada Apodaca had died. The elderly woman's panties had been found next to her body and her nightgown had been pulled up, just like Lucas had said.

The seventy-two-year-old, known as "Grandma" to her large family, had been brutally slain by multiple blows to her head with a small ax or hatchet. She'd been sexually assaulted after her death. She died sometime between 9 P.M. and midnight on May 27, 1983. A neighbor found her body sprawled on the living room floor the following morning and called the El Paso Police Department.

In America's largest border city, where almost two-thirds of the population is of Hispanic descent, Apodaca is not an uncommon surname. The El Paso telephone directory listed more than a column with nearly as many listings in Juárez. In this instance, however, the fact that both the victim and the investigating officer had the same last name was more than a coincidence. Jimmy Apodaca was a nephew of the slain woman.

After viewing the crime scene at the home he knew

so well, Sergeant Apodaca approached Lt. John Lanahan, chief of his Crimes Against Persons division, and requested permission to stay on the case in spite of the family relationship.

"Can you treat it like any other case?" Lanahan asked.

"Yes," Apodaca replied.

The detectives called Assistant D.A. Moody to fill him in on Lucas's statement.

"Bring Lucas to El Paso to see if he can direct you to the crime scene," the prosecutor recommended.

Ranger Clayton Smith told the El Paso detectives Lucas was being flown to Brownfield that night for a court appearance the next day.

"But I'll make arrangements for Lucas to be taken to El Paso as soon as they're through with him in Brownfield," the Ranger promised.

Shortly after Perez and Apodaca finished their interview, the Department of Public Safety plane carrying Lucas and the Ranger left Sierra Blanca. They arrived in Brownfield, southwest of Lubbock, a few minutes after midnight.

The next day, under heavy security, Lucas was escorted into the courtroom of District Judge Ray Anderson. He pleaded guilty to the April 26, 1981, murder of seventeen-year-old Brownfield high school student Dianna Bryant.

The teenager, who worked at a fried chicken franchise, had taken a last-minute baby-sitting job for her younger sister, who had not been available that night. When the mother of the two young children Dianna had been taking care of came home around midnight, she found the teenager dead in her bedroom. The children, a four-year-old boy and a two-year-old girl, were asleep in their beds, unharmed. Dianna, fully clothed except for her shoes and socks, was lying facedown between a chest of drawers and the doorway of the room. She had been strangled with a vacuum cleaner cord.

The murder had gone unsolved until May 17, 1984, when Lucas—who was being taken through West Texas on a case-clearing swing—led a Brownfield officer and a Texas Ranger to the apartments where the murder had occurred. He was unable to point out the exact apartment, but he had directed the officers to the complex with ease. Back at the police station, Lucas said he had killed Dianna while passing through Brownfield with Toole, Becky, and her little brother, Frank Powell.

They had stopped at a barbeque restaurant for coffee, a restaurant Lucas had described before arriving in Brownfield. He and Toole decided to look for a place to break in. They drove around town until they came to the apartment complex, picked a door, and knocked. When a teenage girl answered the door, he said, he asked for something to eat. She let them inside, he said, and made him and Toole a sandwich while pouring cereal for Becky and Frank. Officers had found a bowl of cereal overturned on the kitchen floor.

In his confession Lucas said he used his knife to cut a piece of cord from a vacuum cleaner in the apartment and choked the teenager. Officers had found a vacuum cleaner in the apartment that someone had cut the cord from. After she was dead, he said, he undressed her and had sex with her. For reasons he didn't explain, he said he then put her clothes back on the body. The autopsy indicated she had had sexual intercourse shortly before her death.

A month after his visit to Brownfield, Lucas was interviewed again and signed a written confession. Now, four months after leading officers to the apartment complex where Dianna was killed, Lucas was back to plead guilty to the case. Judge Anderson accepted the plea and sentenced Lucas to seventy-five years in prison. At the task force office in Georgetown, the Bryant case was listed as the 150th homicide attributed to the Lucas-Toole crime spree.

By midday that Thursday, pilot-investigator Jim Field and Ranger Smith had Lucas back in El Paso. After meeting up with Benny Perez, Jimmy Apodaca, and detective Ed Uribe, the men got into two un-marked police cars. Lucas said he could direct the officers to the house where he killed the woman. Perez drove one car, with Lucas sitting in the front. Detective Uribe and Ranger Smith sat in the back. Field rode with Jimmy Apodaca in the second car.

"Where do you want to start?" Perez asked.

"Let's go to the truck stop," Lucas said.

The detective got onto I-10, which cuts across El Paso, and headed east.

Lucas swung his head back and forth, surveying the route with his one eye.

"How fast should I drive?" Perez asked.

"You're fast enough."

The detective was in the right-hand lane, doing about forty-five miles an hour.

"Get off here," Lucas said, pointing to the Lomaland exit.

Perez drove toward a school.

"This is the wrong way," Lucas said. "Get back on the access road."

Suddenly, Perez sensed that Lucas was tensing up. For a second, he wondered if Lucas was going to make a foolish grab for his gun. Then he saw the hitchhikers—a man and a woman. Lucas had snapped his attention on them like a birddog coming to point.

"She would have been mine," Lucas said, his good eye zeroed in on the woman.

Perez shook his head, fascinated by the little man sitting next to him in the police car.

Farther east, Lucas told Perez to turn. They headed

south, toward the Spanish settlement of Ysleta, the oldest town in Texas, a community long-since absorbed by the city of El Paso.

Lucas's head continued to move back and forth, like a radar antenna. Lucas told the detective to keep driving around the area. They passed Irma, the short street where Mrs. Apodaca had lived.

"Stop," Lucas told Perez about a block from the crime scene.

Lucas got out of the car and started walking toward the house. The officers followed closely behind.

As Lucas and the officers walked down the unpaved street, several dogs started barking. Perez looked around for a stick in case one of the strays attacked.

"Dogs don't bother me—you watch," Lucas said.

As Lucas approached, the dogs fell silent.

Lucas looked around for a moment and then walked directly to 144 Irma. Only three structures were on the street; Lucas went straight to the one that had been Librada Apodaca's home.

Lucas pointed to a window.

"That's the room that had a light on," he said. "This is the house, but something's changed."

The two officers had been to the house many times in the eighteen months since the murder. In May 1983, when Mrs. Apodaca was killed, there had been a picket fence around her house. Now the property was enclosed by a chainlink fence. Something else had changed—the house was occupied again.

Before letting Lucas in the house, Perez and Apodaca asked him to draw them a diagram of the house's interior. Lucas reversed the location of two rooms in the house, but otherwise his drawing matched very closely, even to the location of furniture.

When the officers knocked, a little girl came to the front door. Perez showed the child his badge.

"Call your mother and ask if it's all right if we come inside."

The mother, who worked nearby, came home immediately.

Inside, Lucas led the officers step-by-step through what he remembered of the murder. Standing in the hall, Lucas said, "This is where I got her." The spot Lucas indicated was where officers had found blood on the ceiling, as if someone had swung a wet paintbrush in an arc. The stains were gone now. Perez noted that Lucas was off by four or five feet in showing them where he had left Mrs. Apodaca's body.

The officers took Lucas back downtown to the police station and Perez called Assistant D.A. Moody.

"Jeez, he got us to the exact house," Perez told the prosecutor.

Moody was impressed. He had not expected Lucas to be able to take officers to the street, much less the house. He doubted he could have driven to the crime scene, though he had been in El Paso many years.

Lucas's account of the crime to Perez and Apodaca varied in some details from the story he'd told Lt. Jerry Smith in Odessa.

Standing in the victim's house, Lucas recalled that Mrs. Apodaca had confronted him in the kitchen. He'd grabbed a hatchet located near the refrigerator and started swinging at her. She ran from him, Lucas said, and he chased her from the kitchen to the bedroom to the living room.

In the living room, he said, he hit her in the back of the head "four or five times." He pulled off her pants and "had sex with her."

Lucas had told Lieutenant Smith he'd heard a noise in the bedroom, found Mrs. Apodaca there, and that an ax "fell on me" during the struggle that followed.

"Okay, let's do a video confession," Moody said. "I'm going to come watch."

Later that day, Moody sat behind a one-way mirror. He watched and listened as Lucas told his story once again, this time before a video camera.

Moody had been skeptical since first hearing that Lucas had claimed Mrs. Apodaca's murder. But after viewing Lucas's confession, he was convinced that the slight, one-eyed man on the other side of the mirror knew things about the case no one but the killer could have known.

The problem now was how to prove that to a jury.

On September 21, 1984, based on Lucas's admission to Lieutenant Smith in Odessa, his taped statement to Benny Perez and Jimmy Apodaca in Sierra Blanca, the fact that he had been able to lead officers to Mrs. Apodaca's house, and his detailed videotaped confession, Lucas was charged with capital murder in Mrs. Apodaca's death.

Despite Lucas's willingness to confess to Mrs. Apodaca's murder, Moody wanted his case to stand on more than the word of a convicted killer. On instructions from Moody, the detectives had fished for more detailed information in their videotaped interview with Lucas.

When they asked Lucas what he had done after the murder, he offered some interesting information not previously mentioned.

"After leaving the house, I did go back to the truck stop and sat in there talking to a girl . . . trying to get her to go with me. She wouldn't go."

Lucas said he talked with a couple of waitresses at the truck stop and sold them some household items he had taken from Mrs. Apodaca's house. He was hazy on what he'd sold, but he remembered one of the waitresses well, describing her as "real foxy."

As Perez listened to Lucas he realized there were three truck stops on the eastern edge of El Paso where Lucas could have gone. In an effort to pin down the right one, Perez asked Lucas to draw a sketch of the truck stop. Lucas did two drawings: one of the interior, indicating where he'd sat to drink coffee, and one of the exterior, showing where he'd parked his car. The sketches were remarkably similar to a Chevron truck stop at 6666 Gateway East and I-10, the truck stop closest to the scene of the crime.

On the way back to police headquarters with Lucas, Perez drove past the Chevron truck stop. "I think I sold some of the stuff there," Lucas said. "I'm not sure what it was. Something fairly large. But the girl was real foxy."

Lucas's statement was Detective Perez's first clue regarding the disposition of property stolen from the home of Mrs. Apodaca.

As soon as he could, Perez went to the truck stop and talked to the manager, who was able to give him the names of the waitresses who had been working for him in the spring of 1983. All of them had since moved on to other jobs. Perez and the manager spent most of a day digging around in a storage shed for payroll records that would document who had been on duty around the time of Mrs. Apodaca's murder.

Within a few days, Perez found one of the women, twenty-seven-year-old Katherine Watson, in El Paso, working for another restaurant. He called her and asked if she would come down to the police station to look at some pictures as part of an investigation. She agreed and they set up an appointment.

Katherine Watson had seen some of the newspaper and TV coverage of Lucas and his mass murder confessions, but she had not paid much attention to the stories. When she went to the police station on October 4, she had no idea that she might somehow figure into one of his cases. That's the way Detective Perez had wanted it. The detective asked her if she remembered ever having been approached at the truck stop where she used to work by someone trying to sell her something. She immediately recalled an incident around Memorial Day weekend in 1983.

She had been working a 6:00 P.M. to 4:00 A.M. shift on May 28 that year, she told the detective. Sometime after midnight on the morning of May 29 she saw a man sitting at the counter in the restaurant drinking coffee. She didn't pay much attention to him, but recalled later that the place was pretty quiet. The normal rush that came after the bars closed had not yet materialized and never did that night.

Kelly McMurray, one of the waitresses, came back to the restaurant office and told Katherine that a man out front had some things for sale cheap, including a vacuum cleaner. Kelly said she wanted a vacuum cleaner but didn't know anything about them and asked if Katherine would take a look at the one the man had for sale.

"So I told her sure," Katherine later recalled. "So I went on up front . . . and talked to him. And then he went out to get the vacuum cleaner and bring it in."

The two women took the vacuum back to the office, plugged it in, and turned it on. Seeing that it worked fine, Katherine told Kelly it seemed like a good deal.

When they went back out in the restaurant, the man said he also had a portable stereo for sale. Katherine said she was interested, but the man said it was too bulky to carry into the restaurant.

"So I told him I'd go on out to his car and look at it with him," Katherine recalled. "So we went out to the car, and he pulled the stereo out, and I took a look at it."

She described the stereo as "kind of old with speakers that folded out and a turntable that came down, and it was a blackish gray color with specks."

The man, who hadn't given them his name, took the stereo out of his car and set it down in the parking lot. Katherine noticed the large-size car, an older model, was full of trash. She thought someone must have been living in it.

Katherine decided to pass on the stereo, but Kelly bought the vacuum cleaner and a Crockpot. Back inside, Katherine told another waitress "there's a guy up there that's got an iron for sale." The waitress went out and looked at it and decided to buy it.

Now, eighteen months later, Detective Perez showed Katherine a collection of six photographs. She looked at the half-dozen male faces for a moment, then pointed to one of them. That was the man who had been in the truck stop that night, she was pretty sure. Perez tried not to show his elation. The man she had picked was Henry Lee Lucas.

Assistant D. A. Moody, too, was delighted with the development. The state now had an eyewitness placing Lucas in El Paso around the time of the murder. If they could find Kelly McMurray, there was a chance she still might have the items she bought that night. If those items could be identified as having belonged to Mrs. Apodaca, Moody would have physical evidence to take to court.

Later that month, on October 26, Moody arranged for Lucas to appear before the El Paso County grand jury. Lucas again freely admitted the ax murder of the elderly woman, though it was not admissible as evidence. He was the only witness to testify, but his twenty-minute testimony was enough to convince the twelve members of the panel that Lucas needed to be tried for the murder—they returned an indictment against him.

Moody realized that Lucas's lawyers had received a tremendous boost with the massive publicity surrounding their client's recanting of his confessions and the attorney general's investigation into the handling of the whole affair. When Lucas went to trial in

El Paso, for all practical purposes he would be on trial for all of his confessed murders. To counter the hoax defense Moody decided to bring to El Paso officers from across the country who believed they had strong cases against Lucas. That would make for a long trial, but in the end, Moody felt, it would tear down Lucas's defense.

In June, Moody, Simmons, Joe Avalos, chief investigator for the D. A.'s office, and Texas Ranger Calvin Collins, the Ranger stationed in El Paso, left on a multistate fact-finding trip. Moody already had been collecting everything he could get on Lucas by mail, including a transcript of his 1960 trial for his mother's murder.

The four El Paso men went to Austin, Georgetown, Waco, Dallas, and Longview in Texas before crossing over into Louisiana to meet with officers in Monroe. From there they went to Vicksburg, Mississippi, and then back to Louisiana for a visit with detectives in New Orleans. Back in Texas, they stopped in Houston, Waco, Lubbock, and Midland before returning to El Paso.

Armed with case reports and commitments from more than a score of peace officers willing to testify if they were needed, Moody ended the trip with a feeling of confidence that he had more than enough evidence to contest the hoax allegations. Moody felt that Lucas had tried to claim some cases that weren't his, but the prosecutor was convinced the one-eyed little man had killed many people, including Mrs. Apodaca. In fact, the deeper he got into the preparation of his case, the more he came to believe that the ax murder had probably been Lucas's last bloody fling before his arrest in Montague County. Even though he felt good about his case, he was realistic enough to realize it was not going to be an easy conviction. He didn't like it, but he was dealing with more than a set of disputed facts and points of law. With the state attorney general involved, and the lure of statewide and national publicity, the Lucas case had become more than a mass murder investigation. It was a political issue, in El Paso County and statewide.

The small, bare room had pale blue walls. Sheriff Leo Samaniego's jail was overflowing, but he had allowed this little room to be converted into a chapel, a dust speck of tranquility amid the constant swirl of chaos at the county lockup.

Lucas had complained almost constantly since his September 7 transfer from Huntsville to El Paso to prepare for his trial. He had finally asked for something Sheriff Samaniego could easily allow: he wanted to be baptized.

Sister Clemmie Schroeder worked with a local pastor who conducted an interdenominational ministry at the jail to arrange for the ceremony. On Sunday, December 1, 1985, Lucas, clad in an orange county jail uniform, presented himself to receive the sacrament of baptism. As three jail guards, a newspaper reporter, several members of Lucas's defense team, and Sister Clemmie looked on, the minister fully immersed Lucas in the baptismal font. Carefully raising the dripping Lucas from the water, the minister then gave him his first communion as a new Christian.

For his Bible reading, the minister selected a passage from Acts 16:26, which deals with the Apostle Paul's imprisonment in Macedonia.

"And suddenly there was a great earthquake, so that the foundations of the prison were shaken; and immediately all the doors were opened, and every one's bands were loosed."

After the half-hour ceremony, the guards hurried Lucas out of the chapel and back to his eighth-floor cell, where he was being kept in solitary confinement.

* * *

On August 9, 1986, more than three years after Mrs. Apodaca's murder, the public learned something that El Paso police and the D.A.'s office had known for some time: Henry Lucas was not the only person who had confessed to the old woman's murder. Moody put no stock in it, but it was a wonderful development for Lucas's defense lawyers and it made a sensational newspaper story: LUCAS CASE GETS BIZARRE TWIST.

In the first few months after the murder, Mrs. Apodaca's nephew, Sgt. Jimmy Apodaca, and other detectives worked their way down a long list of possible suspects in the murder.

One who had looked promising at first was a Mexican national, Geovany Chavez, who had done some gardening work for Mrs. Apodaca the week of her murder. Sgt. Apodaca contacted a counterpart with the Juárez, Mexico, police and asked him to check the man out. Hauled in for questioning, Chavez denied any involvement in the case. Since Chavez was a homosexual, and because the murder victim had been sexually assaulted, the detective tended to believe the man was telling the truth when he denied all knowledge of the ax murder. Still, just to examine every possible lead, Sergeant Apodaca and another El Paso detective, Joe Bailon, crossed the Rio Grande to talk with the man themselves.

This time Chavez was arrested for questioning by Chihuahua State Judicial Police. They drove him to an area of sand hills near the city dump, west of Juárez, with the two El Paso city officers following in their vehicle.

Chavez was pulled from the car still denying he was involved in Mrs. Apodaca's murder.

"Then they told him to take his pants down and one of the Juárez policemen took an electric cattle prod from the trunk of his car," Apodaca recalled in a deposition taken by Lucas's lawyers. "The Juárez officer held the cattle prod against [the suspect's] genitals and he screamed, 'I did it, I did it, I did it.'"

Apodaca asked the Mexican officers to stop and then asked the half-naked man to give him the details of the murder.

"I went in through the window," the man gasped. "I went to where the old lady was in bed and I killed her."

Chavez told Apodaca he stabbed the woman to death, stole a television set, and left the house.

As much as the El Paso detective wanted to believe that the man actually did what he was claiming, what he said did not match the facts of the case. For one thing, Chavez said he stabbed the woman with a knife. The El Paso officers knew she had been killed with an ax.

"Did you really kill her?" Apodaca asked the man when the Mexican officers had finished with him.

"I did not commit the murder," he panted in Spanish. "I swear on my mother. I swear to God, I swear to all the saints. The only reason I said that I had killed the old lady was because they put that thing on me just now."

"We took him back to the Juárez police station and released him," Sgt. Apodaca said in the deposition.

Three days later, Geovany Chavez was dead, kicked and beaten to death in Juárez after he had broken into a home and stolen a shirt and 10,000 pesos, about $15.

Sergeant Apodaca, notified of the death, said Chavez's slaying was not related to the investigation of Mrs. Apodaca's murder.

"As far as I know, he [Chavez] died after fighting with another man," Apodaca said.

In most murder trials pretrial hearings are dispensed with in fairly short order. But when another round of hearings began on September 8, 1986, Judge Brunson Moore, who was eager "to get the case tried and over with," estimated the process might take up to ten weeks. Between them, the defense and the prosecution had subpoenaed 350 witnesses.

Court-appointed attorneys for Lucas filed a motion protesting the fact that the slain woman's nephew, Sergeant Jimmy Apodaca, was one of the principal investigating officers. The defense also moved to have Lucas's confessions to the slaying of Librada Apodaca ruled inadmissible.

The hearings were crucial for both sides in the Lucas case. The defense believed that if the motion to suppress Lucas's confessions were granted, the prosecution's case would virtually be gutted.

Since Lucas began spewing out his grisly stream of confessions, he had been convicted in ten cases, beginning with the murder of eighty-year-old Kate Rich. In addition to his convictions in the murder of Becky Powell and Orange Socks, he was under a life sentence on a guilty plea to the August 9, 1970, stabbing death of twenty-six-year-old math teacher Linda Phillips in Kaufman County, Texas; a life sentence for the August 3, 1976, shooting death of Clemmie E. Curtis, a Cabell County, West Virginia, police officer; a sixty-year sentence for the November 1, 1977, rape and fatal shooting of eighteen-year-old Lillie Pearl Darty in Harrison County, Texas; seventy-five years for the strangulation of Dianna Bryant in Brownfield, Texas; life for the December 19, 1982, stabbing death in Hale County, Texas, of sixty-six-year-old Glenna Biggers, who had been found with a 14-inch knife impaled in her lower abdomen and a three-pronged fork protruding from her neck; life for the March 17, 1983, murder of an unidentified female in Montgomery County, Texas, and life for the April 18, 1983, murder of sixteen-year-old Laura Jean Domez, also in Montgomery County. Including his mother's murder, Henry Lee Lucas had been convicted in eleven homicides. Bill Moody hoped the Librada Apodaca case would be conviction number twelve.

A few days before testimony was to begin in the hearings, a reporter for the El Paso *Times* got a telephone interview with Lucas. In a statement that sounded like it had been scripted for him, Lucas said, "This is the most important part for me because this is my first trial after I recanted my confessions, and I feel that the truth will finally be brought forward."

Prosecutor Moody had a statement of his own: "This may be the last Lucas trial. We're going for the death penalty."

As part of his preparation for Lucas's trial, Moody had gone over the transcript of the "Orange Socks" trial. The rules of impeachment, he felt, had been stretched to the limit when the criminal records of the former roofing company employees had been allowed into evidence. He was fearful the only capital case against Lucas might be reversed on appeal. The El Paso case, he believed, was insurance against even the faint possibility that Henry Lee Lucas would ever be set free.

Extraordinary precautions were taken to assure Lucas's safety in the courtroom. Sheriff's deputies searched everyone who entered and plainclothes deputies were posted throughout the room.

Lucas watched with one eye and a smile that seemed almost gentle as the courtroom drama played out around him. Dressed in gray pants, navy blazer, and navy sneakers, he appeared to distance himself from the proceedings.

The hearing continued through Monday, November 3. Judge Moore set jury selection in the trial for January 12, 1987, but made no immediate ruling in the defense's motion to suppress Lucas's confession, asking for briefs from both sides.

Seventy-five witnesses, including El Paso officers, Lucas task force members, Sister Clemmie, Vic Feazell, and finally the victim's daughter, had testified during the long hearing. At one point the defense had issued a subpoena for Governor Mark White to testify about the task force, but it was later withdrawn. In addition to the witnesses, 153 exhibits were introduced.

"I think every legal, criminal question has been brought up in this case so far," Moore said at the conclusion of the hearing.

Indeed, the pretrial proceedings had covered much of the ground that would be expected to come up in Lucas's trial. Not only had the admissibility of his confessions been explored, various other defense points had been developed, including the possibility that Lucas had still been at the House of Prayer in Montague County when Librada Apodaca was murdered.

Rueben Moore and the former Faye Munnerlyn, whom he had married since Lucas's 1983 arrest, had testified that Lucas did not leave the House of Prayer until sometime in early June 1982—after the Apodaca murder. They had produced crude work records showing Lucas was helping Moore on a roofing job in north Texas around the time of the ax slaying in El Paso.

However, when Moody and Simmons had talked with Moore while preparing the state's case, Moore had not offered any work records and had said he could not remember the exact date Lucas left the House of Prayer. The work records had not come up until an investigator for Lucas's defense lawyers went to Stoneburg.

A hope for more physical evidence in the case had died with a Department of Public Safety laboratory report which said semen traces found on Librada Apodaca's underwear could not be matched to Lucas, since, as a nonsecretor, his blood type could not be determined from body fluids.

Other items of evidence were more promising. The Crockpot had still been in the possession of the waitress who said she bought it from Lucas; family members had identified it as having belonged to Librada Apodaca. Though the stereo had not been found, family members would be able to testify that the elderly woman had owned a portable stereo that resembled the one Lucas had tried to sell and that the stereo was not in the house when they went through Apodaca's effects after her death. The vacuum cleaner was never located.

Moody also had the odometer removed from the car Lucas had abandoned in New Mexico, which had been impounded and was still in storage. A comparison with the mileage on the car when Lucas left it and the mileage recorded when Lucas took the car in for inspection in May 1982 showed he had traveled many miles in a short period of time—enough for several trips from Stoneburg to El Paso.

But as he completed his brief, Moody worried not so much about the facts of the case as he did about the perceptions created and questions raised during all the pretrial maneuvering. The $500,000 cost to the County of El Paso in prosecuting Lucas and paying for his defense had become a political issue, duly reported in the press. The defense had succeeding in raising the issue of other possible suspects in the ax murder, suspects previously considered and rejected by El Paso police. The controversy over Lucas's claims that he had pulled a massive scam on the law enforcement community by falsely confessing to scores of murders was also of great concern. Picking a jury would be a nightmare after all the publicity—if the case ever got to a jury.

The heart of Moody's brief was the state's contention that Lucas, a hardened criminal, was well aware of his legal rights and that Lucas "knowingly, voluntarily, and intelligently waived his rights to an attorney" in making his confessions in the Apodaca case. "The record," Moody continued, "is replete with sworn testimony to the effect that on many occasions Lucas stated that he did not desire the services of an attorney prior to or during questioning as he did not like attorneys."

Moody had introduced tapes of radio evangelist Bob Larsen's jail interview with Lucas in April 1985 in which he said, "I have lawyers. I don't talk to them. I don't communicate with them. I don't have a reason for a lawyer. Jesus is my lawyer. He's the one that guides me—he tells me what to do and what not to do."

The prosecutor concluded his brief with the plea that the court allow a jury to determine "once and for all time if Henry Lee Lucas is guilty or not guilty."

Either way it turned out, Moody's brief was his last official connection to the case. On December 1, he was sworn in as judge of the 34th Judicial District in El Paso County, appointed by Governor Mark White to fill an unexpired term vacated with the previous judge's appointment to an appeal's court seat. Someone else in the D.A.'s office would continue with the Lucas case.

On December 19, Judge Moore ruled that Lucas's confessions to the murder of Librada Apodaca were not admissible as evidence. Lucas's confessions, Moore ruled, had been "obtained from him without the knowing and voluntary waiver by the defendant of his right to counsel and his right to remain silent. . . ."

In addition, the judge said, "The benefits Lucas received while a prisoner of the Lucas Task Force were positive and apparently were a reward to him for his continued confessions. It seems clear to this court that many of his confessions are false."

Judge Moore, it seemed, had made up his mind

about Henry Lee Lucas. He just did not believe the one-time drifter had killed Apodaca. To allow a jury a chance at reaching the same conclusion would take a lot of his time, a lot of the state's time, and a lot of the county's money.

After Moore handed down the ruling, a reporter asked assistant prosecutor Richard Jewkes where the case stood without Lucas's confessions.

"We're going to have to sit down and evaluate this case based on what we have left," Jewkes said. "We'll have to see where we stand."

Everyone connected to the case already knew the answer, though Jewkes had chosen not to say it publicly just yet. The hope of getting a capital murder conviction on Lucas in El Paso County was dead.

Eleven days later, Judge Moore provided the judicial coup de grace by signing an order dismissing the murder complaint against Lucas. That didn't make him a free man, but Lucas had no more legal problems in El Paso County.

"This case is over and we're kind of glad it is," Moore told a reporter later that day.

Not everyone was glad the case was over, particularly in the part of the courthouse occupied by District Attorney Steve Simmons and his staff. On January 22, 1987, the El Paso *Herald-Post* published one of the more remarkable essays in Texas legal history: NO DOUBTS: DISTRICT ATTORNEY STEVE SIMMONS SPEAKS OUT ON HENRY LEE LUCAS CASE.

"El Paso juries have sentenced several defendants to their deaths on less evidence that we had in the Apodaca case," the D.A. wrote. "It was a solid case, based on extensive corroboration of Lucas's confession, coupled with eyewitnesses and physical evidence linking Lucas to the crime."

The D.A. proceeded to outline his case against Lucas, including fifteen corroborated elements in Lucas's confessions: 1) Lucas led officers to the crime scene; 2) he knew there had been an old wooden fence next to the house, a fence that had been removed by the time he took officers there; 3) he said he stole turquoise jewelry from the house—shortly after the murder, officers had found a turquoise earring near the fence; 4) he said he took a silver box containing coins from the chest of drawers in Apodaca's room, and family members confirmed the box and coins were missing and that Mrs. Apodaca had kept them in her dresser; 5) from outside the house he correctly pointed out the room where the assault had occurred; 6) he correctly showed officers where he left the ax; 7) he did an accurate drawing of the house before seeing it; 8) he correctly described the Ysleta area of El Paso before he led officers there; 9) he recalled pulling down a bedcover in a spare bedroom, which was the way officers found it; 10) he accurately described the truck stop waitresses he said he sold some of Apodaca's property to, enabling police to locate the witnesses and recover some of the property; 11) he knew Apodaca had been attacked first in her bedroom and fled to the living room; 12) he said Apodaca fell over something as he struck her with the ax, and police found a small broken bench with a lot of blood around it; 13) Lucas accurately described Apodaca's clothing; 14) he correctly described pulling up her gown and throwing her panties on the floor next to her body; and 15) he correctly recalled that one light had been on inside the house at the time of the murder.

"While Lucas may have fabricated or falsely confessed to some other murders," Simmons wrote, "there is no doubt in my mind that Lucas killed Apodaca and dozens of other innocent women throughout the United States, his first murder being that of his own mother. . . . I shall not apologize for doing my sworn duty in prosecuting a convicted serial murderer."

* * *

More than 750 miles from El Paso, in his cell on death row, Henry Lee Lucas raised nicotine-stained fingers to his mouth and took a drag off one of the many Pall Malls he smoked every day. His good eye stared off into space, as empty of any emotion as death itself.

EPILOGUE

On July 7, 1988—more than three years after he claimed all his confessions were a hoax—Henry Lee Lucas started talking about murders again.

Since his transfer from Williamson County to death row at the state prison in Huntsville in the summer of 1985, Lucas had virtually disappeared from the headlines. And in the aftermath of the unsuccessful effort to prosecute Lucas in the Librada Apodaca murder, no other jurisdiction chose to attempt another prosecution. But despite his contention that the only person he ever really killed was his mother, not all law enforcement agencies lost interest in him.

Florida Department of Law Enforcement Special Agent Joe Mitchell of Tallahassee, one of the department's first six agents when it was created in 1959, remained particularly keen on Lucas and Toole and their possible connection to several unsolved homicides in the Florida panhandle.

Mitchell was especially interested in a case in Holmes County. On February 10, 1981, nineteen-year-old Jerilyn Murphy Peoples, married only a year, dropped her husband off at a neighbor's house after they'd gone to the grocery store together. She went on to their rural residence to unload the groceries.

Her husband got a ride home a short time later with

a friend. When he arrived, he was startled to find their front door ajar. Groceries were scattered on the floor and a trail of blood led outside. He rushed back out, yelling to stop his friend from driving away. They began a frantic search for Jerilyn Peoples. Moments later, her husband found her slumped over in the passenger side of their car, shot several times.

Peoples was rushed to a hospital in Bonifay, Florida, but attempts to revive her were unsuccessful. She had not been able to say who attacked her.

Sheriff's deputies and FDLE agents surmised that Mrs. Peoples had startled an intruder when she came home. She was shot inside the residence and then dragged back to her car, the killer evidently planning to steal the car and take her, too. When the killer saw the vehicle with her husband and his friend approaching, he slipped off into the nearby woods, they believed.

The investigation stalled out, but in March 1988, Agent Mitchell, who had been asked to take a look at the seven-year-old case, met with the Holmes County sheriff and his chief deputy. After reading the original offense reports, Mitchell and the sheriff's chief deputy concluded the killer—or killers—of Mrs. Peoples had not been from Holmes County.

In looking over a summary of Florida cases claimed by Ottis Toole, Mitchell saw one that looked similar to the Peoples slaying, but the location was off. He knew that in 1981 Lucas and Toole had traveled with Becky Powell and her younger brother, Frank. Mitchell also knew what had happened to Becky. Frank, on the other hand, had ended up in a foster home. The veteran investigator began to wonder if Frank could shed any light on the case.

As long as Frank was a minor, the identity of his foster parents was not even available to law enforcement officers. But now that Frank had turned eighteen, state juvenile officials were free to disclose where he could be located. On May 21, 1988, agent Mitchell had his first meeting with Frank Powell; ten days later, they met again. It was clear to Mitchell that Frank Powell's travels with Lucas and Toole had left him traumatized. The young man's foster father told Mitchell he had frequently awakened his adopted son from screaming nightmares. When Mitchell talked with Powell, he moved slowly, building the young man's trust.

Mitchell's next step was a prison visit with Toole. Prison life had not been easy on Ottis Elwood Toole. Other prisoners, knowing of Toole's claim to have killed young Adam Walsh, a six-year-old Florida boy who vanished in 1981, urinated on Toole through the bars of his cell or tossed food on him. (Walsh was the son of John Walsh, who would become the host of the "America's Most Wanted" crime-stopper TV series. Toole's confession to the celebrated murder, which was the basis of a television docudrama, was never taken seriously by Hollywood, Florida, police and the case remains unsolved.) With Toole's prison treatment in mind, Special Agent Mitchell tried to treat Toole with respect. When Mitchell left the prison, he had a signed confession to Peoples's murder. In his statement Toole recalled that Peoples had been carrying a bag of groceries and that he shot her with a rifle. Lucas, Becky, and Frank Powell were present at the time, he said.

On June 30, 1988, Mitchell, having won Frank Powell's confidence, took a statement from the young man in which he "advised that he was present during the burglary of the Peoples home. Powell further stated that Lucas and Toole are responsible for Peoples's death inasmuch as Peoples surprised Lucas and Toole during the burglary."

Finally, Mitchell and another agent came to Texas and talked with Lucas in prison. He, too, confessed to his role in the Peoples case.

Armed with information developed by Mitchell and other Florida officers, Jim Appleman, state attorney for the 14th Judicial Circuit, obtained grand jury indictments against Lucas and Toole in four Florida murders, including the slaying of Jerilyn Peoples. Lucas also was indicted for first-degree murder in the slayings of John Perry McDaniel, Jr., in a gas station robbery near Campbellton, Florida, on December 15, 1980, and in the March 25, 1981 slaying of Brenda Jo Burton, twenty-one, of Bonifay, Florida, who was found strangled and stabbed in her home. Toole was indicted in those cases and one other, the slaying of seventy-one-year-old Ruby McCary on April 9, 1981, in her home in Washington County, Florida.

Lucas's court-appointed attorneys fought extradition proceedings in Texas, but on December 7, 1990, the former drifter was taken from death row and flown by Florida officers back to Tallahassee.

Tim Moore, commissioner of the Florida Department of Law Enforcement, said Lucas and Toole would be tried in all the cases. "We are gratified that this brutal [Peoples] case will finally come to trial, allowing the communities and families involved to once and for all put this matter behind them," the commissioner said.

Whatever the outcome of the Florida cases, Lucas's Texas death sentence still stands.

On March 22, 1989, the Texas Court of Criminal Appeals affirmed Lucas's conviction in the "Orange Socks" murder case. In appealing Lucas's case, his lawyer argued that Judge Carter had erred in allowing Lucas's written statement to be entered as evidence, saying it was obtained without him having had benefit of counsel.

"Appellant's is admittedly a rare case in the annals of state jurisprudence," wrote Judge W. C. Davis in his opinion upholding the judgment. "While his various appointed attorneys cautioned discretion and silence, Lucas appears to have been determined to speak to the authorities. . . . Indeed, as in the case before us, appellant made what can only be termed a conscious practice of informing on himself as to crimes which, up until that point in time, remained unsolved."

Judge Davis ruled Lucas "appears to have rejected his right to remain silent."

Lucas's first execution date was set for December 3, 1990. But on November 29, only four days before Lucas's scheduled lethal injection, the Court of Criminal Appeals granted a stay. That came as no surprise to Williamson County officials, who had not expected Lucas to die on his first scheduled execution date.

If convicted in one of the cases pending against him in early 1991, Ottis Toole could find himself back on Florida's death row, where he had awaited execution for the arson murder of George Sonenberg until his death sentence was reversed. On April 28, 1984, a Duval County, Florida, jury had found Toole guilty of the 1982 arson murder of Sonenberg. Toole was formally sentenced to death in Florida's electric chair on May 18, 1984. But in November 1985 the Florida Supreme Court reversed Toole's death sentence, finding that the trial court had erred when it did not tell jurors that they could consider it as mitigating evidence that Toole had been under extreme or emotional disturbance when he set the fatal fire. In June 1986, state prosecutors decided not to try for the death penalty in a new hearing. Duval County Circuit Judge James Harrison then resentenced Toole to life in prison.

Toole also is serving a life sentence in the 1983 murder of Ada Mildred Johnson, nineteen, of Tallahassee, Florida. In addition to the more recent indictments pending against him, jurisdictions in Arapahoe County, Colorado; Norfolk, Virginia; Chathen County, Georgia; and Smith County and Williamson County in Texas still have detainers against him on pending murder cases in the unlikely event he were ever released from custody in Florida.

Texas Ranger Phil Ryan was named Peace Officer of the Year by the North Texas Criminal Justice Association on January 9, 1986. He retired from the Texas Department of Public Safety in 1989 to devote full time to a business in which he had ownership. In early 1991 the former Ranger became an investigator for the 235th Judicial District Attorney, with jurisdiction in Wise and Jack Counties.

W. F. ("Hound Dog") Conway was in the middle of his second term as sheriff of Montague County when eighty-year-old Kate Rich disappeared in September 1982. On May 5, 1984, Conway was defeated in the Democratic primary in his bid for reelection. Later that year, the Sheriff's Association of Texas named Conway 1984 Texas Lawman of the Year. Then Texas Governor Mark White sent Conway a personal letter of commendation: "By gathering sufficient legal evidence to bring about the arrest, trial, and conviction of Henry Lee Lucas, you have contributed to the safety of countless citizens throughout Texas."

The three-member Public Safety Commission, which oversees the Department of Public Safety and the Texas Rangers, issued a written statement on January 30, 1986, saying it had found no evidence of wrongdoing on the part of the Rangers in the Lucas affair and that no disciplinary action was warranted.

On July 1, 1986, Bob Prince was promoted to captain of Texas Ranger Company A and moved from Waco to Houston. He kept copies of records developed by the Lucas Task Force and still occasionally receives telephone calls from law enforcement officers or reporters interested in Henry Lee Lucas or Ottis Toole.

Ranger Clayton Smith transferred from Williamson County to Waco to be closer to his home county of

Navarro and the family farm where he spends much of his off-duty time.

Bob Werner, who for a time was a member of the task force, retired as assistant chief of Criminal Law Enforcement for the DPS and is now police chief in Fredericksburg, Texas.

Col. Jim Adams retired as director of the DPS on May 31, 1987. The civil rights lawsuit filed by Lucas against him and other figures in the case was dismissed.

Ed Walsh campaigned unsuccessfully as a Republican candidate for state attorney general in 1986. He now has a private law practice in Williamson County. Ken Anderson, who took part in the prosecution of the "Orange Socks" case as Walsh's first assistant, is now Williamson County District Attorney.

Vic Feazell, who launched the grand jury investigation into the three McLennan County murder confessions Lucas made, was named in a sealed twelve-count racketeering indictment under the federal Racketeering Influenced and Corrupt Organizations Act (RICO) returned in U.S. District Court on September 16, 1986. The following morning, Feazell was led from his office in handcuffs by FBI agents and DPS officers. But that November voters returned the D.A. to office. On June 29, 1987, Feazell was acquitted in U.S. District Court on two counts alleging he accepted $19,000 in payments from Waco defense attorneys in exchange for reducing or dismissing driving while intoxicated and drug charges against some of their clients. The other ten counts of the indictment had been dismissed by U.S. District Judge James Nowlin on the basis of a U.S. Supreme Court decision regarding the federal mail fraud statute. In January 1988 Feazell agreed to a two-year probational suspension of his law license in action by a grievance committee of the state bar. On September 17, 1988, two years to the day after his arrest for racketeering,

Feazell resigned as district attorney to become general counsel for a Waco energy company.

Jan Patterson, who as an assistant U.S. Attorney coordinated the investigation that led to Feazell's indictment, left her prosecutor's job for private practice and part-time instruction at the University of Texas School of Law prior to Feazell's trial.

Jim Mattox, who as state attorney general investigated the circumstances of Lucas's confessions, was defeated in a gubernatorial bid in the 1990 Texas Democratic primary by Ann Richards. Richards went on to defeat her Republican opponent in the November general election and was sworn in as governor on January 15, 1991.

Divorced from her husband during the height of the Lucas investigations, Sister Clemmie Schroeder continues to conduct her jail ministry in Williamson County. She continued to visit Lucas occasionally while he was on death row in Huntsville.

Buddy Terry, who investigated Lucas and Toole's claims of homicides in Jacksonville, Florida, and put together the case against Toole in the arson murder of George Sonenberg, was transferred from the Duval County Sheriff's Department homicide division back to uniform patrol. His beat includes the Springfield neighborhood where Lucas and Toole used to live. The Jacksonville murders Lucas initially confessed to remain unsolved.

Florida Department of Law Enforcement Special Agent Joe Mitchell, nearing retirement from the state law enforcement agency, was called to active duty as an Army Reservist during the Operation Desert Storm troop buildup.

Bill Moody, who tried to get Lucas convicted in the Librada Apodaca case, remains on the bench in El Paso County as 34th District judge.

Brunson Moore, who ruled Lucas's confessions inadmissible, was publicly reprimanded on April 20,

1988, by the Texas Commission on Judicial Conduct. The reprimand came after the Commission found Moore had used his position on the bench to retaliate against lawyers who opposed him politically or were supporters of his political opponents; often displayed an "explosive temperament and vindictive attitude" that was "egregious and injudicious"; and retaliated against an attorney who had filed a complaint on the judge with the Commission. In 1990, Moore was defeated in a reelection bid and left the bench when his term expired in January 1991.

Steve Simmons continues to serve as El Paso County District Attorney.

No other arrests have been made in the ax murder of Librada Apodaca. Her nephew, Jimmy Apodaca, retired from the El Paso Police Department and is now project director of the West Texas Multi County Task Force, a drug-enforcement operation. Sgt. Benito Perez, Jr., is still a detective with the El Paso Police.

Jim Boutwell is still sheriff of Williamson County. He has never faced an opponent and plans to run again in 1992. The century-old jail where Lucas lived for a year and a half now stands empty, replaced by a larger, modern jail and sheriff's office.

The young woman known only as "Orange Socks" has never been identified.

Lucas's place in the annals of mass murder is still undecided. If, as he once claimed, he killed 360, or even 200 or more people, he would be, to use his words, "the world's most worse mass murderer."

If Lucas killed fewer than two hundred people, this title probably belongs to Herman Webster Mudgett, better known as "Dr. Holmes," who in 1893 ran a boardinghouse in Chicago for single women. Scores of the women who took a room at his place were never seen again. Chicago police found that Mudgett had been gassing them, dissecting their bodies, and burying them in a pit near the boardinghouse. Police estimated he had killed two hundred women.

The worst serial killer of modern times—if Lucas's previous claim of hundreds of murders is never substantiated—is John Wayne Gacy, Jr., of Des Plaines, Illinois, who in 1978–79 is said to have killed thirty-eight young men. Ted Bundy murdered up to thirty-six people. If the "Green River Killer" is ever located and linked to the forty-eight murders he is suspected of, he would become the worst serial killer of this century.

How many people did Henry Lee Lucas and Ottis Elwood Toole actually murder? The answer depends on who is asked.

On May 7, 1986, then still in office, Attorney General Mattox released a lengthy investigative report prepared by his staff. The inch-thick document is careful not to give a specific number of homicides believed to have been committed by the pair. At a press conference the day the report was released, Mattox said he generally believed Lucas was responsible for the death of his mother and the murders of Becky Powell and Kate Rich.

"I do believe that Henry Lee Lucas is a murderer," Mattox said. "I could not tell you how many cases he is good for. I think if you really and truly look at the report you could not attribute very many cases to him."

The report added that "Some of Lucas's confessions cannot be affirmatively disproved but, in light of the investigation, should be considered highly suspect. In several homicides, the date of death, as well as the manner of death and the identity of the victim, are unknown. It is, therefore, impossible to refute Lucas's confession by establishing his whereabouts on a particular date."

Col. Jim Adams, then Department of Public Safety director, said after the release of the report that twenty-six murder charges were pending against Lucas and that the DPS still felt he was responsible for more than a hundred homicides.

Attacking the attorney general's report, Adams said, "Little effort appears to have been made to explore and report on those many cases where the investigative agency involved still believes Lucas to be a prime suspect."

Six murder charges were later dropped against Lucas, including his indictment in the 1975 murder of Deborah Sue Williamson, the Lubbock newlywed whose parents, Bob and Joyce Lemons, were convinced Lucas was not their daughter's killer. However, he remains charged or indicted in twenty other murders, according to Texas Ranger Captain Prince. During the eighteen-month period the Lucas Task Force was in operation, the Ranger said, investigators representing a thousand different law enforcement agencies from forty states and Canada questioned Lucas about approximately three thousand homicides. Of that number, Prince said, Lucas was considered a suspect in about 150 murders.

The Lucas case generated considerable controversy in Texas, and it brought at least one distinct change in the law. In light of the Lucas confessions, the Texas Legislature passed a law that made serial murder a capital crime. Until that time the law had reserved the death penalty only for cases involving the commission of another felony or for the murder of a police officer.

Former Lucas Task Force members were pleased to see the renewed interest on the part of Florida authorities. Boutwell and Prince in particular are hopeful that his upcoming prosecution will shed more light on his travels and other suspected crimes.

Is Lucas a modern-day Scheherazade, the woman who had to tell a new, fascinating story every night for 1,001 nights or else have her head chopped off by the King? Or is he the most prolific serial killer of his time? Sheriff Boutwell, to the soles of his cowboy boots, believes Lucas is a murderer who probably killed between one hundred and two hundred people.

Indeed, it seems hard to believe that Lucas's mother, his teenage lover, and an old woman in North Texas could be the only three people he ever killed, especially in light of his extensive travels.

And after eight years, no other suspects have been charged in any of the murders he once claimed.

In the final analysis, the only person who really knows the truth is Henry Lee Lucas.

MIKE COX is a former award-winning reporter who worked on three Texas newspapers, including 15 years with the Austin *American-Statesman,* before joining the Texas Department of Public Safety as a public information officer in 1985. He is the author of five other books and numerous magazine articles. He lives in Austin, Texas, with his wife, Linda.